PROPHECY
FOR
JUDAH

A VERSE-BY-VERSE PROPHECY STUDY

Joel-Zephaniah-Haggai-Zechariah-Malachi

Virtually all Scripture references are quoted from the King James translation of the Holy Bible.

Prophecy for Judah
Copyright © 2017 by Midnight Call Ministries

Published by The Olive Press, a division of Midnight Call, Inc.
West Columbia, SC 29170 U.S.A.

Copy Typists:	Lynn Jeffcoat and Kathy Roland
Copy Editor:	Kimberly Farmer
Layout/Design:	Michelle Kim
Cover Design:	Michelle Kim

Froese, Arno
    Prophecy for Judah
    ISBN #9780937422724

    1. Bible--Prophecy

Printed in the United States of America

The sole purpose of publishing this book is to encourage the readers to surrender and consecrate their lives to Christ.

All funds received from the sale of this book will be used exclusively for the furtherance of the Gospel.

No one associated with this ministry receives a royalty for any of the literature published by Midnight Call Ministries, Inc.

CONTENTS

JOEL

Jehovah Is God

Chapter 3   36

JOEL

Book of the Bible	God's Directly Spoken Words (%)	Prophecy %*	Significant Names Listed in Each Book						
			Judah	Israel	Ephraim	Jerusalem	Zion	Heathen	Samaria
Hosea	93.32	56	15	44	37	0	0	0	6
Joel	**57.70**	**68**	**6**	**3**	**0**	**6**	**7**	**5**	**0**
Amos	80.95	58	4	30	0	2	2	1	5
Obadiah	97.69	81	1	1	1	2	2	4	1
Jonah	7.39	10	0	0	0	0	0	0	0
Micah	44.88	70	4	12	0	8	9	1	3
Nahum	40.30	74	1	1	0	0	0	0	0
Habakkuk	47.84	41	0	0	0	0	0	2	0
Zephaniah	96.92	89	3	4	0	4	2	1	0
Haggai	67.61	39	4	0	0	0	0	1	0
Zechariah	77.38	69	22	5	3	41	8	5	0
Malachi	93.80	56	3	5	0	2	0	2	0

* Percentage of book as prophecy according to *Tim LaHaye Prophecy Study Bible*

Introduction to Joel

Joel means in English, "Jehovah is God." He is identified as the son of Pethuel, but nothing more definite is known about him. This is typical of many prophets of God. They identified with the message they proclaimed; subsequently, their own person became of lesser significance. We may assume that he comes from Jerusalem, because of the repeated reference to that city in all three chapters.

We divide this book into three parts:

Part 1: Proclamation of Judgment upon the Land

Part 2: Comforting Promises of God

Part 3: The Day of the Lord

The prophecies of Joel are directed to Judah, the royal tribe.

Also, Joel specifically emphasizes "the day of the Lord"; that prophecy is repeated by the Apostle Peter at the very beginning of the Church.

11

Chapter 1

Introduction

This chapter proclaims absolute judgment of the people, the vegetation, and the livestock. We may call it the dark chapter, with no hope.

Proclamation of Judgment upon the Land

Joel 1:1-2: "The word of the LORD that came to Joel the son of Pethuel. 2 Hear this, ye old men, and give ear, all ye inhabitants of the land. Hath this been in your days, or even in the days of your fathers?"

(See) Deuteronomy 4:32; Isaiah 7:17; Daniel 12:1; Matthew 24:21; Hebrews 1:1; 2 Peter 1:21

Doubtless, something unprecedented was happening. This is not simply a random natural catastrophe; it was definitely the worst ever. "Has this been in your days, or even in the days of your fathers?" That means these people were eyewitnesses of the things that transpired during those days. They were even instructed to pass on the memory of this catastrophe:

Joel 1:3: "Tell ye your children of it, and let your children tell their children, and their children another generation."

(See) Psalm 78:4

Unprecedented judgment points to the Great Tribulation Jesus spoke about in Matthew 24:21, "For then shall be great tribulation, such as was not since the beginning of the world to this time, no, nor ever shall be." But this is different; we may call it a pre-fulfillment of the Great Tribulation.

Devastation of the Land

Joel 1:4: "That which the palmerworm hath left hath the locust eaten; and that which the locust hath left hath the cankerworm eaten; and that which the cankerworm hath left hath the caterpiller eaten."

A catastrophic invasion of insects upon the crops virtually devoured everything. Nothing of significance seems to be left to sustain life for man and beast.

This also applies to our days. In spite of our technological advances, inventions, and the fact that in the progressive industrial nations, only about 2 percent of the population is involved in agriculture, we are still dependent upon God's grace when it comes to food. Just think for a moment what would happen if rain ceased for the next three years. We could probably stay alive for a year, maybe even two, in those nations with a large reserve of stockpiled food. There is also the possibility of irrigation, but that is very limited. Without rain, life on earth would come to an end.

Intoxication

In the midst of these calamities, there is a warning:

Joel 1:5: "Awake, ye drunkards, and weep; and howl, all ye drinkers of wine, because of the new wine; for it is cut off from your mouth."

(See) Isaiah 32:10

Apparently, people lived in a state of intoxication. They did not know what was going on; they were removed from reality due to drunkenness. This is the case literally and spiritually. An intoxicated person is removed from reality; he is no longer capable of reasoning properly.

Unknown Enemy

If that wasn't enough, next in line comes the enemy:

Joel 1:6: "For a nation is come up upon my land, strong, and without number, whose teeth are the teeth of a lion, and he hath the cheek teeth of a great lion."

(See) Revelation 9:8

The enemy nation is not named; thus, we may take it to be demonic forces. The enemy has "lion teeth" and "cheek teeth of a great lion"; therefore, not human. We must take this literally because it does not say "teeth as of a lion." This is not an allegorical statement.

Fig and Vine Destroyed

Next, favored food trees are destroyed:

Joel 1:7: "He hath laid my vine waste, and barked my fig tree: he hath made it clean bare, and cast it away; the branches thereof are made white."

(See) Isaiah 5:6

The vine symbolizes peace and relaxation; the fig tree rest, shade and food. All is now gone; that's total judgment.

Priests and Farmers Mourn

Joel 1:8-12: "Lament like a virgin girded with sackcloth for the husband of her youth. 9 The meat offering and the drink offering is cut off from the house of the LORD; the priests, the LORD'S ministers, mourn. 10 The field is wasted, the land mourneth; for the corn is wasted: the new wine is dried up, the oil languisheth. 11 Be ye ashamed, O ye husbandmen; howl, O ye vinedressers, for the wheat and for the barley; because the harvest of the field is perished. 12 The vine is dried up, and the fig tree languisheth; the pomegranate tree, the palm tree also, and the apple tree, even all the trees of the field, are withered: because joy is withered away from the sons of men."

(See) Proverbs 2:17; Isaiah 22:12; 24:7; Jeremiah 12:11; 14:3; 48:33;
Hosea 9:1-2

This does not indicate a limited form of judgment, but total devastation of the land of Judah. No future, no restoration is promised. The people and the priests mourn, for the land and the fruit have "withered away."

Rejection of Prophecy

Reading these prophecies reveals why Churchianity, even Bible-believing Christianity, has so little interest in the prophetic Word. After all, who wants to talk about mourning, catastrophes, destruction and death? Don't we all have our plans for the future? Young people dream of careers, marriage, children and prosperity. The older ones plan their golden years. Prophecy, no doubt, is a "monkey wrench" to those plans. It just doesn't fit into our way of life. Subsequently, the instruction to "awake...be ashamed...gird yourself..." no longer reaches the heart of the people. Bible prophecy becomes a hindering element to self-indulgence, the religious philosophy of health, wealth and prosperity. We live in a time where the words of Revelation 3:17 are relevant: "I am rich, and increased with goods, and have need of nothing." That is the Church's response to Bible prophecy in most cases.

Religion Targeted

Joel 1:13-16: "Gird yourselves, and lament, ye priests: howl, ye ministers of the altar: come, lie all night in sackcloth, ye ministers of my God: for the meat offering and the drink offering is withholden from the house of your God. 14 Sanctify ye a fast, call a solemn assembly, gather the elders and all the inhabitants of the land into the house of the LORD your God, and cry unto the LORD, 15 Alas for the day! for the day of the LORD is at hand,

16

and as a destruction from the Almighty shall it come. 16 Is not the meat cut off before our eyes, yea, joy and gladness from the house of our God?"

(See) Deuteronomy 12:7, 12; 2 Chronicles 20:3, 13; Jeremiah 4:8; 39:7; Amos 5:16-18

Israel-Judah is not invited to rejoice in the Lord, but to "Sanctify ye a fast...cry unto the Lord...." They are to recognize the approaching "day of the Lord."

Great Tribulation

Yet, even in the midst of judgment, God's grace breaks through with an invitation to "sanctify a fast" and "cry unto the Lord." The prophet identifies the extent of judgment, particularly the religious failure at that time, and reaches far beyond into the final days.

With this prophecy, Joel not only reveals human history, limited to Israel-Judah, but also the very end, when the day of wrath comes upon all nations on planet Earth.

Livestock Perplexed

Nothing will escape God's judgment. It includes the soil, vegetation and livestock.

Joel 1:17-18: "The seed is rotten under their clods, the garners are laid desolate, the barns are broken down; for the corn is withered. 18 How do the beasts groan! the herds of cattle are perplexed, because they have no pasture; yea, the flocks of sheep are made desolate."

17

(See) 1 Kings 18:5; Hosea 4:3

The prophet Joel is not excluded. He is part of his people and his land; thus, we read his prayer:

Joel 1:19-20: "O LORD, to thee will I cry: for the fire hath devoured the pastures of the wilderness, and the flame hath burned all the trees of the field. 20 The beasts of the field cry also unto thee: for the rivers of waters are dried up, and the fire hath devoured the pastures of the wilderness."

(See) 1 Kings 17:7; Job 38:41; Psalm 104:21

God's Grace Revealed

As we read of these horrific calamities, it seems difficult to grasp in our days. We can go to a supermarket, stocked with an abundance of delicacies, and buy as we please. However, the few and the wise recognize that the abundance offered to us in attractive packages, is only an extension of God's grace and His promise to all mankind, "While the earth remaineth, seedtime and harvest, and cold and heat, and summer and winter, and day and night shall not cease" (Genesis 8:22). That's why believers continue to pray, "Give us this day our daily bread."

18

Chapter 2

Introduction

While chapter 2 continues pronouncing terrible judgment and the day of the Lord in the first 11 verses, hope is revealed to Israel. The Lord makes a specific promise; namely, the restoration of the land of Israel and the people. The center of this hope is revealed with the words, "My people shall never be ashamed."

Joel then reaches into the time of the New Covenant, the pouring out of the Holy Spirit upon the Jews in Jerusalem, and the final judgment, climaxing in the Great Tribulation, "the terrible day of the Lord."

Coming Global Judgment

Joel 2:1: "Blow ye the trumpet in Zion, and sound an alarm in my holy mountain: let all the inhabitants of the land tremble: for the day of the LORD cometh, for it is nigh at hand;"

(See) Numbers 10:5; Psalm 87:1; Obadiah 15; Zephaniah 1:14

Zion is the immediate target, which corresponds with the New Testament Scripture written by the Apostle Peter: "For the time is come that judgment must begin at the house of God" (1 Peter 4:17).

Unprecedented Disaster

Joel 2:2: "A day of darkness and of gloominess, a day of clouds and of thick darkness, as the morning spread upon the mountains: a great people and a strong; there hath not been ever the like, neither shall be any more after it, even to the years of many generations."

(See) Exodus 10:14; Amos 5:18

This is unique because it says: "hath not been ever the like, neither shall be any more after it." It is incomparable in history; it is unprecedented, and will never occur again. We are reminded of the Lord Jesus Christ's words recorded in Matthew 24:21: "For then shall be great tribulation, such as was not since the beginning of the world to this time, no, nor ever shall be."

Who are the "great people and strong"? We presume they are not humans but unidentified demonic entities. We are concerned here with God's ultimate judgment against a rebellious world, and the executor of judgment is not identified, humanly speaking.

Destruction from the Almighty

What kind of judgment is this? Earlier we read, "as a destruction from the Almighty shall it come" (Joel 1:15). This is clearly God's doing. Based on these and other facts we will reveal later, we must allow for the possibility that this is not dealing with an earthly army, but "destruction from the Almighty."

20

Joel 2:3-5: "A fire devoureth before them; and behind them a flame burneth: the land is as the garden of Eden before them, and behind them a desolate wilderness; yea, and nothing shall escape them. 4 The appearance of them is as the appearance of horses; and as horsemen, so shall they run. 5 Like the noise of chariots on the tops of mountains shall they leap, like the noise of a flame of fire that devoureth the stubble, as a strong people set in battle array."

(See) Zechariah 7:14

Who is this destructive force? Is it a nation? Not likely. These are creatures, unknown to us, who seem to appear as horses and horsemen, but they are neither horses nor horsemen. Why? Because we note the words, "like... chariots...like...flame of fire..." These aren't chariots, nor is this a flame of fire. The words "as" and "like" make it clear: we are dealing with demonic forces. Yet these powers are in the hand of God Almighty. They are His tools of judgment; they are executing the "destruction from the Almighty."

Demonic Entities

Next comes a detailed description of the activity of this army: "a great people and strong." This reveals that they are entities out of this world, unknown to us.

Joel 2:6-9: "Before their face the people shall be much pained: all faces shall gather blackness. 7 They shall run like mighty men; they shall climb the wall like men of

21

war; and they shall march every one on his ways, and they shall not break their ranks: 8 Neither shall one thrust another; they shall walk every one in his path: and when they fall upon the sword, they shall not be wounded. 9 They shall run to and fro in the city; they shall run upon the wall, they shall climb up upon the houses; they shall enter in at the windows like a thief."

(See) Jeremiah 8:21

This will be the most shocking event people have ever experienced. We are reminded of the words Jesus used when He spoke about the endtimes: "Men's hearts failing them for fear, and for looking after those things which are coming on the earth: for the powers of heaven shall be shaken" (Luke 21:26).

Doubtless, we are concerned here with the Great Tribulation, the judgment upon the nations God the Almighty will execute by utilizing powers of darkness unknown to us, literally out of this world.

Invincible Creatures

Verse 7 reveals an additional clue to their identity: "run like mighty men" and, "climb the wall like men of war." These are not mighty men, nor are they men of war, but entities different from anything else we have ever seen on planet Earth. In modern language, we can call these frightening beings "Super Creatures": "when they fall upon the sword, they shall not be wounded."

Something is happening on earth that no one has experienced, nor will ever experience again. It is the time

22

when Satan and his angels are expelled out of heaven and are "cast out into the earth" (Revelation 12:9). What is the result? "Therefore rejoice, ye heavens, and ye that dwell in them. Woe to the inhabiters of the earth and of the sea! for the devil is come down unto you, having great wrath, because he knoweth that he hath but a short time" (Revelation 12:12).

Another clue, which reinforces our understanding that we are dealing with demonic forces, is the description of weapons and casualties; there are none. No killing, no death, no ravaging, and no plunder. Although these creatures enter into the houses "like thieves," we don't read of anything being stolen.

When asked what type of war is this, we would venture to say it is a war of darkness from which no one can escape.

The Universe Trembles

Joel 2:10-11: "The earth shall quake before them; the heavens shall tremble: the sun and the moon shall be dark, and the stars shall withdraw their shining: 11 And the LORD shall utter his voice before his army: for his camp is very great: for he is strong that executeth his word: for the day of the LORD is great and very terrible; and who can abide it?"

(See) Numbers 24:23; Jeremiah 50:34; Malachi 3:2

There is no army in the world that can cause the earth to quake, much less the heavens to tremble or affect the

23

shining of the moon and the stars. Thus, we have confirmation that the demonic forces God has authorized will be allowed to fully possess planet Earth and its inhabitants. If we ask why God allows this to happen, we find the answer in John 1:5: "And the light shineth in darkness; and the darkness comprehended it not."

The Wrath of the Lamb

This is God's doing, not that of human beings. When His judgment comes upon planet Earth, the people will recognize that it is not from men but from the hand of God. Here is the testimony about the people of the world: "And the kings of the earth, and the great men, and the rich men, and the chief captains, and the mighty men, and every bondman, and every free man, hid themselves in the dens and in the rocks of the mountains; And said to the mountains and rocks, Fall on us, and hide us from the face of him that sitteth on the throne and from the wrath of the Lamb" (Revelation 6:15-16). There is no repentance and no conversion; only a vain attempt to hide from "him that sitteth on the throne, and from the wrath of the Lamb." People will be fully conscious that this judgment originates from God Almighty.

Many Trumpets

All of this is initiated by "the trumpet in Zion." Many trumpets are mentioned throughout Scripture, beginning in Exodus 19:13 and ending in Revelation 9:14. But most of these trumpets are specific; they serve a certain purpose and must not be confused with one another. There are trumpets of gathering and war, of jubilation and rejoicing, of peace and merry-making; and then there are trumpets of judgment, which we read of in the book of Revelation.

Trump of Grace

Here the trumpet that is blown in Zion is addressed to the people of Israel; it is a trumpet of grace, a trumpet of invitation, a trumpet of reconciliation. It indicates a window of grace for His people.

Doubtless, this is what Jeremiah revealed in chapter 30, verse 7: "Alas! for that day is great, so that none is like it: it is even the time of Jacob's trouble; but he shall be saved out of it." Thus, the judgment is directed in the first place toward "Jacob," but during judgment, "he shall be saved out of it." That is not the case when judgment comes upon the world.

Invitation to Repent

Joel 2:12-14: "Therefore also now, saith the LORD, turn ye even to me with all your heart, and with fasting, and with weeping, and with mourning: 13 And rend your heart, and not your garments, and turn unto the LORD your God: for he is gracious and merciful, slow to anger, and of great kindness, and repenteth him of the evil. 14 Who knoweth if he will return and repent, and leave a blessing behind him; even a meat offering and a drink offering unto the LORD your God?"

(See) Exodus 34:6; 2 Kings 22:19; Psalm 34:18; Isaiah 57:15; 65:8; Jeremiah 4:1; Hosea 12:6; Jonah 4:2; Zephaniah 2:3; Haggai 2:19; Matthew 5:3-4

Israel is admonished to turn to the Lord and seek Him. This clearly is a two-way street: if Israel reacts, God will react on behalf of Israel.

Grace upon Israel

But we must note here that Israel's reaction is God-initiated. Thus, we read in Zechariah 12:9-10: "And it shall come to pass in that day, that I will seek to destroy all the nations that come against Jerusalem. And I will pour upon the house of David, and upon the inhabitants of Jerusalem, the spirit of grace and of supplications: and they shall look upon me whom they have pierced, and they shall mourn for him, as one mourneth for his only son, and shall be in bitterness for him, as one that is in bitterness for his firstborn." At the very moment when Israel is at their wit's end, when the whole world openly turns against the Jewish people, God will intervene. He will pour out "the spirit of grace and supplication" upon Israel. In turn, they will suddenly recognize the Lord at His coming, "they shall look upon me whom they have pierced."

Comforting Promises of God

Joel 2:15-17: "Blow the trumpet in Zion, sanctify a fast, call a solemn assembly: 16 Gather the people, sanctify the congregation, assemble the elders, gather the children, and those that suck the breasts: let the bridegroom go forth of his chamber, and the bride out of her closet. 17 Let the priests, the ministers of the LORD, weep between the porch and the altar, and let them say, Spare thy people, O LORD, and give not thine heritage to reproach, that the heathen should rule over them: wherefore should they say among the people, Where is their God?"

(See) Exodus 19:10; 2 Chronicles 20:13; Isaiah 37:20

Again, it begins with the blowing of the trumpet in Zion; that's always an indication that something new, something extraordinary is going to transpire. This spirit of grace and supplication will be poured out upon the whole house of Israel; the elders, the children, and the infants are addressed. Even the bridegroom and the bride will interrupt their honeymoon.

The Coming Peace

When the ministers of the Lord begin to plead with the God of Israel, it results in a wonderful promise:

Joel 2:18-20: "Then will the LORD be jealous for his land, and pity his people. 19 Yea, the LORD will answer and say unto his people, Behold, I will send you corn, and wine, and oil, and ye shall be satisfied therewith: and I will no more make you a reproach among the heathen: 20 But I will remove far off from you the northern army, and will drive him into a land barren and desolate, with his face toward the east sea, and his hinder part toward the utmost sea, and his stink shall come up, and his ill savour shall come up, because he hath done great things."

(See) Exodus 10:12; Deuteronomy 11:24; Psalm 103:13; Isaiah 42:13; Zechariah 1:14; Malachi 3:10

A Land Reborn

Not only does Israel receive a glorious promise about the Lord being on their side and the defeat of the terrible northern army, but also total restoration of the destroyed land, vegetation and animals is included:

Joel 2:21-24: "Fear not, O land; be glad and rejoice: for the LORD will do great things. 22 Be not afraid, ye beasts of the field: for the pastures of the wilderness do spring, for the tree beareth her fruit, the fig tree and the vine do yield their strength. 23 Be glad then, ye children of Zion, and rejoice in the LORD your God: for he hath given you the former rain moderately, and he will cause to come down for you the rain, the former rain, and the latter rain in the first month. 24 And the floors shall be full of wheat, and the vats shall overflow with wine and oil."

(See) Leviticus 26:4; Psalm 28:7; Isaiah 12:2-6; Habakkuk 3:17-18; Zechariah 8:12; 10:7; James 5:7

We read in chapter 1 about the total desolation of Israel's agriculture: "The field is wasted...corn is wasted...new wine is dried up...oil languisheth...the beasts groan... cattle are perplexed...sheep are made desolate." Now the curse is replaced with the comforting words: "Be not afraid, ye beasts of the field." Why not? Because, "the pastures of the wilderness do spring, for the tree beareth her fruit." This is nothing less than the rebirth of the land of Israel.

While the world will experience God's wrath, and indeed Israel will experience terrible destruction, we must keep in mind that Israel "shall be saved out of it."

Restoration

There is more to come:

Joel 2:25: "And I will restore to you the years that the locust hath eaten, the cankerworm, and the caterpillar, and
the palmerworm, my great army which I sent among
you."

This is an unconditional promise, not dependent on the
people of Israel. God says: "I will restore." The terrible
destruction and suffering due to famine, pestilence and
other catastrophes will not only come to an end, but also
the Lord says, "I will restore to you the years." That
means God will do something unprecedented in history:
Israel's agricultural industry will experience a miraculous
restoration to the level of the Garden of Eden.

Although in our time we see Israel already leading the
world in several aspects of agricultural science, particularly computer-assisted irrigation, we may consider this
only a foreshadowing of things to come.

His Great Army

It is significant that God identifies Himself as the ultimate author of this destruction, with the words, "my
great army which I sent among you." Who is this great
army? We already spoke about it in the first part of chapter 2; it is the army of darkness, a demonic entity suffocating the land of Israel. When God says "my great
army," we realize that God is omnipotent; He is sover-

eign, even over the forces of darkness. Thus, He calls them "my great army." This reminds us of the words in Amos 3:6, "…shall there be evil in a city, and the LORD hath not done it?"

His People "Shall Never Be Ashamed"

Now God sends blessings, overwhelming, all-inclusive and irresistible:

Joel 2:26-27: "And ye shall eat in plenty, and be satisfied, and praise the name of the LORD your God, that hath dealt wondrously with you: and my people shall never be ashamed. 27 And ye shall know that I am in the midst of Israel, and that I am the LORD your God, and none else: and my people shall never be ashamed."

(See) Leviticus 26:11; Isaiah 45:5; Micah 6:14

The terrible Great Tribulation will lead Israel into their darkest hour, but will end in great glory: "my people shall never be ashamed."

Israel's Dilemma Today

We do well to fully and consciously realize that what is happening in Israel today is part of God's sovereign plan. He is in the process of restoring His people. We need not be alarmed at the present day circumstances Israel find herself in. Much is being written about Israel's precarious situation in relationship to the Palestinian Arabs. Hamas has sworn to eliminate Israel; Iran publicly declares its intention to wipe Israel off the map. Even the so-called friendly countries—which see Israel as an extension of

Western culture—all will be put to shame in the end. None has the power to change God's eternal resolutions regarding Israel.

God's Chosen People

When we deal with Israel, the land and the people, we are dealing with the eternal God, who has chosen this tiny piece of land and the most controversial people on earth, for His own specific purpose. What God has promised will come to pass: judgment and comfort, destruction and restoration. We must learn to understand God's intentions as revealed in prophetic Scripture.

This fact also penetrates our hearts deeply, with the assurance that for us who believe in Jesus Christ, God's eternal resolution will be fulfilled, as we read in 2 Corinthians 4:17: "For our light affliction, which is but for a moment, worketh for us a far more exceeding and eternal weight of glory."

Salvation Is of the Jews

Salvation is related to a geographical area: "in mount Zion and in Jerusalem." This verse is uncomfortable for those who believe God has no geographical or physical preference on planet Earth. It is most difficult to spiritualize these things, because they are identified by name. We read in verse 27: "I am in the midst of Israel... and my people shall never be ashamed." Realizing this important fact leads us to the conclusion that the words Jesus spoke, "Salvation is of the Jews," are to be taken very literally.

Pentecost Prophecy

Joel 2:28-29: "And it shall come to pass afterward, that I will pour out my spirit upon all flesh; and your sons and your daughters shall prophesy, your old men shall dream dreams, your young men shall see visions: 29 And also upon the servants and upon the handmaids in those days will I pour out my spirit."

(See) Isaiah 44:3; John 7:39; Acts 21:9; 1 Corinthians 12:13; Galatians 3:28

Scholars differ as to the timeframe of the statement, "it shall come to pass afterward." After what is the question here. Additional information is found in Zechariah 12:9-10: "And it shall come to pass in that day, that I will seek to destroy all the nations that come against Jerusalem. And I will pour upon the house of David, and upon the inhabitants of Jerusalem, the spirit of grace and of supplications: and they shall look upon me whom they have pierced, and they shall mourn for him, as one mourneth for his only son, and shall be in bitterness for him, as one that is in bitterness for his firstborn."

This speaks of the pouring out of His Spirit upon those who had previously rejected the Lord. This is evident from the words, "Look upon me whom they have pierced." Therefore, "it shall come to pass afterward" means after the Old Covenant is fulfilled and the New Covenant is initiated.

First Fulfillment
We are all familiar with the first phase of the fulfillment

recorded in Acts 2. Peter testifies to those who are witnesses of the happening, the 120 disciples upon whom the Spirit of God was poured out, "...this is that which was spoken by the prophet Joel" (Acts 2:16). Let us read again the promise Joel made and which was quoted at the beginning of the Church: "And it shall come to pass in the last days, saith God, I will pour out of my Spirit upon all flesh: and your sons and your daughters shall prophesy, and your young men shall see visions, and your old men shall dream dreams: And on my servants and on my handmaidens I will pour out in those days of my Spirit; and they shall prophesy" (Acts 2:17-18). We call this the birth of the Church.

Fulfilled "in the Last Days"

When will this take place? Answer: "in the last days." Thus, the words, "it shall come to pass afterward" are within the timeframe of the last days. When did the last days begin? We find the answer in Hebrews 1:2: "Hath in these last days spoken unto us by his Son, whom he hath appointed heir of all things, by whom also he made the worlds." The last days began with the speaking of the Son, who was made flesh. Therefore, the beginning of the Church in Jerusalem at Pentecost occurred in the timeframe of "in the last days."

Those who received the Spirit of God prophesied and had visions and dreams. If we carefully check Scripture, we will notice that indeed dreams, visions and prophecies are documented in the New Testament. The Lord spoke to Joseph in a dream (Matthew 1:20). To Ananias, the Lord gave His message in a vision (Acts 9:10). Timothy received gifts by prophecy (1 Timothy 4:14). However, this prophecy will continue to be fulfilled.

Prophecy Not Fulfilled

Joel 2:30-31: "And I will show wonders in the heavens and in the earth, blood, and fire, and pillars of smoke. 31 The sun shall be turned into darkness, and the moon into blood, before the great and terrible day of the LORD come."

(See) Mark 13:24

If we consider Pentecost to be the fulfillment of Joel's prophecy, then we must leave out the following: "And I will show wonders in heaven above, and signs in the earth beneath; blood, and fire, and vapour of smoke: The sun shall be turned into darkness, and the moon into blood, before that great and notable day of the Lord come: And it shall come to pass, that whosoever shall call on the name of the Lord shall be saved" (Acts 2:19-21). Thus, this part of prophecy has not been fulfilled. There is no debate needed; the sun has not turned into darkness, nor the moon into blood. That hasn't happened—it is future.

The Apostle Peter quotes Scripture to signify that God's plan of salvation is not limited to the Jewish church, but applies to the Jews and Gentiles collectively, "And it shall come to pass, that whosoever shall call on the name of the Lord shall be saved" (Acts 2:21).

Joel 2:32: "And it shall come to pass, that whosoever shall call on the name of the LORD shall be delivered: for in mount Zion and in Jerusalem shall be deliverance, as the LORD hath said, and in the remnant whom the LORD shall call."

(See) Psalm 50:15; Isaiah 11:11; 46:13; Jeremiah 33:3; Obadiah 17; Acts 2:21; Romans 9:27; 10:13; 1 Corinthians 1:2

We from among the Gentiles do not have to go to Jerusalem or to mount Zion to be delivered; however, we must understand that salvation came to us from Jerusalem, and from there went to the uttermost parts of the world. In the end, deliverance/salvation will return to its beginning—Jerusalem.

To the Jews First

The fact that this is addressed to the Jews in the land of Israel in the first place is self-evident. Those who were baptized with the Holy Spirit at Pentecost are the ones who qualify under the definition "your sons," "your daughters," "your young men," and "your old men."

Chapter 3

Introduction

While the first chapter proclaimed horrendous judgment upon the land of Israel, the second chapter reported of a supernatural, out-of-this-world armed force. But finally, Israel recognizes their Messiah and the land is miraculously restored. Now with this last chapter, the prophet turns to the Gentile world. While the entire heathen world has greatly benefited from the Jewish people during these last 2,500 years, the Jews, to a greater or lesser degree, were rejected, particularly now as they have returned to their own land. The Gentile nations, without exception, insist that Israel should not take possession of the Promised Land as outlined in Genesis 15:18. That's the point where they interfere with the God of Israel.

Restoration of the Promised Land

Joel 3:1: "For, behold, in those days, and in that time, when I shall bring again the captivity of Judah and Jerusalem,"

This cannot be misunderstood. We are to take these names literally: Judah, Jerusalem, all nations, valley of Jehoshaphat, Israel. There is no way to spiritualize this and apply it to the Church. This is literally the land of Israel, with its capital city Jerusalem. "My people" are clearly identified as the Jewish people. These are our days; the Lord is bringing back the Jews to the land of Israel.

"Parted My Land"

Joel 3:2: "I will also gather all nations, and will bring them down into the valley of Jehoshaphat, and will plead with them there for my people and for my heritage Israel, whom they have scattered among the nations, and parted my land."

(See) 2 Chronicles 20:26; Isaiah 66:16; Zechariah 14:12

This Scripture is extremely topical today because we see the nation of the world, for the first time in history, literally parting the land of Israel. While all countries were established by military force—with the winner determining the borders—such is not the case with Israel. They could not take possession of the land conquered, because the nations wouldn't allow it. All nations, without exception, do not recognize Jerusalem as the capital city of Israel, yet Israel won the city in battle in June 1967.

One more thought about the statement, "parted my land." Take, for example, the USA; the nation was established by force of weapons. The original inhabitants, the Indians, were either killed or placed in reservation camps, where they became powerless and virtually lost their identity. This is true about all new nations established the past 500 years or so. However, the "old nations" by whatever name, were also established by the power of war. That is how it always has been.

But Satan, the god of this world who rules the nations, has no intention of letting God have His way; thus, he vehemently opposes the fulfillment of prophecy. He does not want the Jews to return to their land, Israel.

If we want to know what's going on in Israel, in the Middle East and the rest of the world, we need not look further than Israel. The real reason for the world's chaos is and always will be Israel. Here is where the powers of darkness and the power of light collide. It is the god of this world who causes the nations to part, to cut up the land of Israel.

We have emphasized the three words, "parted my land" many times on various occasions and in different messages, but I think we can't emphasize it enough because that is the actual source of the world's conflicts. It's not because of the political conflict in the Middle East, the Arab world or Islam; it's all because of Jerusalem and the land of Israel.

God Gathers the Nations

"I shall bring again the captivity of Judah and Jerusalem," means the Jews are coming back to the land of Israel. Parallel to it, God says, "I will also gather all nations."

I think many of us don't realize what is happening in the invisible world. There is a battle raging between the powers of darkness and God's intention to fulfill His promises to His people Israel. If we disregard the sovereign declaration of the prophetic Word, "I shall bring again the captivity of Judah and Jerusalem, I will also gather all nations," we really miss the point. God is act-ing and man is reacting.

The nations of the world are just running in circles, blaming each other, making great speeches, signing peace agreements one after the other, but nothing helps. Why not? Because the world simply disregards the "I will" of God.

The Greatest Controversy for the World

Think for a moment: was there ever a people and a city in the world as controversial as the Jews and Jerusalem? Why are they so controversial? Because unknowingly, they are being led by God in the process of finally establishing peace on earth, goodwill to mankind. That is part of the fulfillment of innumerable prophecies, including Daniel 2:44: "And in the days of these kings shall the God of heaven set up a kingdom, which shall never be destroyed: and the kingdom shall not be left to other people, but it shall break in pieces and consume all these kingdoms, and it shall stand for ever." There is no political evidence to show God's work, but that does not change God's intentions and actions.

Times of the Gentiles

When God says, "In the days of these kings shall the God of heaven set up a kingdom, which shall never be destroyed," then we realize that "in the days" means about 2,600 years; that's from the time of Nebuchadnezzar, about 600 B.C., to our time.

Although there is no visible evidence of the establishment of this indestructible kingdom, it has nevertheless continued to be established throughout the ages till now.

Here we learn how to understand the seemingly contradictory statement, that with God a thousand years is as one day and one day as a thousand years. That statement demolishes our mathematical configuration about the end times and the second coming of Christ.

So, the commotion and rumors of wars, famines, pestilences, and earthquakes are part of the package, but they all serve toward the fulfillment to set up His kingdom, which shall never be destroyed.

Building His Church

Spiritually speaking, this applies to the Church; she is the elect, purchased with the blood of the Lamb, an eternal identity. The process of building this Church continues until this very day. Thus, we see a parallel in the building of the kingdom of God on earth and the building of the invisible kingdom, His Church.

Nevertheless, when reading the words of the prophet Joel, we understand that this Scripture deals with Israel, Jerusalem and the Jewish people—not the Church.

Israel's Victory Denied

Back to Israel: Since 1948, they have fought several wars against Arab nations, and always came out victorious. Their armed forces conquered large territories. At one time, they were standing at the gates of Damascus in the north and Cairo in the south. What happened next? The nations, the USA and the USSR, which themselves were established by conquering territory by force, told Israel to cease immediately and surrender the territory they had conquered from their enemies.

But that's not all: these nations continue to insist that Israel must now surrender parts of the Promised Land to their Arab neighbors in the name of a so-called peace process. That is the official policy of all the nations of the world. They are all guilty of the three words, "parted my land."

The Guilt of the Nations

There is more: the Bible gives us a more detailed picture regarding the guilt of the nations concerning Israel:

Joel 3:3-6: "And they have cast lots for my people; and have given a boy for an harlot, and sold a girl for wine, that they might drink. 4 Yea, and what have ye to do with me, O Tyre, and Zidon, and all the coasts of Palestine? will ye render me a recompence? and if ye recompense me, swiftly and speedily will I return your recompence upon your own head; 5 Because ye have taken my silver and my gold, and have carried into your temples my goodly pleasant things: 6 The children also of Judah and the children of Jerusalem have ye sold unto the Grecians, that ye might remove them far from their border."

(See) Deuteronomy 32:25; Ezekiel 25:15; Amos 6:1; Obadiah 11; Luke 18:7; James 2:13

We all know this is not happening today. No Jewish people are being sold into slavery. The time has passed when enemies could take the trophies of war: silver, gold and pleasant things for themselves. But these things happened during the process of 2,600 years. The Jewish people were dispersed literally into the whole world. There is not one nation on earth that does not have Jewish people in their midst. That was fulfillment of prophecy, "they have cast lots for my people."

The Global Church

Here we see a similar picture relating to the Church of Jesus Christ. There isn't a nation that does not have members of the living Church of God in their midst. We may think that the Church is non-existent in some of the fundamental Muslim countries, such as Saudi Arabia, Iran, Sudan, and others, but that's only on the surface. The visible manifestation of the Church through infra-structure, such as church buildings, schools, seminaries, etc., does not necessarily reveal the Church Jesus spoke of when He said, "I will build my church." The true Church, the body of Christ, continues to be built. Believers will be added to the body of Christ until the Church is complete. Then when the last from among the Gentiles is added, the Rapture will take place. That will be a tremendous surprise; millions upon millions, from all parts of the world, will be suddenly raptured, vanishing from planet Earth. That will create a vacuum to force all religions into global unity.

Judgment of the Nations

In the meantime, the nations are uniting against Israel. Some openly and aggressively, such as Iran; others friendly and helpful, such as the USA. But all belong to the enemies, of whom the Lord says, "I will also gather all nations, and will bring them down into the valley of Jehoshaphat." The Bible calls this the Battle of Armageddon: the confrontation between the powers of the Creator of heaven and earth, and the powers of darkness, the god of this world and all his nations.

Joel 3:7-8: "Behold, I will raise them out of the place whither ye have sold them, and will return your recompence upon your own head: 8 And I will sell your sons and your daughters into the hand of the children of Judah, and they shall sell them to the Sabeans, to a people far off: for the LORD hath spoken it."

(See) Ezekiel 23:42

Today, God has begun to interfere with the affairs of man on behalf of Israel. While the whole world has plans for Israel, God says, "I will establish my kingdom, and I will destroy yours." The Gentiles took advantage of the Jews; the day will come when the Jews will take advantage of the Gentiles, as documented in verse 8.

An Admonition

In view of this extremely serious message, I pray that you have made the decision to be a member of the Church of Jesus Christ. No matter which nation you belong to, you will be ashamed of your nationality, of your flag and your national anthem, but you will not be ashamed when you put all of your faith and trust in Him, of whom we read in Matthew 28:18: "All power is given unto me in heaven and in earth."

Prepare for War

Joel 3:9: "Proclaim ye this among the Gentiles; Prepare war, wake up the mighty men, let all the men of war draw near; let them come up:"

This is instruction for preparation of war. It is addressed to the Gentiles. Is this in the future? Yes and no. "Yes," because the battle of Armageddon has not taken place. But "No," because this statement is valid for the entire time of the Gentiles: from Babylon (600 BC) until *Rome* in our days. That's a time span of about 2,600 years.

The Gentiles always stand in opposition to Israel. Here we must quote Isaiah 40:17: "All nations before him are as nothing; and they are counted to him less than nothing, and vanity." This is quite incomprehensible to our mind, that the whole world, all 200 plus nations, amounts to nothing: as a matter of fact, "less than nothing" when compared to His people, His plan and His land.

The Wrong Way of the Gentiles

The next verse reveals the world's true spirit:

Joel 3:10: "Beat your plowshares into swords, and your pruninghooks into spears: let the weak say, I am strong."

(See) Isaiah 2:4; Zechariah 12:8

Here I am reminded of the words Hitler asked the German people, "Do you want butter or canons?" The German people overwhelmingly responded, "Canons!" As a result, the whole world got involved: World War II. In plain words, all nations at all times wanted war in order to achieve their own imagined peace. But the Lord answers, "There is no peace for the wicked." Why not? First John 5:19 answers: "The whole world lieth in wickedness."

Peace through War

I venture to depart from the standard interpretation of this Scripture, which applies this verse strictly to the Battle of Armageddon. Why? Because innumerable wars have been fought in the past. Reading Israel's history, we are confronted with war after war. I believe that all of this is part of the Battle of Armageddon.

Take, for example, Europe. The European nations have warred against each other for thousands of years. That is clearly documented history. Therefore, we must apply this Scripture to the past, the present and the future.

No More War

Today, it is virtually impossible to imagine war between the industrialized nations. The progressive nations of the world have already entered the dispensation of manmade peace. Can you imagine England attacking the Netherlands, or Germany invading France? Such thoughts are ludicrous. They fully depend on each other; they have become more or less one nation, although distinct from one another.

The European Union insists that each member nation should treasure its own culture, holidays, traditions and language. Today the political and economic integration process has virtually invalidated the existence of national borders. Europe is leading the way. We will see this development with the rest of the world as time goes by.

Peace Must Come

Furthermore, in 1 Thessalonians 5:2-3 we read: "For yourselves know perfectly that the day of the Lord so cometh as a thief in the night. For when they shall say, Peace and safety; then sudden destruction cometh upon them, as travail upon a woman with child; and they shall not escape." That means before "the day of the Lord" comes, the people on planet Earth will live in peace; they will say, "Peace and safety."

To understand verse 10 of Joel 3 better, let's take a panoramic look at history from Nebuchadnezzar until today. The nations of the world occupied themselves continuously with war, "swords and spears," rather than with "plowshares" and "pruning hooks." War was on equal footing with agriculture. It was because of war that the Europeans discovered, conquered and settled the two new continents—America and Australia.

Israel, Enemy of the Gentiles

However, that does not change the nations' conflict with the one nation—Israel. Thus, God caused Joel to write down precisely what will transpire:

Joel 3:11-13: "Assemble yourselves, and come, all ye heathen, and gather yourselves together round about: thither cause thy mighty ones to come down, O LORD. 12 Let the heathen be wakened, and come up to the valley of Jehoshaphat: for there will I sit to judge all the heathen round about. 13 Put ye in the sickle, for the harvest is ripe: come, get you down; for the press is full, the fats overflow; for their wickedness is great."

(See) 2 Chronicles 20:26; Psalm 96:13; Jeremiah 51:33; Revelation 14:15

Irreversible Judgment

Notice the gathering of all nations, and the judgment upon "all ye heathen." This simply speaks of the heathen, the nations of the world; they are ripe for judgment.

It is not a light thing that the nations of the world have spurned God's gracious offer of salvation in Jesus Christ for about two millennia, but they also collectively oppose God's promises to Israel—they continue to divide the land, divide the city, and trample down the eternal Word of prophecy. Judgment is irrevocable.

Universal Participation

The final confrontation between light and darkness will not be limited to Israel and the nations, but the universe will participate:

Joel 3:14-15: "Multitudes, multitudes in the valley of decision: for the day of the LORD is near in the valley of decision. 15 The sun and the moon shall be darkened, and the stars shall withdraw their shining."

The sun, the moon and the stars will be involved. This is

judgment upon the nations unto destruction. That's what the prophets proclaimed to Israel, and through Israel to the rest of the world.

When Sin Was Judged

We are reminded here of the judgment upon sin. When Jesus was judged, the earth and the universe were involved: "Now from the sixth hour there was darkness over all the land unto the ninth hour...And, behold, the veil of the temple was rent in twain from the top to the bottom; and the earth did quake, and the rocks rent" (Matthew 27:45, 51).

Battle of Armageddon

Doubtless, these verses in Joel 3 speak of the Battle of Armageddon, the confrontation between the Bright and Morning Star, and the fallen morning star, Lucifer.

The actual confrontation is revealed for us in 2 Thessalonians 2:8: "And then shall that Wicked be revealed, whom the Lord shall consume with the spirit of his mouth, and shall destroy with the brightness of his coming." In plain words, truth confronts the lie, and light destroys darkness. This is the clearest description of the Battle of Armageddon. There is no need for nuclear bombs, planes, tanks or armed forces; this is God's judgment upon the nations unto destruction—it is God-made, not manmade.

Wrath of the Lamb

When we read of God's judgments being executed upon the world, something very strange happens: "And the kings of the earth, and the great men, and the rich men, and the chief captains, and the mighty men, and every bondman, and every free man, hid themselves in the dens and in the rocks of the mountains; And said to the mountains and rocks, Fall on us, and hide us from the face of him that sitteth on the throne, and from the wrath of the Lamb" (Revelation 6:15-16). What are they afraid of? "The wrath of the Lamb." The world will no longer see Jesus, the Lamb of God sacrificed for their sins, the only way to escape from the wrath to come. They will see the other side of the Lamb of God: now it is too late to be saved, forever and ever. There is no repentance or crying for forgiveness; they are just hiding behind the materials, the rocks and mountains, from which they extracted the minerals to build their modern society. They outright and blatantly rejected the Creator and His provision for salvation.

No More Repentance

This is especially highlighted in Revelation 9:20-21: "And the rest of the men which were not killed by these plagues yet repented not of the works of their hands, that they should not worship devils, and idols of gold, and silver, and brass, and stone, and of wood: which neither can see, nor hear, nor walk: Neither repented they of their murders, nor of their sorceries, nor of their fornication, nor of their thefts."

Total reliance upon materialism is the great sin of the endtimes. People of all walks of life have created their own little idols by which they oppose the Creator, the living God of heaven and earth, the Lord Jesus Christ.

The end result? "Neither repented they...."

Furthermore, in chapter 16, verses 9 and 11 we read, "And men were scorched with great heat, and blasphemed the name of God, which hath power over these plagues: and they repented not to give him glory...And blasphemed the God of heaven because of their pains and their sores, and repented not of their deeds." In other words, they recognized that this is not an enemy who is sending nuclear missiles against them, but this judgment is of God. There is no room for true repentance; instead, they blasphemed God.

The World against Zion

All the mighty powers on earth, which had so arrogantly lifted themselves up with lofty words—"We are the greatest...We are the best"—will now meet Him of whom we read:

Joel 3:16: "The LORD also shall roar out of Zion, and utter his voice from Jerusalem; and the heavens and the earth shall shake: but the LORD will be the hope of his people, and the strength of the children of Israel."

Very plainly, there is judgment upon the nations, but hope and strength for the children of Israel. We note that He does not roar *out of heaven*, but *out of Zion*. This geographic reference surely points to the universal importance of Zion—Jerusalem.

Jerusalem's Future

Finally, the question regarding Judah and Zion will be

settled:

Joel 3:17: "So shall ye know that I am the LORD your God dwelling in Zion, my holy mountain: then shall Jerusalem be holy, and there shall no strangers pass through her any more."

(See) Isaiah 35:8; Nahum 1:15; Revelation 21:27

The Europeans and Asians, Africans, Americans and Australians, will be banished from Jerusalem: "no strangers [shall] pass through her any more."

Now the time has come for the initiation of the thousand-year kingdom of peace, beginning with Jerusalem:

Joel 3:18: "And it shall come to pass in that day, that the mountains shall drop down new wine, and the hills shall flow with milk, and all the rivers of Judah shall flow with waters, and a fountain shall come forth of the house of the LORD, and shall water the valley of Shittim."

(See) Ezekiel 47:1; Zechariah 13:1; Revelation 22:1

Egypt and Edom Judged

Two more enemies, however, have to be dealt with in a special way:

Joel 3:19: "Egypt shall be a desolation, and Edom shall be a desolate wilderness, for the violence against the children of Judah, because they have shed innocent blood in their land."

51

Ezekiel 29 also reports of the judgment of Egypt: "And I will make the land of Egypt desolate in the midst of the countries that are desolate, and her cities among the cities that are laid waste shall be desolate forty years: and I will scatter the Egyptians among the nations, and will disperse them through the countries" (verse 12).

Judgment against Edom is detailed by the prophet Obadiah: "For thy violence against thy brother Jacob shame shall cover thee, and thou shalt be cut off for ever...But thou shouldest not have looked on the day of thy brother in the day that he became a stranger; neither shouldest thou have rejoiced over the children of Judah in the day of their destruction; neither shouldest thou have spoken proudly in the day of distress" (verses 10, 12).

Judah and Jerusalem Cleansed

Now, God turns to the Jewish people with this solemn proclamation:

Joel 3:20: "But Judah shall dwell for ever, and Jerusalem from generation to generation."

This is not an automatic thing; it is the result of God's unspeakable grace for His people and His city.

Joel 3:21: "For I will cleanse their blood that I have not cleansed: for the LORD dwelleth in Zion."

Our Glorious Hope

What a marvelous book we have at our disposal. The Bible testifies quite plainly that Jesus is the only way to salvation, and that "Salvation is of the Jews." Also, He is coming again; His return is guaranteed with His statement, "I will come again."

The prophet Joel gives a compact message to Israel and to the world. Israel is the beginning of salvation, and Israel is also the ending—which means the return of Jesus, the King of the Jews, the Messiah of Israel and the Savior of the world.

Conclusion

As believers in the Lord Jesus Christ, we can rejoice with Judah and Jerusalem, because we are the recipients of unspeakable grace through our Savior. We are not saved based on our merits, but it is grace upon grace, and nothing more.

I close this study with the testimony of the songwriter: "Amazing grace, how sweet the sound, that saved a wretch like me; I once was lost, but now am found, was blind but now I see."

Zephaniah

Jehovah Conceals

Chapter 3   79

ZEPHANIAH

Book of the Bible	God's Directly Spoken Words (%)	Prophecy %*	Significant Names Listed in Each Book						
			Judah	Israel	Ephraim	Jerusalem	Zion	Heathen	Samaria
Hosea	93.32	56	15	44	37	0	0	0	6
Joel	57.70	68	6	3	0	6	7	5	0
Amos	80.95	58	4	30	0	2	2	1	5
Obadiah	97.69	81	1	1	1	2	2	4	1
Jonah	7.39	10	0	0	0	0	0	0	0
Micah	44.88	70	4	12	0	8	9	1	3
Nahum	40.30	74	1	1	0	0	0	0	0
Habakkuk	47.84	41	0	0	0	0	0	2	0
Zephaniah	96.92	89	3	4	0	4	2	1	0
Haggai	67.61	39	4	0	0	0	0	1	0
Zechariah	77.38	69	22	5	3	41	8	5	0
Malachi	93.80	56	3	5	0	2	0	2	0

* Percentage of book as prophecy according to *Tim LaHaye Prophecy Study Bible*

Introduction to Zephaniah

Zephaniah can be translated with the words "Hidden of the Lord" or "Jehovah Conceals." He is a descendant from the royal house of Judah, and very determinedly directs his message against Judah.

For 8 days in March or April, Jews celebrate Passover. Israel remembers the day when they were redeemed from the slavery of Egypt. God gave the instruction to His people through Moses, "And this day shall be unto you for a memorial; and ye shall keep it a feast to the LORD throughout your generations; ye shall keep it a feast by an ordinance for ever" (Exodus 12:14). Until this day, almost 3,500 years later, Jews all over the world celebrate Passover, a feast to remember how God had redeemed His people from slavery, based on the substance of the blood of a lamb.

When we read Scripture, we note over and again that this event is recounted by the prophets and the apostles. Hebrews 11:28-29 recalls this mighty event in Israel's history: "Through faith he kept the passover, and the sprinkling of blood, lest he that destroyed the firstborn should touch them. By faith they passed through the Red sea as by dry land: which the Egyptians assaying to do were drowned."

In the New Testament, something different is observed: not the remembering of the exodus, but the memory of the ultimate sacrifice, the perfect Lamb of God. We read the instruction for the Church in 1 Corinthians 11:23-26: "For I have received of the Lord that which also I delivered unto you, That the Lord Jesus the same night in which he was betrayed took bread: And when he had given thanks, he brake it, and said, Take, eat: this is my body, which is broken for you: this do in remembrance of me. After the same manner also he took the cup, when he had supped, saying, This cup is the new testament in my blood: this do ye, as oft as ye drink it, in remembrance of me. For as often as ye eat this bread, and drink this cup, ye do show the Lord's death till he come." The central point of the Lord's Table is for it to be a feast of memory and our demonstration to "show the Lord's death till he come." Without death, there is no resurrection; without resurrection, our faith is in vain. We remember Jesus Christ and Him crucified as a total, absolute and once-and-for-all sacrifice, when we partake of the broken bread and the wine.

Chapter 1

Introduction

While the prophet Zephaniah specifically addresses the house of Judah, he does not fail to include the whole world. This is evident in chapter 3, verse 8: "...for my determination is to gather the nations, that I may assemble the kingdoms, to pour upon them mine indignation, even all my fierce anger: for all the earth shall be devoured with the fire of my jealousy."

Who is Zephaniah? Contrary to most of the other prophets, Zephaniah goes into detail regarding his identity, which determines that he is of the royal house of Judah. The name Zephaniah means, "Jehovah conceals, protects, and hides."

Total Destruction

Zephaniah 1:1: "The word of the LORD which came unto Zephaniah the son of Cushi, the son of Gedaliah, the son of Amariah, the son of Hizkiah, in the days of Josiah the son of Amon, king of Judah."

(See) 2 Kings 22:1; Jeremiah 1:2

Then without further warning, and with no introduction or explanation, he proclaims irreversible destruction upon the land of Judah:

Zephaniah 1:2-3: "I will utterly consume all things from off the land, saith the LORD. 3 I will consume man and beast; I will consume the fowls of the heaven, and the fishes of the sea, and the stumblingblocks with the wicked; and I will cut off man from off the land, saith the LORD."

(See) Genesis 6:7; Jeremiah 7:20; Ezekiel 33:27-28

There is no grace, no compassion, no future; total and absolute destruction is clearly proclaimed.

Judah and Jerusalem

Zephaniah 1:4-5: "I will also stretch out mine hand upon Judah, and upon all the inhabitants of Jerusalem; and I will cut off the remnant of Baal from this place, and the name of the Chemarims with the priests; 5 And them that worship the host of heaven upon the housetops; and them that worship and that swear by the LORD, and that swear by Malcham;"

(See) 1 Kings 11:33; Hosea 10:5

The royal tribe of Israel, Judah, and God's residence, Jerusalem, are mentioned in the same line with Baal, Chemarims, and Malcham—Baal, the god of the heathen; Chemarims, the idolatrous priests; and Malcham, an idol. Quite apparently, Israel had erased the border between good and evil, between holy and profane, between the divine and the occult, between Jews and Gentiles.

61

Baal and Idols

This truly reminds us of our time. The distinction between following Christ and following any religion is being speedily erased. "God bless this and that" has become common language, is considered politically appropriate, and is supported by Churchianity.

The mixture is evident from the words, "that swear by the Lord, and that swear by Malcham." Apparently, they were teaching that there is only one true God, yet there are many ways by which we may reach Him. Here we are reminded of John 14:6, "Jesus saith unto him, I am the way, the truth, and the life: no man cometh unto the Father, but by me."

The rejection of the God of Israel is evident from verse 6:

Zephaniah 1:6: "And them that are turned back from the LORD; and those that have not sought the LORD, nor enquired for him."

(See) Isaiah 1:4; 9:13; Hosea 7:10

These were people who once believed in the Lord and inquired of Him, but no longer. Now the time has come when prayer will not help. Actually, God rejects it.

Truth Mixed with Lies

Zephaniah 1:7: "Hold thy peace at the presence of the Lord GOD: for the day of the LORD is at hand: for the LORD hath prepared a sacrifice, he hath bid his guests."

(See) Isaiah 34:6; Jeremiah 46:10; Habakkuk 2:20; Zechariah 2:13

The time has come for total judgment. We must take careful notice that the prophet leaves nothing out; he enumerates every detail in the next verse. The political leaders, the princes, are mentioned:

Zephaniah 1:8: "And it shall come to pass in the day of the LORD'S sacrifice, that I will punish the princes, and the king's children, and all such as are clothed with strange apparel."

(See) Isaiah 24:21

What is this strange apparel? There is a difference of opinion among scholars. But one thing is clear: it is apparel which is misused, and apparently does not serve to identify the real person. The clothing designed for women, worn by men, or vice versa, falls in the category of "strange apparel."

Zephaniah 1:9: "In the same day also will I punish all those that leap on the threshold, which fill their masters' houses with violence and deceit."

(See) Jeremiah 5:27; Amos 3:10

Here we are reminded of 1 Samuel 5, when the Philistines took the Ark of the Covenant into their idol temple. In verses 4-5 we read: "And when they arose early on the morrow morning, behold, Dagon was fallen upon his face to the ground before the ark of the LORD; and the head of Dagon and both the palms of his hands were cut off upon the threshold; only the stump of Dagon was left to him. Therefore neither the priests of Dagon, nor any that come into Dagon's house, tread on the threshold of Dagon in Ashdod unto this day." This superstition (not to tread on the threshold) had taken hold of Israel. But superstition did not cover up their dishonesty, violence and deceit. Even until this day, we find those who practice superstition; for example, the bridegroom will carry his bride over the threshold to avoid "bad luck."

Jerusalem Searched

Again, the prophet turns to Jerusalem in particular:

Zephaniah 1:10-12: "And it shall come to pass in that day, saith the LORD, that there shall be the noise of a cry from the fish gate, and an howling from the second, and a great crashing from the hills. 11 Howl, ye inhabitants of Maktesh, for all the merchant people are cut down; all they that bear silver are cut off. 12 And it shall come to pass at that time, that I will search Jerusalem with candles, and punish the men that are settled on their lees: that say in their heart, The LORD will not do good, neither will he do evil."

(See) 2 Chronicles 33:14; Nehemiah 3:3; Job 21:15; Psalm 10:11, 13; James 5:1; Revelation 18:11-12

Judgment has come, that's for sure. The fish gate is not

clearly identifiable in our days. It is assumed that it was in the western part of Jerusalem, on the way to the Mediterranean. However, that part of the city, the fish gate, is not isolated—the other part of Jerusalem is included. "From the second" is translated by Luther with the words, "the other part of the city." This simply means, no exception.

Commerce Condemned

"Howl, ye inhabitants of Maktesh" (verse 11). Maktesh can be translated in today's language as "Market Street" or "Main Street." Again, we see nothing and no one is exempt; judgment is at hand. This is highlighted in verse 12: "I will search Jerusalem with candles." There is no hiding or escape: even the very religious ones are exposed, in spite of their apparent knowledge of the Lord.

Zephaniah 1:13: "Therefore their goods shall become a booty, and their houses a desolation: they shall also build houses, but not inhabit them; and they shall plant vineyards, but not drink the wine thereof."

(See) Deuteronomy 28:30; Amos 5:11; Micah 6:15

The Day of the Lord

When you build and do not inhabit, when you plant and do not harvest, then the end has come. Note, however, that this is not limited to the land of Judah, or the city of Jerusalem, because the Day of the Lord is much more. As we read in the next verse, it includes planet Earth.

Zephaniah 1:14-16: "The great day of the LORD is near, it is near, and hasteth greatly, even the voice of the day of the LORD: the mighty man shall cry there bitterly. 15 That day is a day of wrath, a day of trouble and distress, a day of wasteness and desolation, a day of darkness and gloominess, a day of clouds and thick darkness, 16 A day of the trumpet and alarm against the fenced cities, and against the high towers."

(See) Jeremiah 30:7; 4:19; 8:16; Hosea 5:8; Joel 2:1, 11; Amos 3:6; Malachi 4:5; Revelation 6:17

There is no doubt that this speaks of the Great Tribulation. But at the time of Zephaniah, judgment upon the house of Judah and the city of Jerusalem was the immediate issue.

The testimony of the destruction is recorded for us by various prophets, such as Ezra and Nehemiah. Jesus spoke of it as well, in Matthew 24:21: "For then shall be great tribulation, such as was not since the beginning of the world to this time, no, nor ever shall be." We know that judgment upon the land of Israel, and Jerusalem in particular, had come true many times. Some historians speak of Jerusalem being destroyed 14 times. But the final judgment is yet to come.

God's Wrath

The exhibition of the wrath of God is something that will include all of the earth. We will see it confirmed as we continue this study. The combined message to Judah and Israel is unmistakably clear. The reasons are enumerated and the sin is exposed. It makes no difference how strong the defense is, whether it is "fenced cities" or "high towers"; when God's judgment comes, there is no power to command it to halt.

The End of Judah

Zephaniah 1:17-18: "And I will bring distress upon men, that they shall walk like blind men, because they have sinned against the LORD: and their blood shall be poured out as dust, and their flesh as the dung. 18 Neither their silver nor their gold shall be able to deliver them in the day of the LORD'S wrath; but the whole land shall be devoured by the fire of his jealousy: for he shall make even a speedy riddance of all them that dwell in the land."

(See) Ezekiel 7:19; Zephaniah 3:8

This is the total destruction of all who oppose the Lord. There is no more mercy or grace, only judgment. Neither silver nor gold can deliver.

However, at the time of this prophecy, there was no reason for them to be alarmed; they were accumulating riches. The economy was doing just fine, and their investments were growing. Because they were religious, they thought, why would the Lord do anything that we deem unreasonable? "The Lord will not do good, neither will he do evil."

The Coming False Peace

Today, such religious philosophy has been well established within Churchianity. Although signs of the times are everywhere, we still hear positive messages proclaimed from thousands of pulpits, week-after-week. We note that television and radio programs, which promise to be very beneficial to the listeners, are prospering. Christian bookstores are filled with titles that give instructions to the reader on how to attain more happiness, more joy, more security, and more possessions. That is the great tragedy of our times. Collectively, the church and the world have determined to work toward a peaceful and secure world, but without remembering the price paid—the death on the cross of Jesus Christ our Lord, which we are admonished to remember until He comes. Only when He comes will true peace be established—He is the only One who paid the price for peace.

Never must we attempt to degrade or cheapen the peace of God with military victories or governmental authority, outside the accomplished work of Jesus Christ on Calvary's cross.

Many think that God will unilaterally pardon all sins. After all, the Bible says, "For God so loved the world." But, if that were the case, then the atonement of Jesus would be nothing more than a mockery. Jesus had to die to pay for our peace. Therefore, let us reconfirm our faith and determination to follow the Lord and proclaim Him crucified. That is the only way to remain in Him, "And the peace of God, which passeth all understanding, shall keep your hearts and minds through Christ Jesus" (Philippians 4:7). That is my prayer for you.

The royal tribe of Judah was self-assured; they believed in a secure future. After all, they were the chosen tribe; the keystone to a prosperous, secure and peaceful Israel. But, as we can see in this chapter of Zephaniah, they had not counted on the holiness of God.

Chapter 2

Introduction

Studying prophetic Scripture is vitally important in our days. The prophets proclaim severe judgment upon the people of Israel in general and Judah in particular, yet the Gentiles are not excluded.

What is evident is that the signs of the times for the world are definitely negative. However, we must not overlook the fact that the majority of people in the industrialized world are still doing rather well.

The Economist, 1 June 2013 headlines the issue, "Towards the end of poverty." A graph shows that in 1990, almost 2 billion people were living on $1.25 per day or less. For 2010, that number went to just over 1 billion people; that means from 43 percent poverty in 1990, to 21 percent in 2010. When things improve for the betterment of mankind, then there is no reason for humanity to seek the countenance of God. That, doubtless, was the case during the times of the prophets in the land of Israel.

In our study of the other prophets, we noticed how horribly Israel treated their poor (see Amos 2:6-7; 4:1; 5:11, etc.). When the judgment of God comes, riches will no longer help. We saw this in chapter 1, verse 18: "Neither their silver nor their gold shall be able to deliver them...." This warning is also given in the New Testament: "Go to now, ye rich men, weep and howl for your miseries that shall come upon you. Your riches are corrupted, and your garments are motheaten. Your gold and silver is cankered; and the rust of them shall be a witness against you, and shall eat your flesh as it were fire. Ye have heaped treasure together for the last days" (James 5:1-3). Note particularly the words, "the last days." The obsession for more possessions is playing a major role in these end times, particularly in the developed world.

Invitation for Change

Zephaniah 2:1-2: "Gather yourselves together, yea, gather together, O nation not desired; 2 Before the decree bring forth, before the day pass as the chaff, before the fierce anger of the LORD come upon you, before the day of the LORD'S anger come upon you."

(See) 2 Kings 23:26; Joel 2:16

Who is this nation not desired? It is Israel collectively, and Judah in particular. Why should they gather themselves together? Because God is giving them the opportunity to repent before judgment comes. Here something marvelous is being said; namely, God's wonderful grace and mercy breaks through in the midst of judgment. Note the word "before" is listed four times. What are they to do *before* the Lord's fierce anger?

Zephaniah 2:3: "Seek ye the LORD, all ye meek of the earth, which have wrought his judgment; seek righteousness, seek meekness: it may be ye shall be hid in the day of the LORD'S anger."

(See) Psalm 76:9; Joel 2:14; Amos 5:6, 15

Quite apparently, there was a remnant within the land of Judah who was admonished to seek the Lord, to seek righteousness, to seek meekness. These are the ones that would escape the destructive judgment that was to come upon the land.

Gaza, Ashdod and Ashkelon

The next verse reminds us of the place often in the media:

Zephaniah 2:4: "For Gaza shall be forsaken, and Ashkelon a desolation: they shall drive out Ashdod at the noon day, and Ekron shall be rooted up."

(See) Jeremiah 6:4; Amos 1:7-8; Zechariah 9:5-7

Gaza is one of the oldest cities in the world. Biblically speaking, she has been associated with Israel's fiercest enemies, the Philistines. The cities of Ashkelon and Ashdod have been newly established by the State of Israel in the same location. But the ancient Gaza, Ashkelon, Ashdod and Ekron were destroyed. The desolation and destruction are testified to by ancient ruins now uncovered by archeologists.

Zephaniah 2:5: "Woe unto the inhabitants of the sea coast, the nation of the Cherethites! the word of the LORD is against you; O Canaan, the land of the Philistines, I will even destroy thee, that there shall be no inhabitant."

(See) Joshua 13:3; Ezekiel 25:16

The cities on the Mediterranean coast experienced the fulfillment. The land was deserted with few inhabitants. This changed when the Jews returned to the land of Israel and rebuilt the country. Tel Aviv for example, was established in 1909. The city was literally built on sand dunes. In 2015, the Tel Aviv metropolitan area was listed with a population of approximately 3,460,346. The virtually miraculous success of the Jews in the land of Israel has become the envy of the Arab world. Israel's success has also contributed toward the often unexplained fierce hatred of the Jewish people by Arab nationalists, and lately Europe.

The Remnant

In spite of severe judgment, in spite of total destruction and desolation, there is a remnant:

Zephaniah 2:6-7: "And the sea coast shall be dwellings and cottages for shepherds, and folds for flocks. 7 And the coast shall be for the remnant of the house of Judah; they shall feed thereupon: in the houses of Ashkelon shall they lie down in the evening: for the LORD their God shall visit them, and turn away their captivity."

(See) Psalm 126:4; Isaiah 11:11; 17:2; Jeremiah 23:3; Ezekiel 39:25; Micah 4:10; Luke 1:68

Ashkelon is a modern-day miracle; it is a thriving, prosperous city. Driving to Ashkelon from Tel Aviv or

Jerusalem, one is confronted with another miracle; namely, the restoration and resurrection of agriculture. Before the Jews came, the land of Israel was nothing more than a semi-desert, mostly unsuitable for agriculture. Today, anyone passing through can testify: "...This land that was desolate is become like the garden of Eden; and the waste and desolate and ruined cities are become fenced, and are inhabited" (Ezekiel 36:35).

Ammon and Moab Judged

Zephaniah 2:8-9: "I have heard the reproach of Moab, and the revilings of the children of Ammon, whereby they have reproached my people, and magnified themselves against their border. 9 Therefore as I live, saith the LORD of hosts, the God of Israel, Surely Moab shall be as Sodom, and the children of Ammon as Gomorrah, even the breeding of nettles, and saltpits, and a perpetual desolation: the residue of my people shall spoil them, and the remnant of my people shall possess them."

(See) Isaiah 15:1; Jeremiah 48:27; 49:1; Ezekiel 25:8; Amos 1:13; 2:1

When reading these verses, we are surprised at an apparent change in God's declaration. Chapter two started with the degrading statement, "O nation not desired," meaning Israel. But now God pronounces judgment against Israel's neighbors. Why? Because nations such as Moab and Ammon had no right to reproach God's chosen. Three times we read the words "my people" in these two verses. God is watching over His own. He will fulfill

His promises in due time. He does not permit others to judge Israel. Actually, He condemns those who rejoice over Israel's misfortune, although Israel had brought the horrible judgment upon themselves.

Zephaniah 2:10-11: "This shall they have for their pride, because they have reproached and magnified themselves against the people of the LORD of hosts. 11 The LORD will be terrible unto them: for he will famish all the gods of the earth; and men shall worship him, every one from his place, even all the isles of the heathen."

(See) Genesis 10:5; 49:10; Psalm 2:8; 22:27; Isaiah 2:2-3; 11:9-10; Malachi 1:11; John 4:21

Ethiopia Judged

Zephaniah 2:12: "Ye Ethiopians also, ye shall be slain by my sword."

(See) Isaiah 18:1

Ethiopia plays a significant role in the Bible. The queen of Sheba came to King Solomon, and confessed that the God of Israel is the God of heaven and earth. Later, we read of the Ethiopian finance minister, who came to the temple in Jerusalem to worship. On his way back to Ethiopia, the Spirit of God caused Philip to preach unto him that Jesus Christ is the Son of God. The Ethiopian's heart was opened; he received the truth and asked, "What doth hinder me to be baptized?" (Acts 8:36).

"And Philip said, If thou believest with all thine heart, thou mayest. And he answered and said, I believe that Jesus Christ is the Son of God" (verse 37). There is a clear relationship between Ethiopia and Israel. Even in modern times, thousands of Ethiopians have been recognized as Jews and have received Israeli citizenship.

Assyria Judged

Another nation mentioned is Assyria. Here is what we read:

Zephaniah 2:13-15: "And he will stretch out his hand against the north, and destroy Assyria; and will make Nineveh a desolation, and dry like a wilderness. 14 And flocks shall lie down in the midst of her, all the beasts of the nations: both the cormorant and the bittern shall lodge in the upper lintels of it; their voice shall sing in the windows; desolation shall be in the thresholds: for he shall uncover the cedar work. 15 This is the rejoicing city that dwelt carelessly, that said in her heart, I am, and there is none beside me: how is she become a desolation, a place for beasts to lie down in! every one that passeth by her shall hiss, and wag his hand."

(See) Isaiah 13:21; 47:8; Revelation 18:7

Destructive judgment has been experienced by Israel's northern neighbors for millennia. Even in our days, Lebanon, Syria and Iraq are under judgment. The epitome of rebellion against God is exposed with their own words, "I am, and there is none beside me." This also reminds us of the church of the Laodiceans, where she exclaims, "I am rich, and increased with goods, and have need of nothing" (Revelation 3:17a).

Jesus Builds His Church

What a fitting picture of our days. Churchianity is suffocating in riches and luxuries, while members of the true Church are oppressed, disregarded, rejected, mocked, and often persecuted. I take this opportunity to call your attention to our brothers and sisters who are in deep tribulation and extreme persecution in countries such as Iraq, Sudan, Afghanistan, and recently, in Syria. But we must not overlook what our Lord said, "I will build my church." He has His children in the midst of chaos in many places on earth. From confidential sources, we receive reports that many fear for their lives.

Unfortunately, the general attitude is that the Church is a visible manifestation in the world. Subsequently, it is believed that the Church is somehow limited to Christianized Europe and the new countries. I venture to say that this is a great mistake. While Christian activity is monopolized by the European (Western) world, particularly by the USA, that in no way means the Church is headquartered there. His Church is global and alive and well on all five continents. It is the Church Jesus Himself built; the real Church is independent of the nations of the world.

Let's assume all churches the world over were closed tomorrow; that all mission organizations, missionaries, radio, television, publishing houses, etc. ceased their work. Would that change His Church? I don't think so. While all these works are important and we must do our utmost to propagate the Gospel of Jesus Christ to people everywhere, never must we be high-minded and presume that God depends on us. When the Rapture takes place, it may well be that a relatively small number will be raptured from the so-called "Christian world"; and, surprisingly, great numbers from the Muslim, Hindu, and communist world.

After the true Church is gone, religious unity will be established among Churchianity, Muslims, Hindus, Buddhists, etc. That will add to the foundation for the fulfillment of Revelation 13:8: "And all that dwell upon the earth shall worship him [the Antichrist]."

Today, everything is in full swing of preparation. Politicians, bankers, financial managers, and global economists are feverishly working to establish a unified world; one that is controlled, regulated, and readily prepared for one person to rule—Antichrist.

Chapter 3

Introduction

The target of Zephaniah's prophetic message is the house of Judah. Mercilessly, the prophet exposes the horrendous sins of the princes, judges, prophets, and priests. Yet, the thundering message of the coming judgment is ignored, "...But they rose early, and corrupted all their doings."

Nevertheless, the rest of the world is not exempt. Verse 8 is directed toward the nations, the kingdoms, "for all the earth." This is consistent with all the prophets; while their message is primarily focused on either the house of Judah or the ten-tribe rebellious Israel, the nations of the world are not spared. The distinct difference, however, lies in the fact that there is no hope for the nations, yet in the midst of the most horrendous judgment, there is hope for Israel.

We see this beginning with verse 9. It is an act of grace for His chosen people. It does not say, they will do this or that, but we read, "For then will I turn to the people a pure language." This is the work of the grace of God for the descendants of Abraham.

The presence of the Lord among His people is emphasized, "The LORD thy God in the midst of thee is mighty; he will save, he will rejoice over thee with joy; he will rest in his love, he will joy over thee with singing" (verse 17).

79

The end of Israel's oppression, suffering, and persecution, but also of their disobedience is vividly expressed in the last verse, "At that time will I bring you again, even in the time that I gather you: for I will make you a name and a praise among all people of the earth, when I turn back your captivity before your eyes, saith the LORD" (verse 20).

We can be assured that this word awaits fulfillment. Although the Jews have been returning to the land of their fathers, beginning with the first massive immigration in 1882, they are not "a praise among all people of the earth." When we observe the often heard and read anti-Israel rhetoric, "The Jews are no different from any other people on earth," then we have the confirmation that the Word of God, His prophetic Word, is accurate. What He promised many millennia ago will be fulfilled to its smallest detail in due time. Hatred for Israel will be turned to praise; subsequently, a tremendous change will be experienced by all Gentile nations of the world.

Jerusalem Polluted

Zephaniah 3:1: "Woe to her that is filthy and polluted, to the oppressing city!"

(See) Jeremiah 6:6; Ezekiel 23:30

These are brutal words, "filthy...polluted...oppressing." But, these words clearly define Jerusalem in her spiritual state. Of course, this could also be said about any other city in the world, but Jerusalem is special: it is the only city on earth that God chose to have a sanctuary built where His name would dwell. In the fullness of time, in accordance with His prophetic Word, He sent His Son Jesus to the city of Jerusalem, where He was taken and crucified. Yet we read the last four words of the prophet Joel, "for the Lord dwelleth in Zion."

It's the same city Jesus speaks of in Matthew 23, pronouncing His eightfold "woes" against the city and the religious authority: "O Jerusalem, Jerusalem, thou that killest the prophets, and stonest them which are sent unto thee, how often would I have gathered thy children together, even as a hen gathereth her chickens under her wings, and ye would not!" (Matthew 23:37).

Princes, Judges, Prophets and Priests Polluted

Zephaniah 3:2: "She obeyed not the voice; she received not correction; she trusted not in the LORD; she drew not near to her God."

(See) Psalm 78:22; Jeremiah 5:3; 7:23-28; 22:21

This Scripture clearly details four sins of negligence: 1. not obeying the voice of God; 2. not receiving correction; 3. not trusting in the Lord; and 4. not drawing near to God.

Zephaniah 3:3-4: "Her princes within her are roaring lions; her judges are evening wolves; they gnaw not the bones till the morrow. 4 Her prophets are light and treacherous

81

persons: her priests have polluted the sanctuary, they have done violence to the law."

(See) Jeremiah 5:6; Ezekiel 22:26

Here we have the princes, the political authority; the judges, the executors of the law; the prophets, who are supposed to make God's will known to the people; and the priests, who should stand for the people before God—all polluted.

Ezekiel also exposes the sins of the priests: "Her priests have violated my law, and have profaned mine holy things: they have put no difference between the holy and profane, neither have they showed difference between the unclean and the clean, and have hid their eyes from my sabbaths, and I am profaned among them" (Ezekiel 22:26).

Does that mean they had ceased to declare the Word of God and did not implement God's law? Not really. The princes and the judges were doing their job, but in a corrupt manner. The prophets continued to prophesy and the priests continued their service in the sanctuary, but sin had darkened them to such an extent that they were no longer capable of distinguishing between the law of God and their own interpretation. They actually thought they were doing the right thing. Everything was going smoothly. There was prosperity and peace, but there was also deceit.

Verse 5 makes it clear that the law was present:

Zephaniah 3:5: "The just LORD is in the midst thereof; he will not do iniquity: every morning doth he bring his judgment to light, he faileth not; but the unjust knoweth no shame."

(See) Deuteronomy 32:4; Psalm 99:3-4

When the priests and prophets read the law, the very truth was present in their midst. But religious practice without true faith in the living God can only bring about confusion and judgment in the end.

Nations Destroyed

Zephaniah 3:6: "I have cut off the nations: their towers are desolate; I made their streets waste, that none passeth by: their cities are destroyed, so that there is no man, that there is none inhabitant."

(See) Leviticus 26:31; Isaiah 6:11; Jeremiah 9:12; Zechariah 7:14; Matthew 23:38

Corruption Continues

God gives testimony through His prophet Zephaniah about what He had done to other nations, with the hope that they would repent:

Zephaniah 3:7: "I said, Surely thou wilt fear me, thou wilt receive instruction; so their dwelling should not be cut off, howsoever I punished them: but they rose early, and corrupted all their doings."

83

(See) Genesis 6:12; Job 36:10; Hosea 9:9

These seven verses speak of those who outright and consciously rejected God's sovereign rulership, His holiness, and His law. For such people, no hope is given, and no future is promised. Utter destruction is the end.

Waiting for the Lord

Zephaniah 3:8: "Therefore wait ye upon me, saith the LORD, until the day that I rise up to the prey: for my determination is to gather the nations, that I may assemble the kingdoms, to pour upon them mine indignation, even all my fierce anger: for all the earth shall be devoured with the fire of my jealousy."

(See) Psalm 27:14; Proverbs 20:22; Isaiah 30:18; Joel 3:2

This speaks of the final judgment, the end of the Great Tribulation, when God will gather all the nations of the world for one purpose: condemnation. In Revelation 16:16 we read: "And he gathered them together into a place called in the Hebrew tongue Armageddon." That is the time when the Lord Himself shall return to execute judgment upon the nations of the world, and in particular, their leader, the Antichrist: "And then shall that Wicked be revealed, whom the Lord shall consume with the spirit of his mouth, and shall destroy with the brightness of his coming" (2 Thessalonians 2:8).

The Work of Amazing Grace

Zephaniah 3:9: "For then will I turn to the people a pure language, that they may all call upon the name of the LORD, to serve him with one consent."

(See) Psalm 22:27; 86:9; Isaiah 19:18; 57:19; Habakkuk 2:14

When the Great Tribulation has ended, when Armageddon is past, the nations of the world will then speak truth. This does not mean a new kind of language, or, as some scholars say, Hebrew. Actually, the opposite is true: the people who are saved during the Great Tribulation are described in Revelation 7:9: "...a great multitude, which no man could number, of all nations, and kindreds, and people, and tongues, stood before the throne, and before the Lamb, clothed with white robes, and palms in their hands." These are believers from all the nations and languages (tongues). However, they do not belong to the Church, i.e. the Bride of Christ. The Church will be raptured before the Great Tribulation begins. This is absolutely necessary; otherwise, the Great Tribulation cannot take place. Darkness cannot overwhelm light; and light, as we all know, is stronger than darkness. The true Church is the light of the world.

Zephaniah 3:10: "From beyond the rivers of Ethiopia my suppliants, even the daughter of my dispersed, shall bring mine offering."

(See) Psalm 68:31; Isaiah 18:1; Malachi 1:11; Acts 8:27

85

Here Ethiopia is mentioned again. We already noticed that this country has a special relationship with Israel. The queen of Ethiopia came to witness the glory of Solomon. Later, the Ethiopian eunuch went to the temple in Jerusalem to seek the God of Israel. But he found more on his way back: He found Jesus Christ, the Son of God. The man was baptized and returned to Ethiopia, testifying that Jesus is Lord and Savior.

Pride Eliminated

Zephaniah 3:11: "In that day shalt thou not be ashamed for all thy doings, wherein thou hast transgressed against me: for then I will take away out of the midst of thee them that rejoice in thy pride, and thou shalt no more be haughty because of my holy mountain."

(See) Isaiah 2:12, 5:15; 11:9; 45:17; 54:4; 56:7; Ezekiel 20:40; Joel 2:26-27; Matthew 3:9

This is amazing grace, undeserved favor—sin will be forgiven, transgression pardoned. But there is more; those who persistently "rejoice in pride" will be taken out by the Lord. Only a remnant remains. Who are these people?

Zephaniah 3:12: "I will also leave in the midst of thee an afflicted and poor people, and they shall trust in the name of the LORD."

(See) Isaiah 14:32; 50:10; 57:15; Matthew 5:3; Luke 6:20

Jerusalem Renewed

In verse 2, we emphasized that Jerusalem did not trust in the Lord, but now these people "shall trust in the name of the Lord." That will be the time when truth has taken hold of the people of Israel. They will be converted, their sins forgiven, and will now exemplify the new life:

Zephaniah 3:13: "The remnant of Israel shall not do iniquity, nor speak lies; neither shall a deceitful tongue be found in their mouth: for they shall feed and lie down, and none shall make them afraid."

(See) Isaiah 10:20-22; Ezekiel 34:13-15; Micah 4:7; Revelation 14:5

Jerusalem is now viewed from the opposite direction—no longer "filthy and polluted."

Zephaniah 3:14: "Sing, O daughter of Zion; shout, O Israel; be glad and rejoice with all the heart, O daughter of Jerusalem."

(See) Psalm 14:7; Zechariah 9:9

From God's view, they are encouraged to rejoice, but from the world's view, Zion, Israel, and Jerusalem have become the great stumbling stone for all people. Zionism is not a popular word among the nations, and Israel is a difficult issue for the leaders of the world. Jerusalem is the most divisive city for all the nations of planet Earth. But when these prophecies are fulfilled, Zionism, Israel and Jerusalem will rejoice.

The Presence of the Lord

Zephaniah 3:15: "The LORD hath taken away thy judgments, he hath cast out thine enemy: the king of Israel, even the LORD, is in the midst of thee: thou shalt not see evil any more."

(See) Isaiah 54:14; Ezekiel 37:26-28; 48:35; John 1:49; Revelation 21:3

We read in verse 5 that the Lord was in their midst, but this time as the Savior, Redeemer and King.

Zephaniah 3:16-17: "In that day it shall be said to Jerusalem, Fear thou not: and to Zion, Let not thine hands be slack. 17 The LORD thy God in the midst of thee is mighty; he will save, he will rejoice over thee with joy; he will rest in his love, he will joy over thee with singing."

(See) Isaiah 25:9; 35:3-4; 62:5; 63:1

Here we see the fulfillment of the prophecies of Zechariah, the father of John the Baptist, "Blessed be the Lord God of Israel; for he hath visited and redeemed his people, And hath raised up an horn of salvation for us in the house of his servant David; As he spake by the mouth of his holy prophets, which have been since the world began: That we should be saved from our enemies, and from the hand of all that hate us; To perform the mercy promised to our fathers, and to remember his holy

88

covenant; The oath which he sware to our father Abraham, That he would grant unto us, that we being delivered out of the hand of our enemies might serve him without fear" (Luke 1:68-74).

When Zechariah spoke this prophecy, Israel did not experience the fulfillment. They were not saved from their enemies and from the hand of all that hate them. But there is hope, "The Lord thy God in the midst of thee." This is not a democratically elected authority, but the Almighty, the everlasting One.

Isaiah 9:6 gives us a fuller definition: "For unto us a child is born, unto us a son is given: and the government shall be upon his shoulder: and his name shall be called Wonderful, Counsellor, The mighty God, The everlasting Father, The Prince of Peace."

Regathering the Outcasts

Zephaniah 3:18: "I will gather them that are sorrowful for the solemn assembly, who are of thee, to whom the reproach of it was a burden."

(See) Psalm 42:2-4; Lamentations 2:6; Ezekiel 9:4

The reproached, the rejected and the sorrowful will be elevated in the presence of the Lord. Now the tables are turned; judgment will be executed against those who oppressed Israel:

Zephaniah 3:19: "Behold, at that time I will undo all that afflict thee: and I will save her that halteth, and gather her that was driven out; and I will get them praise and fame in every land where they have been put to shame."

(See) Isaiah 60:14,18; 62:7; Ezekiel 34:16; Micah 4:6; Zechariah 8:23

What a tremendous act of grace, from being afflicted and despised to "praise and fame."

Zephaniah 3:20: "At that time will I bring you again, even in the time that I gather you: for I will make you a name and a praise among all people of the earth, when I turn back your captivity before your eyes, saith the LORD."

(See) Deuteronomy 26:18-19; Psalm 22:27; Jeremiah 29:14;
Ezekiel 37:12, 21

Israel's Glory

Finally, Israel will have attained the glory of their original calling. Moses spoke of it: "For thou art an holy people unto the LORD thy God, and the LORD hath chosen thee to be a peculiar people unto himself, above all the nations that are upon the earth" (Deuteronomy 14:2). Israel's position will be attained exclusively due to the grace of God. He will cause their conversion; He will take away their sins; and He will place them above all the nations on planet Earth.

Conclusion

At this point in time, Israel knows nothing about the things that will yet take place. They have no idea about the already fulfilled prophecies of the Messiah, the Lord

Jesus Christ. Their greatest worries are security, prosperity and peace. We know from the prophetic books that Israel will attain a degree of peace, under the rulership of Antichrist, but we also know it will be temporary.

May these few words be an encouragement to each of us, knowing that no matter what's happening on earth—no matter the trials, difficulties, sickness, sadness, disappointments and tragedies we experience here—the best for each one who believes in Jesus Christ as their personal Savior, is yet to come. We read in 1 Corinthians 2:9 this glorious statement: "But as it is written, Eye hath not seen, nor ear heard, neither have entered into the heart of man, the things which God hath prepared for them that love him."

HAGGAI

Celebration

HAGGAI

Book of the Bible	God's Directly Spoken Words (%)	Prophecy %*	Significant Names Listed in Each Book						
			Judah	Israel	Ephraim	Jerusalem	Zion	Heathen	Samaria
Hosea	93.32	56	15	44	37	0	0	0	6
Joel	57.70	68	6	3	0	6	7	5	0
Amos	80.95	58	4	30	0	2	2	1	5
Obadiah	97.69	81	1	1	1	2	2	4	1
Jonah	7.39	10	0	0	0	0	0	0	0
Micah	44.88	70	4	12	0	8	9	1	3
Nahum	40.30	74	1	1	0	0	0	0	0
Habakkuk	47.84	41	0	0	0	0	0	2	0
Zephaniah	96.92	89	3	4	0	4	2	1	0
Haggai	67.61	39	4	0	0	0	0	1	0
Zechariah	77.38	69	22	5	3	41	8	5	0
Malachi	93.80	56	3	5	0	2	0	2	0

* Percentage of book as prophecy according to *Tim LaHaye Prophecy Study Bible*

95

Introduction to Haggai

Haggai means "celebration" or "born on a festive day." The time of his appearance is clearly recorded, "In the second year of Darius." It was most likely the year 538 B.C. when King Cyrus gave permission for the Jews to return to Jerusalem. Approximately 42,000 people left for Israel to fulfill the request of King Cyrus to rebuild the temple in Jerusalem. Not much progress was made until 18 years later, when the prophet Haggai appeared. Haggai was a decisive figure in the rebuilding of the temple in Jerusalem, which was completed after four years. The largest part of his writings is not prophetic, rather historical.

The book of Haggai consists of only two chapters and 38 verses. We may call him a prophet of few words. He proclaims judgment and salvation, destruction and restoration. The main target of his prophecies is the people of Judah.

Chapter 1

Introduction

In conjunction with the prophet Zechariah, Haggai passes on the prophetic Word regarding the rebuilding of the temple in Jerusalem. His prophecy is decisive in restarting the construction of the temple.

Haggai 1:1: "In the second year of Darius the king, in the sixth month, in the first day of the month, came the word of the LORD by Haggai the prophet unto Zerubbabel the son of Shealtiel, governor of Judah, and to Joshua the son of Josedech, the high priest, saying,"

(See) 1 Chronicles 3:17; 6:15; Ezra 4:24; Zechariah 4:6

Here we need to take note that a Gentile is mentioned, King Darius. No longer are the kings of Judah or Israel listed. This is the time of the Gentiles. The year is 520 B.C. The Word of the Lord comes to Haggai, addressed to Zerubbabel, the governor of Judah, and Joshua, the high priest. Judah was no longer an independent sovereign nation, but was subject to Gentile power under King Darius.

Israel Today

It should be of interest that modern Israel was established for purely political reasons. On the day before Israel declared the state on 14 May 1948, they still had not agreed on the full wording of the Declaration of Independence, due to two issues: the border and religion. Here is a commentary about the document as listed in Wikipedia under "Israeli Declaration of Independence":

The second major issue was over the inclusion of God in the last section of the document, with the draft using the phrase, "and placing our trust in the Almighty." The two rabbis, Shapira and Yehuda Leib Maimon, argued for its inclusion, saying that it could not be omitted, with Shapira supporting the wording "God of Israel" or "the Almighty and Redeemer of Israel." It was strongly opposed by Zisling, a member of the secularist Mapam. In the end the phrase "Rock of Israel" was used, which could be interpreted as either referring to God, or the land of Eretz Israel, Ben-Gurion saying, "Each of us, in his own way, believes in the 'Rock of Israel' as he conceives it."

This is not surprising because the majority of the People's Council [Moetzet HaAm] were born, raised and educated in the Soviet Union. Thus, religion—in this case, including the name "God" in the Declaration—was of lesser significance. That's the beginning of modern Israel. Thus, we see that Israel's establishment was first of all political.

Abraham's Calling
When we read of the calling of Abraham, which we may call the beginning of Israel, the story is different. It says, "Now the LORD had said unto Abram, Get thee out of thy country, and from thy kindred, and from thy father's

house, unto a land that I will show thee: And I will make of thee a great nation, and I will bless thee, and make thy name great; and thou shalt be a blessing: And I will bless them that bless thee, and curse him that curseth thee: and in thee shall all families of the earth be blessed" (Genesis 12:1-3). Abraham's election is based on God's sovereign "I will." It is the "I will" of the Eternal One against the "I will" of the adversary, Satan, whose will stands diametrically opposed to God's.

The "I Will" of Lucifer

Let's read in Isaiah 14:13-14 the expressed "I will" of the originator of sin: "For thou hast said in thine heart, I will ascend into heaven, I will exalt my throne above the stars of God: I will sit also upon the mount of the congregation, in the sides of the north: I will ascend above the heights of the clouds; I will be like the most High." This great contradiction between the "I will" of God and the "I will" of Satan is manifested throughout the world today. The "I will" of humanity is definitely replacing the "I will" of God more and more; that's a fact.

"The Time Is Not Come"

Haggai 1:2: "Thus speaketh the LORD of hosts, saying, This people say, The time is not come, the time that the LORD's house should be built."

Note the five words, "The time is not come."

Speak to the average church member, even those who

claim to believe in the Bible, and mention that the Rapture is at hand, that signs are being fulfilled, and that we are living in the end stages of the end times. You will most likely receive the answer, "People have always said that." Why do people make such statements? Quite simply, they are not waiting for the coming of the Lord. They are waiting for something else to occur first; they are expecting a tangible sign in order to believe that we are living in the end stages of the end times.

Of course, this is nothing new. Back in the apostles' time, there were believers who disregarded the prophetic Word. It was the Apostle Peter who wrote, inspired by the Holy Spirit: "This second epistle, beloved, I now write unto you; in both which I stir up your pure minds by way of remembrance: That ye may be mindful of the words which were spoken before by the holy prophets, and of the commandment of us the apostles of the Lord and Saviour" (2 Peter 3:1-2). We are to be mindful to remember the words spoken by the holy prophets. Then he describes the opposition to the prophetic Word: "Knowing this first, that there shall come in the last days scoffers, walking after their own lusts, and saying, Where is the promise of his coming? for since the fathers fell asleep, all things continue as they were from the beginning of the creation" (verse 3-4). The voices of those who speak that language—"Where is the promise of his coming?"—are increasing in our days.

If Not Now, When?
What was the reason for Israel to say, "The time is not come, the time that the Lord's house should be built"?

That question is answered in detail in the book of Ezra. We know from the report that King Cyrus of Persia granted permission to the Jews to return to Jerusalem: "Who is there among you of all his people? his God be with him, and let him go up to Jerusalem, which is in Judah, and build the house of the LORD God of Israel, (he is the God,) which is in Jerusalem" (Ezra 1:3). Note, the target was the rebuilding of the temple.

Not only did he encourage the Jews to build the house of the Lord God of Israel, but he also made provision to finance it: "And whosoever remaineth in any place where he sojourneth, let the men of his place help him with silver, and with gold, and with goods, and with beasts, beside the freewill offering for the house of God that is in Jerusalem" (verse 4). Money was not an issue, but readiness to do the work was lacking dangerously: "The time is not come"!

The Adversaries

Many Jews took the long journey to Jerusalem. When they arrived, they first built an altar to offer burnt offerings; they thanked God. Next, the foundation of the house of God was laid. Apparently, everything went well.

But then came the adversaries: "Now when the adversaries of Judah and Benjamin heard that the children of the captivity builded the temple unto the LORD God of Israel" (Ezra 4:1).

Obviously, the Jews heard about the enemies. What next? The target shifted from building the house of God to building the city. That was the mistake the Jews made.

Enemies Mightily Accuse the Jews

The Jews started to build their defense instead of the temple. The enemies of Israel now had a legitimate reason to complain to the king of Persia, and that is exactly what they did. They sent a letter to the king describing the work that was going on in Jerusalem: "Be it known unto the king, that the Jews which came up from thee to us are come unto Jerusalem, building the rebellious and the bad city, and have set up the walls thereof, and joined the foundations. Be it known now unto the king, that, if this city be builded, and the walls set up again, then will they not pay toll, tribute, and custom, and so thou shalt endamage the revenue of the kings" (Ezra 4:12-13).

Interestingly, these enemies do not mention anything about the building of the temple; they only report about the building of the city.

The Jews were building their own houses instead of the temple. Of course, they had plenty of reasons to do so; after all, you must take care of your family, and building the city wall was necessary for security.

But what was the result? "Then ceased the work of the house of God which is at Jerusalem. So it ceased unto the second year of the reign of Darius king of Persia" (Ezra 4:24).

Haggai's Prophetic Message

That is precisely the time, the second year of Darius the king, when the prophet Haggai brought the message of God to Israel:

Haggai 1:3-4: "Then came the word of the LORD by Haggai the prophet, saying, 4 Is it time for you, O ye, to dwell in your cieled houses, and this house lie waste?"

(See) Ezra 5:1; Jeremiah 33:10, 12

In brief, they were rebuilding the city without giving priority to rebuilding the temple.

"Consider Your Ways"
God, through His prophet, explains why they are in such a predicament:

Haggai 1:5-6: "Now therefore thus saith the LORD of hosts; Consider your ways. 6 Ye have sown much, and bring in little; ye eat, but ye have not enough; ye drink, but ye are not filled with drink; ye clothe you, but there is none warm; and he that earneth wages earneth wages to put it into a bag with holes."

(See) Deuteronomy 28:38-40

The Jews were successful in building their economy, prosperity, and defense, but without God's blessing. Israel received a lot of foreign aid from Persia (today's Iran), but that did not satisfy the real need of the people. Why? Because they had reversed their priorities; thus, God's blessing was missing. They placed security and prosperity first; then in second place, the building of the temple.

Jesus our Lord made this profound statement to the people of Israel then and to the Church now: "seek ye

103

first the kingdom of God, and his righteousness; and all these things shall be added unto you" (Matthew 6:31).

Build the House of the Lord

Haggai 1:7-8: "Thus saith the LORD of hosts; Consider your ways. 8 Go up to the mountain, and bring wood, and build the house; and I will take pleasure in it, and I will be glorified, saith the LORD."

(See) 1 Kings 6:1; Psalm 132:13-14

He is simply telling them, first things first: "build the house." Not your house, not your security, not your well-being; the house of God in Jerusalem should have been Israel's first priority, but they ignored this.

Blessing Departed

Haggai 1:9: "Ye looked for much, and, lo, it came to little; and when ye brought it home, I did blow upon it. Why? saith the LORD of hosts. Because of mine house that is waste, and ye run every man unto his own house."

It is of interest that the Jews *did* build, but their priority slightly shifted; they were building the WALL instead of the house of the Lord. Israel's enemies exposed the mistake, as we saw in Ezra 4:12-13.

Will the Church Change the World?

Here we have a prophetic message for the Church. What

is the task of the Church of Jesus Christ on earth? To be witnesses unto Him, thus glorifying God. Ephesians 1:5-6 reads: "Having predestinated us unto the adoption of children by Jesus Christ to himself, according to the good pleasure of his will, To the praise of the glory of his grace, wherein he hath made us accepted in the beloved."

The majority of Christianity has changed this calling to an earthly one. Although noble and well meaning, millions of Christians have taken on all kinds of tasks the Lord has not given them. Instead of being witnesses, they are trying to change the world. This world is not to be changed by the testimony of the Church; sinners should be changed into saints and added to the body of Christ, glorifying Jesus our Lord: "Ye are our epistle written in our hearts, known and read of all men" (2 Corinthians 3:2).

The Priority of the Church

There are a great many speeches, sermons, books and articles that speak about the changing of the world through the Gospel, but in reality it is just wishful thinking. We are not called to change the world. We are not able to change anything—not our nation, our town and, as many of us have experienced, not even our own family. Our task does not consist of changing or influencing this world, but our task is to build "the house of God."

Haven't you read what 1 Peter 2:5 says? "Ye also, as lively stones, are built up a spiritual house, an holy priesthood, to offer up spiritual sacrifices, acceptable to God by Jesus Christ." Ephesians 2:20-22 adds: "And are built upon the foundation of the apostles and prophets,

Jesus Christ himself being the chief corner stone; In whom all the building fitly framed together groweth unto an holy temple in the Lord: In whom ye also are builded together for an habitation of God through the Spirit."

Prepare for Eternity

This leads to an important question: am I building the holy temple of the Lord, or am I building self; that is, the things of this world?

How many dear Christians today have forgotten who they are? We are heavenly citizens! We have no future here on earth. We are just passing through, preparing for eternity. Your family and your country have no direct relationship to the spiritual habitation, which is now in the process of being completed. Therefore, escape from the things of the world and turn decidedly toward the fulfillment of your calling to be a "lively stone," in the building of the "habitation of God through the Spirit"!

Israel Misused Persia's Foreign Aid

God's earthly people, the Jews, had very specific earthly promises. To harvest an abundance, to fill storehouses and barns with the produce of the land, was a sign of God's blessing. Because of disobedience, God's hands were tied, so-to-speak, from blessing His people because they had placed their priority in the wrong direction. The Jews in Jerusalem used the foreign aid package they received from the king of Persia for their own selves. Thus, the pronouncement of judgment:

Haggai 1:10-11: "Therefore the heaven over you is stayed from dew, and the earth is stayed from her fruit. 11 And I called for a drought upon the land, and upon the mountains, and upon the corn, and upon the new wine, and upon the oil, and upon that which the ground bringeth forth, and upon men, and upon cattle, and upon all the labour of the hands."

(See) Deuteronomy 28:23-24; 1 Kings 17:1; 2 Chronicles 6:26; Jeremiah 3:3; Joel 1:18-20

This is a death sentence. When God withholds rain, it's the end of physical existence for vegetation, cattle and men.

Even today, with all our sophistication, our inventions and technology, we could not exist if God were to withhold rain from the earth.

But the Creator God, in His grace, mercy and long-suffering, always made provision for His people and for the rest of the world.

If My People Humble Themselves

Scripture records that the great and glorious King Solomon, who walked with the Lord, was the richest and wisest king there ever was. He prayed a long prayer to God at the dedication of the temple, but one verse stands out: "If my people, which are called by my name, shall humble themselves, and pray, and seek my face, and turn from their wicked ways; then will I hear from heaven, and will forgive their sin, and will heal their land" (2 Chronicles 7:14).

This promise is specifically for the people of Israel,

because they are "my people." Their land is chosen from all the lands of the world. It is Jerusalem where God chose to place His name forever. The Jews have a physical, geographically identifiable land which the Lord calls "my land."

Will God heal the land of Israel? The answer is an unqualified "yes." Israel will humble themselves, they will seek the face of God, and they will repent; and God will hear from heaven, He will forgive their sins, and He will heal their land. The preparation for the fulfillment of that prophecy is now in progress.

Promise for the Church?
Can we not appropriate this promise for ourselves? The answer is an unqualified "yes." However, we must add that from spiritual perspectives, this is applicable only for His Church, not our country. Our country or others are NOT "my people."

Who are we? Ephesians 2:12 describes our position as Gentiles, "That at that time ye were without Christ, being aliens from the commonwealth of Israel, and strangers from the covenants of promise, having no hope, and without God in the world." We can never appropriate the promises given to Israel, but we can be participants of the spiritual blessing through Christ, as we can read in the next verse, "But now in Christ Jesus ye who sometimes were far off are made nigh by the blood of Christ" (verse 13).

Power of the Prophetic Word

Haggai 1:12: "Then Zerubbabel the son of Shealtiel, and Joshua the son of Josedech, the high priest, with all the remnant of the people, obeyed the voice of the LORD their God, and the words of Haggai the prophet, as the LORD their God had sent him, and the people did fear before the LORD."

(See) Psalm 111:10; Proverbs 1:7; Ecclesiastes 12:13

Quite striking to see that suddenly, Zerrubabel the governor, and Joshua the high priest reacted to the prophet's message: "the people did fear before the Lord."

Haggai 1:13-15: "Then spake Haggai the LORD's messenger in the LORD's message unto the people, saying, I am with you, saith the LORD. 14 And the LORD stirred up the spirit of Zerubbabel the son of Shealtiel, governor of Judah, and the spirit of Joshua the son of Josedech, the high priest, and the spirit of all the remnant of the people; and they came and did work in the house of the LORD of hosts, their God, 15 In the four and twentieth day of the sixth month, in the second year of Darius the king."

(See) 2 Chronicles 15:2; Ezra 5:2; Psalm 110:3; Isaiah 41:10; Matthew 28:20; Romans 8:31; 1 Corinthians 15:58

Here we see the active power of the prophetic Word, undergirded by God's grace in stirring the spirit of Zerub-

109

babel and Joshua. They did what they had been instructed to do: build the house of the Lord.

Chapter 2

Introduction

This chapter contains an important prophecy pointing to the future glory of the temple during messianic times.

Proclaiming the Prophetic Word

Haggai the prophet proclaims the prophetic Word. We read the details in the book of Ezra, chapter 5, verse 1: "Then the prophets, Haggai the prophet, and Zechariah the son of Iddo, prophesied unto the Jews that were in Judah and Jerusalem in the name of the God of Israel, even unto them."

This is immensely important, for the previous verse stated, "Then ceased the work of the house of God which is at Jerusalem..." (Ezra 4:24). Now the prophetic Word is proclaimed and a change takes place.

Economic-Political Power of the Church

We should stop here for a moment and contemplate this issue from spiritual perspectives. There is no denying that Christian activity is abounding. We have more churches and more members than ever before. Reliable statistics reveal that church attendance is at an all time high in the USA; about 40 percent of the population attends church weekly. Compare that to the time of the Declaration of Independence; church attendance was less than 10 percent.

111

Today, the evangelical church has become a powerful voice to be reckoned with in the political and economic world. Christian radio, television and publishing houses are seemingly without number. But the prophetic message—the yearning for Jesus to return in the clouds of heaven to call His elect unto Himself—is definitely decreasing.

Prophecy on the Decline

Many remember the excitement among Bible believers after Israel's victory in the Six-Day War in 1967. Christians read the prophetic Scripture; they were eagerly seeking more information about events that were taking place during those days.

We started the US branch of Midnight Call in 1968, publishing the first English language magazine in January 1970. From that time on, we placed small ads in most major Christian publications. The promotion was titled, "Prophecy Fulfilled? See Clearly God's Plan for Today and Tomorrow." We listed several subjects; for example:

- Is the Antichrist Already Among Us?
- Israel and the Bible
- World Currency, World Religion and World Dictator
- The Roman Empire on the Rise

Thousands of responses were received from this small advertisement; people wanted to know more about Bible prophecy. That was in the early 1970s. Later in the early 90s, we repeated the same small advertisement in a major

Christian publication, but the result was shocking: only two people responded.

Of course, our experience is not decisive, but it certainly shows the direction Churchianity is moving; away from the Word of God, toward blessing, success, health, wealth, prosperity and security.

The Inferior New Temple

Haggai 2:1: "In the seventh month, in the one and twentieth day of the month, came the word of the LORD by the prophet Haggai, saying,"

This is now one month later, after they had begun the work on the house of the Lord. Haggai is instructed to ask the old folks a question:

Haggai 2:2-3: "Speak now to Zerubbabel the son of Shealtiel, governor of Judah, and to Joshua the son of Josedech, the high priest, and to the residue of the people, saying, 3 Who is left among you that saw this house in her first glory? and how do ye see it now? Is it not in your eyes in comparison of it as nothing?"

(See) Ezra 3:12; Zechariah 4:10

This new temple was not like the house of God built under Solomon. It was definitely inferior. This is evident from the report in Ezra 3:12: "But many of the priests and Levites and chief of the fathers, who were ancient men, that had seen the first house, when the foundation of this house was laid before their eyes, wept with a loud voice; and many shouted aloud for joy." The laying of the foundation for the new temple resulted in a mixture of sadness and joy: "So that the people could not discern the noise of the shout of joy from the noise of the weeping of the people: for the people shouted with a loud shout, and the noise was heard afar off" (verse 13). In this case, the old folks lamented at the laying of the foundation, while the younger ones rejoiced.

"I Am with You"

Haggai 2:4-5: "Yet now be strong, O Zerubbabel, saith the LORD; and be strong, O Joshua, son of Josedech, the high priest; and be strong, all ye people of the land, saith the LORD, and work: for I am with you, saith the LORD of hosts: 5 According to the word that I covenanted with you when ye came out of Egypt, so my spirit remaineth among you: fear ye not."

(See) Exodus 3:12; 29:45-46; Deuteronomy 31:23; 1 Chronicles 28:20; Ephesians 6:10

These words of encouragement were certainly like fresh water to a dry and thirsty land for Zerubbabel, the political leader, and Joshua the high priest.

Note that the Lord God goes way back to the time when Israel came out of Egypt, to demonstrate that He is the same: the God of Abraham, the God of Isaac, and the God of Jacob.

The words, "fear ye not" are essential for this relatively small group of Jews returning to Jerusalem after 70 years of captivity. Why? Because of the guarantee, "my spirit remaineth among you."

The Day of the Lord
Haggai does not give additional prophecies for Israel in the immediate future, but goes right to the end: the Day of the Lord, when He judges the nations of the world.

Haggai 2:6-7: "For thus saith the LORD of hosts; Yet once, it is a little while, and I will shake the heavens, and the earth, and the sea, and the dry land; 7 And I will shake all nations, and the desire of all nations shall come: and I will fill this house with glory, saith the LORD of hosts."

(See) 1 Kings 8:11; Isaiah 34:4; 60:7; Daniel 2:44; Joel 3:16; Hebrews 12:26

This prophecy reaches directly to the time of the Great Tribulation. It is the Day of the Lord, the judgment of the nations.

The book of Hebrews gives us more information, "Whose voice then shook the earth: but now he hath promised, saying, Yet once more I shake not the earth only, but also heaven. And this word, Yet once more, signifieth the removing of those things that are shaken, as of things that are made, that those things which cannot be shaken may remain" (Hebrews 12:26-27).

The Desire of the Nations
In the midst of the judgment, there is this wonderful promise for the desire of the nations and the glory of the

115

Lord, which will fill the house. We may ask, what is the "desire of all nations"? We receive the answer in Romans 8:19, 22: "For the earnest expectation of the creature waiteth for the manifestation of the sons of God...For we know that the whole creation groaneth and travaileth in pain together until now." We are also reminded of Psalm 102:15-16: "So the heathen shall fear the name of the LORD, and all the kings of the earth thy glory. When the LORD shall build up Zion, he shall appear in his glory."

While the prophet Isaiah speaks of this terrible global judgment, he continues in the same breath to proclaim hope for the Gentiles: "For, behold, the darkness shall cover the earth, and gross darkness the people: but the LORD shall arise upon thee, and his glory shall be seen upon thee. And the Gentiles shall come to thy light, and kings to the brightness of thy rising" (Isaiah 60:2-3).

Prophecy about the Final Temple

The next verse emphasizes an important fact: that the rebuilding of the temple in Jerusalem is not God's ultimate goal. As we have already seen, it was paid for by King Darius of Persia. Thus, the Lord makes it plain:

Haggai 2:8: "The silver is mine, and the gold is mine, saith the LORD of hosts."

(See) 1 Chronicles 29:14, 16; Isaiah 60:17

Then, something else is promised: namely, that the future temple, this house of God, will supersede the glory of

Solomon's temple.

Haggai 2:9: "The glory of this latter house shall be greater than of the former, saith the LORD of hosts: and in this place will I give peace, saith the LORD of hosts."

(See) Psalm 85:8-9; Isaiah 9:6; Zechariah 2:5

We all know that "this place" is the city of Jerusalem, the geographical point of contact between heaven and earth, between God and man. It was there outside the city of Jerusalem that the Son of God, Jesus Christ our Lord, sacrificed Himself on Calvary's cross, when He poured out His life in His blood for the remission of sins.

He in person is our peace. That is much more than we can possibly define with words. It is not a peace that is written on a piece of paper; it is not accomplished by negotiation or by war, but this peace which God gives is above and beyond all measure: "...the peace of God, which passeth all understanding, shall keep your hearts and minds through Christ Jesus" (Philippians 4:7).

Peace for Israel
For Israel, there will be peace; not what Israel hopes for or even imagines, but it will be a peace created by God, based on His grace on the one hand and His righteousness on the other.

No longer will a Jew be despised and rejected; no longer will the nations of the world take it upon themselves to divide the Promised Land; no longer will anyone dare to speak against Israel. Then will be fulfilled what is written in Zechariah 8:23: "Thus saith the LORD of hosts; In those days it shall come to pass, that ten men shall take hold out of all languages of the nations, even shall take hold of the skirt of him that is a Jew, saying, We will go with you: for we have heard that God is with you." What an unspeakable blessing that will be: "God is with you."

Even today, the statement, "God is with you" is applicable to your life. When you place your priority in the crucified One, the One who completed and perfected redemption, then the peace of God rests upon you, your family and your surroundings. They will be drawn to the light you radiate, even without you being conscious of it yourself.

Reinstitution of Temple Service

Haggai 2:10: "In the four and twentieth day of the ninth month, in the second year of Darius, came the word of the LORD by Haggai the prophet, saying,"

We remember that the prophecy began on the first day of the sixth month; now we are at the twenty-fourth day in the ninth month of the same year. This time, the Word of the Lord is specifically addressed to the priests, to those who handle the services of the Lord.

The Law of Purification

Haggai 2:11-12: "Thus saith the LORD of hosts; Ask now the priests concerning the law, saying, 12 If one bear holy

118

flesh in the skirt of his garment, and with his skirt do touch bread, or pottage, or wine, or oil, or any meat, shall it be holy? And the priests answered and said, No."

(See) Leviticus 10:10; Deuteronomy 33:10

The priests answered correctly: "the holy flesh" does not have the power to sanctify or make holy that which is unholy. The *holy flesh* serves only one purpose, and that is the sacrificial element thereof. It is consecrated unto the Lord; it is segregated for that specific purpose alone. The priests were well aware of it and gave the right answer.

Haggai 2:13: "Then said Haggai, If one that is unclean by a dead body touch any of these, shall it be unclean? And the priests answered and said, It shall be unclean."

(See) Leviticus 22:4-6; Numbers 19:11, 22

Here again the priests answered correctly, "It shall be unclean." An unholy people can only offer an unholy sacrifice. They cannot be made clean by the "holy flesh," but are polluted by sin.

The Unclean Remains Unclean

Here in Haggai 2:12, we see the *holy flesh* served a specific purpose and nothing else. That which is unholy can only make things unholy and defiled. Holiness is segregated, set apart, sanctified. Unholiness can bring forth nothing but unholiness. Sin beareth sin.

The answer the priests gave to these two questions is

119

now applied to the people of Israel:

Haggai 2:14: "Then answered Haggai, and said, So is this people, and so is this nation before me, saith the LORD; and so is every work of their hands; and that which they offer there is unclean."

(See) Proverbs 15:8; Titus 1:15

New Testament Consecration

Here we have a prophetic pointer to the Lord Jesus Himself. The knowledge of Jesus alone will not make us holy. We must become one with His body. Colossians 1, verses 20 and 22 say, "And, having made peace through the blood of his cross, by him to reconcile all things unto himself; by him, I say, whether they be things in earth, or things in heaven...In the body of his flesh through death, to present you holy and unblameable and unreproveable in his sight." Notice it says we are reconciled through His blood and through the flesh; that means death.

Jesus made the following statement to the disciples in John 6:56-57, "He that eateth my flesh, and drinketh my blood, dwelleth in me, and I in him. As the living Father hath sent me, and I live by the Father: so he that eateth me, even he shall live by me." What does "eateth my flesh, and drinketh my blood" mean? Quite simply, death. We must become participants in His death.

This was offensive to those who heard it. It says in verse 60, "Many therefore of his disciples, when they had heard this, said, This is an hard saying; who can hear it?"

But then Jesus explains in verse 63, "It is the spirit that quickeneth; the flesh profiteth nothing: the words that I speak unto you, they are spirit, and they are life."

What does it mean? First of all, what it does not mean is important. When we partake of the Lord's Table, we take the broken bread and eat it, and we take the cup and drink from it. Paul explains, "For as often as ye eat this bread, and drink this cup, ye do show the Lord's death till he come" (1 Corinthians 11:26). Communion is the demonstration of the fact that my life identifies with the death of Jesus Christ.

Decrease in Blessings

Haggai 2:15: "And now, I pray you, consider from this day and upward, from before a stone was laid upon a stone in the temple of the LORD:"

(See) Ezra 3:10; 4:24

They should remember what happened before the temple was built:

Haggai 2:16: "Since those days were, when one came to an heap of twenty measures, there were but ten: when one came to the pressfat for to draw out fifty vessels out of the press, there were but twenty."

This is just a different picture of the same cause and effect we read of in chapter 1, verses 6-9.

They were convinced that there was more in their storehouse, but when they got there, instead of twenty measures they found only ten. When they went to the oil press, they were sure they would find fifty vessels, but there were only twenty. Why?

Haggai 2:17: "I smote you with blasting and with mildew and with hail in all the labours of your hands; yet ye turned not to me, saith the LORD."

(See) Deuteronomy 28:22; 1 Kings 8:37; Jeremiah 5:3; Amos 4:6, 8-11

God turned the blessing prepared for His people into a curse.

Consider Again

Haggai 2:18-19: "Consider now from this day and upward, from the four and twentieth day of the ninth month, even from the day that the foundation of the LORD'S temple was laid, consider it. 19 Is the seed yet in the barn? yea, as yet the vine, and the fig tree, and the pomegranate, and the olive tree, hath not brought forth: from this day will I bless you."

(See) Zechariah 8:9

The people were able to compare physical facts. There was no seed in the barn, no fruit on the vine, no figs on the tree, yet from that day, the twenty-fourth day of the ninth month, the Lord says, "From this day will I bless you." Obedience to the prophetic Word to "build the temple" caused grace and blessing to be restored to Israel.

One more time on that very same day, the Lord speaks

to Haggai:

Haggai 2:20-21: "And again the word of the LORD came unto Haggai in the four and twentieth day of the month, saying, 21 Speak to Zerubbabel, governor of Judah, saying, I will shake the heavens and the earth;"

(See) Ezekiel 21:27; Hebrews 12:26

Quite obviously, this is a spiritual matter. Zerubbabel is not the Messiah; he was the governor of Judah. But there was an important thing in Zerubbabel's life: he was obedient.

Let us again read Ezra 5:2: "Then rose up Zerubbabel the son of Shealtiel, and Jeshua the son of Jozadak, and began to build the house of God which is at Jerusalem: and with them were the prophets of God helping them." Because of his obedience, additional revelations were made that reached thousands of years into the future, "I will shake the heavens and the earth."

Shaking the Heavens and Earth

When will this happen? At the time when the Lord shall stand up for His people Israel, "The LORD also shall roar out of Zion, and utter his voice from Jerusalem; and the heavens and the earth shall shake: but the LORD will be the hope of his people, and the strength of the children of Israel" (Joel 3:16).

In the process toward the fulfillment, when God will shake the heavens and the earth, there will be chaos. This has been the case in the past, is now, and will be in the future. Jesus in His prophetic speech alluded to this universal conflict: "And ye shall hear of wars and rumours of wars: see that ye be not troubled: for all these things must come to pass, but the end is not yet. For nation shall rise against nation, and kingdom against kingdom: and there shall be famines, and pestilences, and earthquakes, in divers [various] places" (Matthew 24:6-7). History confirms that numerous wars have been fought, kingdom against kingdom, nation against nation. We have plenty of documentation regarding famines, pestilences and earthquakes. But the finality has not occurred yet, namely, "shaking the heavens and earth."

Enemies Destroyed

Haggai 2:22: "And I will overthrow the throne of kingdoms, and I will destroy the strength of the kingdoms of the heathen; and I will overthrow the chariots, and those that ride in them; and the horses and their riders shall come down, every one by the sword of his brother."

(See) Psalm 46:9; Daniel 2:44; Micah 5:10; Zephaniah 3:8; Matthew 24:7

This is a prophecy against Satan and his kingdoms; he is the god of this world. What is "the strength of the kingdoms..."? One word: war. The process of fulfillment has been in full swing since the time of Haggai until this very day, and will continue until the return of the Lord. What will happen at that time? We may answer in modern terms: total and absolute gun control. There will be no more weapons. The prophet Isaiah proclaims: "And it shall come to pass in the last days, that the mountain of the Lord's house shall be established in the top of the mountains, and shall be exalted above the hills; and all nations shall flow unto it. And many people shall go and say, Come ye, and let us go up to the mountain of the LORD, to the house of the God of Jacob; and he will teach us of his ways, and we will walk in his paths: for out of Zion shall go forth the law, and the word of the LORD from Jerusalem. And he shall judge among the nations, and shall rebuke many people: and they shall beat their swords into plowshares, and their spears into pruninghooks: nation shall not lift up sword against nation, neither shall they learn war any more" (Isaiah 2:2-4).

The Coming Messiah

Haggai 2:23: "In that day, saith the LORD of hosts, will I take thee, O Zerubbabel, my servant, the son of Shealtiel, saith the LORD, and will make thee as a signet: for I have chosen thee, saith the LORD of hosts."

(See) Song of Solomon 8:6; Isaiah 42:1; 43:10; Jeremiah 22:24

Is the prophet speaking of Zerubbabel in the days of King Darius? Not very likely, because this speaks of the end of the world, when the Lord will destroy all the kingdoms of the heathen. This is heralding the great day of God Almighty. He will come in great power and glory to destroy the forces of darkness under the leadership of Satan, his Antichrist and the false prophet. Zerubbabel is mentioned because he pictures the Lord Jesus Christ, who came to do the will of the Father. He was "obedient unto death, even the death of the cross." But Christ's name is hidden; it is only revealed at that moment through Zerubbabel.

Spiritual Understanding

Now someone may object to my interpretation that the Lord's identity is hidden in Zerubbabel; thus, an explanation is necessary. We do believe the Bible literally. It means what it says. But it does need to be understood spiritually.

Here are some examples: Simon Peter made the statement; "Thou art the Christ, the Son of the living God" (Matthew 16:16). Jesus answered, "Blessed art thou, Simon Barjona: for flesh and blood hath not revealed it unto thee, but my Father which is in heaven" (verse 17). Then, Jesus spoke of His suffering and prophesied that He would be killed, yet would be raised on the third day. Peter answered and said, "Be it far from thee, Lord: this shall not be unto thee" (verse 22). How did Jesus answer? "Get thee behind me, Satan..." (verse 23). Did Peter become Satan? Obviously not, but the statement he just made was satanically inspired.

When David uttered the words in Psalm 22, "My God, my God, why hast thou forsaken me?...they pierced my hands and my feet...They part my garments among them, and cast lots upon my vesture" (verses 1, 16, 18), was David speaking about himself? Of course not. David, the faithful servant, was uttering a prophecy of Jesus Christ, who cried out on Calvary's cross, "My God, my God, why hast thou forsaken me?" The hands and feet of David were not pierced, but those of our Lord were. The Roman soldiers indeed did not cast lots for

David's clothing, but for the Lord's vesture.

Who Is Zerubbabel?

In conclusion, let us reread the last verse of the book of Haggai: "In that day, saith the LORD of hosts, will I take thee, O Zerubbabel, my servant, the son of Shealtiel, saith the LORD, and will make thee as a signet: for I have chosen thee, saith the LORD of hosts." Zerubbabel's identity is revealed with the statement, "the son of Shealtiel." It is quite revealing that Zerubbabel is not the priest representing the religious aspect, but he is the politician, the governor of Judah. Modern Israel was not founded because of religious conviction, but by the political-social movement Zionism, which aimed at one specific target: security for Jews in their own land.

God picks up with the nation of Israel where He left off.

With the beginning of the return of the Jews to the land of Israel, God began to reestablish the geographical identity first. That succession is clearly recorded by the prophet Ezekiel. When we read chapter 36, we notice that God speaks to the topographical land of Israel. He tells the mountains, the hills, the rivers, the valleys and the desolate places to get ready, "...Ye shall shoot forth your branches, and yield your fruit to my people of Israel: for they are at hand to come" (verse 8).

Ye Shall Be Clean

The return is documented in Ezekiel 36:24: "For I will take you from among the heathen, and gather you out of all countries, and will bring you into your own land."

Then a change takes place in verse 25: "Then will I sprinkle clean water upon you, and ye shall be clean: from all your filthiness, and from all your idols, will I cleanse you." The Jews ceased to worship idols when they returned to the land of Israel. Idol worship is the culture and tradition of the Gentile nations.

What next? "A new heart also will I give you, and a new spirit will I put within you..." (verse 26). The Jews of Israel are a different people than the Jews in the Diaspora. The Jews who returned to the land of Israel received "a new spirit." They are courageous, strong and self-reliant. Today, they are the best soldiers in the world, and they are the best farmers as well.

But that's not the end. In verse 27 we read: "And I will put *my spirit* within you, and cause you to walk in my statutes, and ye shall keep my judgments, and do them." Israel is in the process of restoration physically and topographically, but spiritual restoration is yet to come.

The Apostle Paul speaks prophetically of this in Romans 11:25-26: "...blindness in part is happened to Israel, until the fulness of the Gentiles be come in. And so all Israel shall be saved...."

ZECHARIAH

Jehovah Remembers

Chapter 10   249

Chapter 11   263

Chapter 14   310

ZECHARIAH

Book of the Bible	God's Directly Spoken Words (%)	Prophecy %*	Significant Names Listed in Each Book						
			Judah	Israel	Ephraim	Jerusalem	Zion	Heathen	Samaria
Hosea	93.32	56	15	44	37	0	0	0	6
Joel	57.70	68	6	3	0	6	7	5	0
Amos	80.95	58	4	30	0	2	2	1	5
Obadiah	97.69	81	1	1	1	2	2	4	1
Jonah	7.39	10	0	0	0	0	0	0	0
Micah	44.88	70	4	12	0	8	9	1	3
Nahum	40.30	74	1	1	0	0	0	0	0
Habakkuk	47.84	41	0	0	0	0	0	2	0
Zephaniah	96.92	89	3	4	0	4	2	1	0
Haggai	67.61	39	4	0	0	0	0	1	0
Zechariah	77.38	69	22	5	3	41	8	5	0
Malachi	93.80	56	3	5	0	2	0	2	0

* Percentage of book as prophecy according to *Tim LaHaye Prophecy Study Bible*

Introduction to Zechariah

The name Zechariah may be interpreted "Jehovah Remembers." He was not only a prophet, but also a priest. His office in the prophetic ministry overlapped that of Haggai, who specifically emphasized the instant blessings for the building of the temple. Zechariah goes far beyond his time and reveals the first and second coming of the Messiah, showing the Lord's ultimate victory expressed particularly with the words found in the last two verses: "holiness unto the Lord."

Zechariah is the 11th of the 12 Minor Prophets and presents us with the largest volume of information. He is the seventh in line of the eight prophets who target Judah in particular. Hosea and Amos are addressed primarily to the ten-tribe Israel, while Jonah and Nahum are the two Minor Prophets whose message is directed toward the Gentiles. The book of Obadiah targets Esau-Edom. The overwhelming content of the 12 Prophets is directed toward Judah. This is not surprising, because Judah is the official representative of the 12 tribes of the children of Israel.

Judah, the Royal Tribe

Although we have dealt with this issue when we studied the other prophets, I think it is beneficial to take a closer look at Judah. The dying Jacob made this prophecy: "Judah, thou art he whom thy brethren shall praise; thy hand shall be in the neck of thine enemies; thy father's children shall bow down before thee. Judah is a lion's whelp: from the prey, my son, thou art gone up: he stooped down, he couched as a lion, and as an old lion; who shall rouse him up? The scepter shall not depart from Judah, nor a lawgiver from between his feet, until Shiloh come; and unto him shall the gathering of the people be" (Genesis 49:8-10). Out of Judah comes "Shiloh," the Messiah.

"Gathering of the People"

Out of Judah came the Jews. What has happened to the rest of the tribes? We know that the tribe of Benjamin was incorporated into the tribe of Judah. The ten-tribe Northern Kingdom rebelled against Judah, was led into Assyrian captivity and vanished. However, before their captivity, remnants of those tribes joined themselves to the tribe of Judah. For example, in 2 Chronicles 11:16: "…out of all the tribes of Israel such as set their hearts to seek the LORD God of Israel came to Jerusalem, to sacrifice unto the LORD God of their fathers." In chapter 15, verse 9 we read: "And he gathered all Judah and Benjamin, and the strangers with them out of Ephraim and Manasseh, and out of Simeon: for they fell to him out of Israel in abundance, when they saw that the LORD his God was with him."

The House of Israel

Often the question is, are the Jews Israel? Long after the ten-tribe Israel disappeared, God spoke through the prophet Ezekiel to the Jews, but defines them as "the house of Israel" several times in chapter 3. You will find this mentioned also in other places. Later, when the apostle Peter addressed the Jews in Israel, he said, "Ye men of Israel" (Acts 2:22). Therefore, all Jews are Israelites, but not all Israelites are Jews. So, what happened to the remnant? They have been dissolved into the Gentiles and no longer are participants in the promises for the people of Israel. Only in "him [Judah] shall the gathering of the people be."

The greatest authority of all is our Lord Jesus Christ. He exclaimed, "Salvation is of the Jews." Later, in the Book of Revelation we read:"And one of the elders saith unto me, Weep not: behold, the Lion of the tribe of Judah, the Root of David, hath prevailed to open the book, and to loose the seven seals thereof" (5:5).

Chapter 1

Introduction

The prophet Zechariah himself plays no significant part. Actually, we don't know the place or the time of his birth. He receives the Word of the Lord, and the Word is plain: God is displeased with Israel's past and present.

Zechariah 1:1-2: "In the eighth month, in the second year of Darius, came the word of the LORD unto Zechariah, the son of Berechiah, the son of Iddo the prophet, saying, 2 The LORD hath been sore displeased with your fathers."

(See) 2 Chronicles 36:16; Ezra 4:24; 5:1; 6:14; Haggai 1:15; Matthew 23:35

Here we have a scant summary of the entire book: the Word of God, the prophet Zechariah, the Lord, and the fathers.

Zechariah 1:3: "Therefore say thou unto them, Thus saith the LORD of hosts; Turn ye unto me, saith the LORD of hosts, and I will turn unto you, saith the LORD of hosts."

(See) Isaiah 31:6; 44:22; Jeremiah 25:5; Micah 7:19; Malachi 3:7; Luke 15:20; James 4:8

God's patience, love and compassion are revealed in these few words. It is up to the people to turn to the God of Israel. If they do so, He will confirm His promise, "I will turn unto you."

Faith of Our Fathers
The faith of the fathers, traditional faith, does not help, does not lead to repentance, does not lead to truth, does not lead to revelation of the Lord. This is evident from the next three verses:

Zechariah 1:4-6: "Be ye not as your fathers, unto whom the former prophets have cried, saying, Thus saith the LORD of hosts; Turn ye now from your evil ways, and from your evil doings: but they did not hear, nor hearken unto me, saith the LORD. 5 Your fathers, where are they? and the prophets, do they live for ever? 6 But my words and my statutes, which I commanded my servants the prophets, did they not take hold of your fathers? and they returned and said, Like as the LORD of hosts thought to do unto us, according to our ways, and according to our doings, so hath he dealt with us."

(See) Psalm 78:8; 106:6-7; Jeremiah 4:1; 6:17; 11:7-8; Ezekiel 33:11

Not tradition, but the absolute authority of the Word of God is, was, and always will be decisive. When reading Holy Scripture, we must consciously realize we are reading the Word of God. Only from that position of faith will we understand the message God intends us to. The Word of God is eternal, and we who believe in

Jesus Christ, the Living Word of God, are eternal citizens; thus, to heed the Word of God is absolutely essential.

The First Night Vision: The Future Revealed

Zechariah 1:7-8: "Upon the four and twentieth day of the eleventh month, which is the month Sebat, in the second year of Darius, came the word of the LORD unto Zechariah, the son of Berechiah, the son of Iddo the prophet, saying, 8 I saw by night, and behold a man riding upon a red horse, and he stood among the myrtle trees that were in the bottom; and behind him were there red horses, speckled, and white."

(See) Joshua 5:13; Zechariah 6:1-8; Revelation 6:4

In the first six verses, the Word of God came to the prophet to reveal the present and the past. Now the future is revealed.

We have to recall the vision of the prophet Daniel, "In the first year of Belshazzar king of Babylon Daniel had a dream and visions of his head upon his bed: then he wrote the dream, and told the sum of the matters. Daniel spake and said, I saw in my vision by night, and, behold, the four winds of the heaven strove upon the great sea" (Daniel 7:1-2). Daniel's vision is directed toward the Gentiles, expressed with the words "the four winds." This reminds us of the four Gentile superpowers: Babylon, Persia, Greece and Rome. It is important to realize that Zechariah is seeing a vision.

146

Who Is the Man?

Zechariah does not receive words about the Gentiles in particular; his vision is targeted toward his people, his land and his city Jerusalem. He sees something very unusual: a man riding on a red horse and standing still among the myrtles. Who is this man? He is unnamed. From verse 11 we learn that he is "the angel of the Lord." Often this phrase is considered to be describing a pre-appearance of the Messiah, the Lord Jesus Christ.

Myrtles

What are the myrtles? Scholars differ in their interpretation. We do know they are beautiful evergreen shrubs, bearing white flowers and producing a black edible fruit. They discharge a pleasant odor. Thus, this rider on the red horse is surrounded by a pleasant aroma, which may signify the prayers of the saints.

More Horses

Other colored horses are mentioned as well. What are they? Zechariah asks the question:

Zechariah 1:9: "Then said I, O my lord, what are these? And the angel that talked with me said unto me, I will show thee what these be."

He does not have to wait long for an answer.

Zechariah 1:10-11: "And the man that stood among the myrtle trees answered and said, These are they whom the LORD hath sent to walk to and fro through the earth.

11 And they answered the angel of the LORD that stood among the myrtle trees, and said, We have walked to and fro through the earth, and, behold, all the earth sitteth still, and is at rest."

(See) Job 1:7; Isaiah 14:7

The Earth at Rest?

Their report is simple, "all the earth sitteth still, and is at rest." That seems to contradict the commotion, confrontation, war and disaster that has plagued planet Earth until this day. The Lord Jesus Himself described planet Earth in His prophetic speech in Matthew 24:6-7: "...Ye shall hear of wars and rumours of wars: see that ye be not troubled: for all these things must come to pass, but the end is not yet. For nation shall rise against nation, and kingdom against kingdom: and there shall be famines, and pestilences, and earthquakes, in divers places."

So what does this "still" and "rest" mean? We will answer it a little later, but first, let's read verse 12:

Zechariah 1:12: "Then the angel of the LORD answered and said, O LORD of hosts, how long wilt thou not have mercy on Jerusalem and on the cities of Judah, against which thou hast had indignation these threescore and ten years?"

(See) Psalm 102:13-14; Daniel 9:2; Revelation 6:10

Here we see the issue is Jerusalem. We receive a glimpse into the spiritual world, during the time Jerusalem was in desolation for 70 years. The angel that talked with Zechariah communes with the angel of the Lord, and he in turn addresses the Lord of hosts, which is the Father in heaven.

No Automatic Fulfillment

We understand that the prophetic Word and its fulfillment is not something that is programmed and works automatically. We learn this from Daniel, who understood that 70 years were to be accomplished in the desolation of Jerusalem, and then said, "I set my face unto the Lord God, to seek by prayer and supplications, with fasting, and sackcloth, and ashes" (Daniel 9:3). He certainly did not believe in automatic fulfillment of prophecy; he got personally involved!

This urges us to be fully involved in the preparation for the liberation of the Church from planet Earth into the presence of the Lord. We are involved, each believer individually. We are to intimately seek the face of the Lord, as the apostle Paul did: "That I may know him, and the power of his resurrection, and the fellowship of his sufferings, being made conformable unto his death" (Philippians 3:10). Did Paul not know the Lord? Of course he did, but this Scripture reveals there is no end in knowing the Lord; He is the embodiment of unsearchable riches, the Eternal One!

Comfort for Jerusalem

Next we see the Lord speaking with the angel that spoke to Zechariah:

149

Zechariah 1:13-14: "And the LORD answered the angel that talked with me with good words and comfortable words. 14 So the angel that communed with me said unto me, Cry thou, saying, Thus saith the LORD of hosts; I am jealous for Jerusalem and for Zion with a great jealousy."

(See) Isaiah 40:1-2; 57:18; Jeremiah 29:10; Joel 2:18; Zechariah 8:2

God's city Jerusalem is much more than the capital city of Israel; it is the residence of God. Zechariah's call was to proclaim God's specific interest in Jerusalem and Zion. It is the city where His holy name shall dwell forever, and that city was trodden down deliberately and intentionally by the Gentiles. Now we should understand why the nations of the world do not recognize Jerusalem as the capital city of the Jewish state of Israel today.

Heathen at Ease

Zechariah 1:15: "And I am very sore displeased with the heathen that are at ease: for I was but a little displeased, and they helped forward the affliction."

(See) Psalm 123:4; Isaiah 47:6; Jeremiah 48:11; Amos 1:11

Not only was the Lord displeased with the fathers, but also He is now displeased with the nations. Why? Because they treat Jerusalem with contempt.

The world is "still" and "at rest" when it comes to Jewish Jerusalem. The official Vatican position is recognized globally: Jerusalem must be an international city. The nations are also at ease when it comes to the persecution of the Jewish people. They have been so throughout the centuries. As a matter of fact, "they helped forward the affliction." This speaks against all nations of the world; there are no exceptions.

Although this prophecy was targeted toward Jerusalem and the Jewish people at the time when the 70 years of Jerusalem's desolation came to an end, it is also applicable in our days as well. Is there any nation that agrees with God's eternal resolutions, declaring the city of Jerusalem as His residence and the capital city of the Jewish state of Israel? There is none.

Jerusalem Established

Because of the world's rejection of God's Word, the Lord will establish Jerusalem nevertheless:

Zechariah 1:16-17: "Therefore thus saith the LORD; I am returned to Jerusalem with mercies: my house shall be built in it, saith the LORD of hosts, and a line shall be stretched forth upon Jerusalem. 17 Cry yet, saying, Thus saith the LORD of hosts; My cities through prosperity shall yet be spread abroad; and the LORD shall yet comfort Zion, and shall yet choose Jerusalem."

(See) Isaiah 12:1; 14:1; 40:1-2; 44:26; 51:3; 61:4

That wonderful promise concludes the first night vision of Zechariah.

The Second Night Vision: The Four Horns

How the Gentile nations are involved in the persecution of the Jews becomes evident when we read the next two verses:

Zechariah 1:18-19: "Then lifted I up mine eyes, and saw, and behold four horns. 19 And I said unto the angel that talked with me, What be these? And he answered me, These are the horns which have scattered Judah, Israel, and Jerusalem."

(See) 1 Kings 22:11; Psalm 75:4-5; Habakkuk 3:14

Zechariah again sees something unusual; thus, he asked the question, "What be these?" He receives the answer right away: these are the horns which have scattered Judah, Israel and Jerusalem. The four horns manifest the Gentile powers: Babylon, Persia, Greece and Rome.

The Four Gentile Empires

This corresponds to Daniel's prophecy, in chapter 2, verses 31-35:

"Thou, O king, sawest, and behold a great image. This great image, whose brightness was excellent, stood before thee; and the form thereof was terrible. This image's head was of fine gold, his breast and his arms of silver, his belly and his thighs of brass, His legs of iron, his feet part of iron and part of clay. Thou sawest till that a stone was cut out without hands, which smote the image upon his feet that were of iron and clay, and brake them to pieces. Then was the iron, the clay, the brass, the silver, and the gold, broken to pieces together, and became like

152

the chaff of the summer threshingfloors; and the wind carried them away, that no place was found for them: and the stone that smote the image became a great mountain, and filled the whole earth."

This means that the four Gentile superpowers have no future. It matters not what birth certificate you have or what passport you carry; it's only "like the chaff of the summer threshingfloors; and the wind carried them away."

It seems like these verses, among many others, would be very difficult to grasp for nationalists and patriots, because they have all been indoctrinated by their respective government with the words, "Our country is different; we are blessed by God; we are the greatest; we love peace and righteousness." But that's precisely what all the nations of the world said and are saying today. However, the end is determined by God. Daniel 2:44 reads, "And in the days of these kings shall the God of heaven set up a kingdom, which shall never be destroyed: and the kingdom shall not be left to other people, but it shall break in pieces and consume all these kingdoms, and it shall stand for ever."

Four Smiths (Carpenters)

The vision continues:

Zechariah 1:20-21: "And the LORD showed me four carpenters. 21 Then said I, What come these to do? And he spake, saying, These are the horns which have scattered Judah, so that no man did lift up his head: but these are come to fray them, to cast out the horns of the Gentiles, which lifted up their horn over the land of Judah to scatter it."

(See) Psalm 75:4-5, 10; Isaiah 44:12; 54:16

The *Tenakh* translates the word "carpenter" with "smith" or "blacksmith." What is the task of these four carpenters/smiths? They will destroy the power structure of the Gentiles.

Zechariah, as virtually all other prophets, proclaims merciless judgment of God upon His nation, but always concludes with comfort and hope for Israel. That, incidentally, applies to each of us who believe that Jesus Christ is the Son of God, who poured out His life in His blood on Calvary's Cross and paid once and for all for our trespasses. Have you received Him?

Chapter 2

Introduction

This chapter begins with the third night vision of Zechariah. Obviously, his first concern was Jerusalem and the temple. Zechariah was a contemporary of Haggai, so he must have been concerned about the present need. But when we read these prophecies, we immediately realize that he also speaks about the future. He sees the time when the Lord will literally and physically dwell in the midst of His people. We must reiterate that time for preparation must be allowed; thus, things that are happening even today are the process of fulfillment of Bible prophecy.

The Third Night Vision: Measuring Jerusalem

Zechariah 2:1: "I lifted up mine eyes again, and looked, and behold a man with a measuring line in his hand."

(See) Jeremiah 31:39; Ezekiel 40:3; 47:3

This man is not identified as an angel or a special messenger; it simply says "a man with a measuring line." Obviously, this was a personality not to be revealed at that time. Some scholars believe that this man is the preincarnate Christ, and that may well be. But we will stick

155

to what is written, "a man."

Zechariah had a question:

Zechariah 2:2: "Then said I, Whither goest thou? And he said unto me, To measure Jerusalem, to see what is the breadth thereof, and what is the length thereof."

(See) Revelation 11:1; 21:15-17

When something is measured, it is done with a specific purpose in mind. Before building a house, one measures the property to determine where the house will be built, how large it should be.

Here the man says that he is measuring Jerusalem. I propose that this is a spiritual issue, a prophetic analysis of a certain territory. For example, the prophet Ezekiel reports of someone using a measuring device in chapter 40, giving details about the temple that is to be erected in the millennium. In Revelation chapter 11, measurement is taken of the temple of God, the altar and the worshipers. Doubtless, these are spiritual dimensions, because God knows the exact measurements of the temple; for that matter, He knows the precise measurement of the universe. But we do not read any more details on this measuring issue.

Another Angel

Next comes an unnamed angel and "another angel." We read in verses 3-4:

Zechariah 2:3-4: "And, behold, the angel that talked with me went forth, and another angel went out to meet him, 4

156

And said unto him, Run, speak to this young man, saying, Jerusalem shall be inhabited as towns without walls for the multitude of men and cattle therein:"

(See) Ezekiel 36:10; 38:11

Who gives the order to whom? The Menge translation confirms it is the "another angel" who is telling the first one to give the message to Zechariah. Interestingly, Zechariah is identified as a "young man"; that means he does not have much experience, yet he reports what he has seen about the future.

Jerusalem Secure

The words "without walls" and "multitude" signify the virtually unlimited abundance with which Jerusalem will be blessed. Security will also be provided, and that guarantee comes directly from the Lord:

Zechariah 2:5: "For I, saith the LORD, will be unto her a wall of fire round about, and will be the glory in the midst of her."

(See) Psalm 46:11; Isaiah 4:5; 26:1; Haggai 2:9; Revelation 21:23

What a wonderful word of comfort for all who are in fear, in great need, and often resigned to hopelessness. The Lord in His grace will never forsake His own children. He will never leave you. He is your greatest security, and that for all eternity. Have you ever felt forsaken? Have problems overwhelmed you? Then do as the Word of God instructs, "Casting all your care upon him; for he careth for you" (1 Peter 5:7).

The Northern People

Now comes the instruction concerning the regathering of the outcast:

> **Zechariah 2:6-7:** "Ho, ho, come forth, and flee from the land of the north, saith the LORD: for I have spread you abroad as the four winds of the heaven, saith the LORD. 7 Deliver thyself, O Zion, that dwellest with the daughter of Babylon."

(See) Deuteronomy 28:64; Isaiah 48:20; Jeremiah 31:10; 51:6; Ezekiel 11:16

Geographical reference is given here: "the north." If we apply this to the modern State of Israel, we cannot be far off the mark. Who were the early pioneers who established the State of Israel? The overwhelming majority came from the former Soviet Union, located directly to the north of Israel. They came and the first thing they did was establish communes, Kibbutzim.

Origin of Kibbutz

It is unfortunate that virtually all Bible scholars and prophecy teachers detour the fact that modern Israel was built on the foundation of communism. Specifically in the USA, the communist system is vehemently opposed; anything that is even vaguely associated with communism is outright condemned. But that does not change the fact that Kibbutzim actually originated in Russia. It described a movement of workers having an undivided interest in land or a manufacturing facility, operating on the principle of collectivism; hence, the name Kolkhoz in Russian and Kibbutz in Hebrew.

There is an abundance of information available regarding the early Zionists who came to the land. It was a hopeless land, desolate and waste, but these Jewish people were convinced that the land would produce food not only to sustain themselves, but also the people that were to come. Thus, the backbone of pre-state Israel was the Kolkhoz-Kibbutz.

Resurrection of the Land

Here we should take a look at Ezekiel 36, beginning with verse 4: "Therefore, ye mountains of Israel, hear the word of the Lord GOD; Thus saith the Lord GOD to the mountains, and to the hills, to the rivers, and to the valleys, to the desolate wastes, and to the cities that are forsaken, which became a prey and derision to the residue of the heathen that are round about."

Why does the Lord speak to the topographical land of Israel first, and not the people? Verse 8 gives us the answer: "But ye, O mountains of Israel, ye shall shoot forth your branches, and yield your fruit to my people of Israel; for they are at hand to come."

What happened as a result of those Jewish communist settlers from the land of the north? "And the desolate land shall be tilled, whereas it lay desolate in the sight of all that passed by. And they shall say, This land that was desolate is become like the garden of Eden; and the waste and desolate and ruined cities are become fenced, and are inhabited" (Ezekiel 36:34-35).

Whenever you have the opportunity to go to Israel, be sure to include the agricultural part of the land, and you will see with amazement that the words we have just read continue to be fulfilled.

Daughter of Babylon

We also note the instruction for Zion to get out of the territory of Babylon: "Deliver thyself, O Zion, that dwellest with the daughter of Babylon" (verse 7).

This does not speak of Babylon per se, but the "daughter of Babylon." Who is she? She is the continuation of Babylon, Medo-Persia, Greece and Rome until our time. The Jews are instructed to "deliver" themselves from all the countries of the world, as revealed in the next verse:

Zechariah 2:8-9: "For thus saith the LORD of hosts; After the glory hath he sent me unto the nations which spoiled you: for he that toucheth you toucheth the apple of his eye. 9 For, behold, I will shake mine hand upon them, and they shall be a spoil to their servants: and ye shall know that the LORD of hosts hath sent me."

(See) Deuteronomy 32:10; Psalm 17:8; Isaiah 14:2; 60:7-9

The Schlachter translation is a little clearer, "To obtain honor, I have sent you to the nations, but they plundered you." Wherever the Jews went, they contributed to prosperity, particularly in science, the arts, and finance. The Gentile nations should have recognized the Jews as God's chosen people, thus giving honor to God. But history proves that the Jews were not honored, nor did God receive honor from the Gentiles. The Jews were discriminated against, persecuted and killed.

The Apple of His Eye

Let's read again Zechariah 1:15: "And I am very sore displeased with the heathen that are at ease: for I was but a little displeased, and they helped forward the affliction." Hence the strong statement, "For he that toucheth you [Jews] touches the apple of his [God's] eye."

Everyone knows how extremely sensitive the eye is. One tiny speck of dust will irritate the eye and can blur one's vision. God uses this statement to show how He considers His people, no matter how Israel behaves toward God. That is God's business, between Him and His people alone.

Israel from God's View

We have the example of the people of Israel when they came out of slavery and wandered in the desert for 40 years. There is ample evidence of their stubbornness, disobedience and outright rebellion against God. Listen to the words God gives to the heathen prophet Balaam, "He hath not beheld iniquity in Jacob, neither hath he seen perverseness in Israel: the LORD his God is with him, and the shout of a king is among them...Surely there is no enchantment against Jacob, neither is there any divination against Israel: according to this time it shall be said of Jacob and of Israel, What hath God wrought!" (Numbers 23:21, 23).

God shields His people Israel from Gentile accusations.

In spite of Israel's rebellion, Moses prophesied of this coming prosperity over the nations of the world: "For the LORD thy God blesseth thee, as he promised thee: and thou shalt lend unto many nations, but thou shalt not borrow; and thou shalt reign over many nations, but they shall not reign over thee" (Deuteronomy 15:6).

"Rejoice, O Daughter of Zion"

Zechariah 2:10: "Sing and rejoice, O daughter of Zion: for, lo, I come, and I will dwell in the midst of thee, saith the LORD."

(See) Leviticus 26:12; Isaiah 65:18-19; 2 Corinthians 6:16

This is the proclamation of the coming of the Lord in three phases.

First Coming

First He came to Bethlehem, born of a virgin in extreme poverty. He started His ministry at about the age of 30. Jesus fulfilled Bible prophecy such as making the blind see, the lame walk, and the dead arise. Then He poured out His life in His blood on Calvary's Cross for the payment of sin for all mankind, was buried, rose again on the third day, and ascended into heaven. That concluded His first coming.

Second Coming

His second coming will be when He gathers the fruit of His Word, His Church, unto Himself. This is documented for us in 1 Thessalonians 4:16-17: "For the Lord himself shall descend from heaven with a shout, with the voice of the archangel, and with the trump of God: and the dead in Christ shall rise first: Then we which are alive and remain shall be caught up together with them in the clouds, to meet the Lord in the air: and so shall we ever be with the Lord."

Note that He will not come to earth, but will meet us in the clouds of the air.

Third Coming

His third coming is when He comes literally and physically to Jerusalem and His feet will stand on the Mount of Olives. At that time, He will overrule all the nations of the world. The first step toward real peace is to implement real gun control; actually, abolishing weapons: "And he shall judge among many people, and rebuke strong nations afar off; and they shall beat their swords into plowshares, and their spears into pruninghooks: nation shall not lift up a sword against nation, neither shall they learn war any more" (Micah 4:3).

From that point on, the Lord will dwell in the midst of His people, the Jews.

Zechariah 2:11: "And many nations shall be joined to the LORD in that day, and shall be my people: and I will dwell in the midst of thee, and thou shalt know that the LORD of hosts hath sent me unto thee."

(See) Exodus 12:49; Isaiah 2:2-3; 11:10: Ezekiel 33:33; Micah 4:2

Many Nations

Who are these "many nations?" They are believers from the Gentiles. For more explanation, let us read Ephesians 2:12: "That at that time ye were without Christ, being aliens from the commonwealth of Israel, and strangers from the covenants of promise, having no hope, and without God in the world." There we have it, "aliens... strangers...no hope...without God." And then in chapter 3, verse 6: "That the Gentiles should be fellowheirs, and of the same body, and partakers of his promise in Christ by the gospel." These Gentiles—these aliens, foreigners and strangers without hope—have been added to Israel.

Amos too speaks about it: "That they may possess the remnant of Edom, and of all the heathen, which are called by my name, saith the LORD that doeth this" (Amos 9:12).

Israel's Future

Zechariah 2:12: "And the LORD shall inherit Judah his portion in the holy land, and shall choose Jerusalem again."

(See) Deuteronomy 32:9; 2 Chronicles 6:6; Psalm 33:12; 132:13-14; Jeremiah 10:16; Zechariah 1:17

God chooses Jerusalem; He calls Israel the Holy Land. The Gentiles, however, call it Palestine, or Israeli-occupied Arab territory. The nations endorse the dividing of the Holy City between Arabs, Jews, and Christians.

But what does God say to the world?

Zechariah 2:13: "Be silent, O all flesh, before the LORD: for he is raised up out of his holy habitation."

(See) Psalm 46:10; Habakkuk 2:20

That's the best we can do: be silent, be still, be in prayer. Our involvement in the political maneuvering of the nations is ineffective interference in the diabolical scheme of Satan and his cohorts. The devil attempts to replace Israel as God's chosen nation. That is the real but hidden goal of Satan. Never must we permit ourselves to be led astray by the cunning devices of the devil, who is busy establishing his false peace, false salvation, and his false savior, the Antichrist.

Chapter 3

Introduction

The third chapter gives us the fourth prophetic night vision of Zechariah. He describes what he sees. Though this may be confusing, when we look at it from spiritual perspectives, we can understand this message much better.

The Fourth Night Vision: Joshua, the High Priest

Zechariah 3:1-2: "And he showed me Joshua the high priest standing before the angel of the LORD, and Satan standing at his right hand to resist him. 2 And the LORD said unto Satan, The LORD rebuke thee, O Satan; even the LORD that hath chosen Jerusalem rebuke thee: is not this a brand plucked out of the fire?"

(See) 1 Chronicles 21:1; Job 1:6; Psalm 109:6; Amos 4:11; Matthew 4:10; Luke 22:31; Romans 16:20; Jude 9; Revelation 12:10

According to the margin of the *Tanakh* Bible, Joshua the high priest was one who returned from Babylonian captivity. His name means "Jehovah remembers," "Jehovah saves," or, as Abraham Meister (*Biblisches Namen-Lexikon*) states, "Jehovah is generous and liberal."

The Right Hand

There is something striking in the sentence, "and Satan standing at his right hand." The right hand signifies strength and defense. We remember from the New Testament that the Lord Jesus Christ set Himself at the right hand of God, according to 1 Peter 3:22. In this case, the opposer, the evil one—Satan—stands at the right hand of Joshua the High Priest, for one purpose: "to resist him." Satan simply is saying, "He is mine." How can he do that? Because the Bible says, "He who sins is of the devil." Sin is clearly revealed in verse 3:

Zechariah 3:3: "Now Joshua was clothed with filthy garments, and stood before the angel of the LORD."

(See) Ezra 9:15; Isaiah 4:4; 64:6

Satan's Right to Sinners

Someone recently asked if the devil can be both on earth and in heaven. Here we have the answer: he has access to heaven, but he can also be on the earth, as is evident in the book of Job: "Now there was a day when the sons of God came to present themselves before the LORD, and Satan came also among them. And the LORD said unto Satan, Whence comest thou? Then Satan answered the LORD, and said, From going to and fro in the earth, and from walking up and down in it" (Job 1:6-7).

How long will he have access to the throne of God? Answer: Until the saints are perfected; that is, until the Church is complete and raptured. This is documented for us in Revelation 12:9-10, where we read: "And the great dragon was cast out, that old serpent, called the Devil, and Satan, which deceiveth the whole world: he was cast out into the earth, and his angels were cast out with him. And I heard a loud voice saying in heaven, Now is come salvation, and strength, and the kingdom of our God, and the power of his Christ: for the accuser of our brethren is cast down, which accused them before our God day and night."

Satan is the legal representative of sin and rebellion; and, because all have sinned and come short of the glory of God, he is the representative of all sinners. He is not the defender but the accuser.

Joshua: Representative of Israel

This vision of Joshua the High Priest as a person, represents the Old Testament priestly service, and all Israel. Israel collectively failed numerous times when it came to keeping the laws and commandments of God. Israel—in this case, Joshua the High Priest—was polluted by sin. Besides, it was impossible for the Old Testament priestly service, demonstrated through the sacrifice of animals, to take away sin; it was only covered. We read, "For it is not possible that the blood of bulls and of goats should take away sins" (Hebrews 10:4).

Satan's Legitimate Claim

So, why does Joshua stand before the Lord? There is only one answer: he is seeking grace. There is no way for him to stand before the holy countenance of God in filthy garments. Satan, therefore, legitimately stands at his right hand, demanding his ownership of the sinner,

Joshua.

Immeasurable Grace

Such is also the case for the believer under the New Covenant. We do need someone who stands at the right hand of God, not to accuse us, but to defend us. We may ask, on what basis is defense possible if the accused party is guilty? Again, there is only one answer—grace! Realizing this fact, it makes my heart sing, "Grace, grace, God's grace, grace that will pardon and cleanse within. Grace, grace, God's grace, grace that is greater than all our sin."

Satan Rebuked

In spite of Satan's legal rights, he is rebuked. Why? Because "the Lord...hath chosen Jerusalem." Interestingly, the High Priest Joshua is ignored but Jerusalem is mentioned first. Why? Because Jerusalem is the city where the greatest act of unrighteousness in all of human history transpired. There Satan, through the hands of sinful man, nailed the sinless One, Jesus Christ, to the cross. There He poured out His life in His blood and died to make grace possible. Satan made his fatal mistake in Jerusalem; he caused the death of the only innocent person, Jesus Christ the righteous one.

Jerusalem, Home of God's Name

Now we should better understand why the whole world is involved in the Jerusalem conflict. Jerusalem is infinitely more than this relatively small city in the mountains of Judea. Jerusalem is His dwelling place; we may call it the residence of God's name.

In relationship to the name of God, one should carefully read 1 Kings chapter 8, where the word "name" appears 13 times. In verse 60, Solomon prays for his nation but includes the Gentiles: "That all the people of the earth may know that the LORD is God, and that there is none else." How does God answer? "And the LORD said unto him, I have heard thy prayer and thy supplication, that thou hast made before me: I have hallowed this house, which thou hast built, to put my name there for ever; and mine eyes and mine heart shall be there perpetually" (1 Kings 9:3).

The leaders of this world and the overwhelming majority of the population do not have the slightest idea about the significance of the city of Jerusalem.

Jerusalem is the geographical point where God touched planet Earth to accomplish redemption for mankind. It is the city of Jerusalem to which Jesus will return, establish peace for Israel, and from there rule the world.

Satan's Claim Invalidated

In relationship to Satan's claim to Joshua, God created a new law that supersedes the old one. The new law is based on the full payment for the sins of mankind, and the substance is the blood of Christ. Joshua's pardon is based on the coming victory of the Son of God and Son of Man, the Messiah of Israel and Savior of the world.

Zechariah 3:4-5: "And he answered and spake unto those that stood before him, saying, Take away the filthy garments from him. And unto him he said, Behold, I have caused thine iniquity to pass from thee, and I will clothe thee with change of raiment. 5 And I said, Let them set a fair mitre upon his head. So they set a fair mitre upon his head, and clothed him with garments. And the angel of the LORD stood by."

(See) Exodus 28:39; 29:6; Job 29:14; Isaiah 43:25; 52:1; 61:3, 10; Ezekiel 36:25; Micah 7:18-19; Revelation 19:8

The high priest with all his services was incapable of bringing about the change from sin to righteousness, from pollution to cleanliness, from the devil's territory to God's heaven. Note that the Lord is the cause of this change. He ordered new "raiment" and "a fair mitre upon his head," or as the NIV says, "a clean turban." This is an act of grace pointing toward the coming grace, which would be accomplished by the Son of God, Jesus Christ.

New Order Given

Zechariah 3:6-7: "And the angel of the LORD protested unto Joshua, saying, 7 Thus saith the LORD of hosts; If thou wilt walk in my ways, and if thou wilt keep my charge, then thou shalt also judge my house, and shalt also keep my courts, and I will give thee places to walk among these that stand by."

(See) 1 Kings 3:14; Deuteronomy 17:9, 12; Psalm 91:11

The command goes out to walk in the Lord's way, to keep His charge, to judge His house, and to keep His courts. "To walk among these that stand by." Who are they? Heavenly beings. The Menge translation reads, "And I will give you free access to these who stand before me as servants."

"My Servant the BRANCH"

How will God accomplish this? How is He to permit a sinful person to come into the presence of God? It will take a miracle.

Zechariah 3:8: "Hear now, O Joshua the high priest, thou, and thy fellows that sit before thee: for they are men wondered at: for, behold, I will bring forth my servant the BRANCH."

(See) Isaiah 8:18; 11:1; 42:1; 53:2; Jeremiah 23:5; 33:15; Zechariah 6:12

David, in his Psalm, describes the action of this servant: "For he shall stand at the right hand of the poor, to save him from those that condemn his soul" (Psalm 109:31). In short, the birth of Jesus in Bethlehem was a miracle. The prophets spoke about it, and we read of the fulfillment in the first book of the New Testament, the Gospel of Matthew. The Branch is the Servant of the Lord. He is none other than Jesus Christ, the Son of God.

The Stone

Then a further prophecy about the coming One is revealed:

Zechariah 3:9: "For behold the stone that I have laid before Joshua; upon one stone shall be seven eyes: behold, I will engrave the graving thereof, saith the LORD of hosts, and I will remove the iniquity of that land in one day."

(See) Isaiah 28:16; Jeremiah 31:34; 50:20; Zechariah 4:10; Revelation 5:6

Here is another symbolic demonstration of the Messiah of Israel and the Savior of the world. He is the stone of which Daniel wrote: "And in the days of these kings shall the God of heaven set up a kingdom, which shall never be destroyed: and the kingdom shall not be left to other people, but it shall break in pieces and consume all these kingdoms, and it shall stand for ever. Forasmuch as thou sawest that the stone was cut out of the mountain without hands, and that it brake in pieces the iron, the brass, the clay, the silver, and the gold; the great God hath made known to the king what shall come to pass hereafter: and the dream is certain, and the interpretation thereof sure" (Daniel 2:44-45).

Seven Eyes

The seven eyes are the perfect and declared intention of God to save, and they are focused upon the one single stone. It is the same stone of which Zechariah writes later in chapter 12:3: "And in that day will I make Jerusalem a burdensome stone for all people: all that burden themselves with it shall be cut in pieces, though all the people of the earth be gathered together against it." It is the stone that the builders rejected, which has become the Chief Cornerstone. Thus, we see Jerusalem being identified with the Messiah, the rejected stone, the One whom

173

the seven eyes of God watched over.

What is the purpose of all of this? "I will remove the iniquity of that land in one day." Reading such a sentence moves our hearts, because it shows that it will be God's infinite love and grace that will cause the repentance and subsequent forgiveness of the sins of the people of Israel. It is based exclusively on His compassion, "I will remove the iniquity." Again, grace, abundant grace!

The World's "No" to Jerusalem

Today we see the nations of the world in their fervent, even fanatical opposition to a Jewish Jerusalem. The world says: under no circumstances must Jerusalem be the undivided capital city of Israel, the Jewish state. When we hear the media and what the various leaders of this world say about Jerusalem, then we would be led to believe there is no hope for the Jews; there is no future for a Jewish Jerusalem. The nations of the world will not permit Jerusalem to be the place God has destined it to be. But this verse tells us the opposite, because it is based on the "I will" of God.

Real Peace to Come

Zechariah 3:10: "In that day, saith the LORD of hosts, shall ye call every man his neighbour under the vine and under the fig tree."

(See) 1 Kings 4:25; Micah 4:4

When this occurs, man, for the first time in history, will live in peace with his neighbor. They will enjoy the fruit of the land; they will invite each other to share in their blessings. This is real peace, such as can never be accomplished with weapons of war, negotiations or peace treaties. As a matter of fact, weapons of war will be abolished when Jesus comes.

That, incidentally, is the only peace worth fighting for. This fight is not with weapons of war, but with the power of a dedicated prayer life in the saints. It is the battle in the invisible world that is raging right now. That battle totally ignores all the political circumstances, agreements and disagreements.

It's the battle the apostle Paul speaks of: "For we wrestle not against flesh and blood, but against principalities, against powers, against the rulers of the darkness of this world, against spiritual wickedness in high places" (Ephesians 6:12).

Chapter 4

Introduction

There are two reasons why Zechariah had to be awoken. First, Zechariah had just received four powerful visions revealing far-reaching consequences; not only for Israel, but also for the entire world. The other reason for the angel to wake him up was to make sure Zechariah was not dreaming. He had to be awake to see and describe the fifth night vision he was about to receive.

The Fifth Night Vision: The Angel Awakens Zechariah

Zechariah 4:1: "And the angel that talked with me came again, and waked me, as a man that is wakened out of his sleep,"

(See) 1 Kings 19:5-7; Jeremiah 31:26

Incidentally, being tired is nothing unusual. The great prophet Elijah had to be awoken twice by the angel of the Lord in order for him to realize that he had not fulfilled his calling yet. This is recorded for us in 1 Kings 19:5-8: "And as he lay and slept under a juniper tree, behold, then an angel touched him, and said unto him, Arise and eat. And he looked, and, behold, there was a cake baken on the coals, and a cruse of water at his head. And he did eat and drink, and laid him down again. And the angel of the LORD came again the second time, and touched him, and said, Arise and eat; because the journey is too great for thee. And he arose, and did eat and drink, and went in the strength of that meat forty days and forty nights unto Horeb the mount of God."

Here is demonstrated for us the limitations of our natural body, and the supernatural process that takes place when we follow the instruction of the Lord.

The Golden Candlestick

Zechariah 4:2-3: "And said unto me, What seest thou? And I said, I have looked, and behold a candlestick all of gold, with a bowl upon the top of it, and his seven lamps thereon, and seven pipes to the seven lamps, which are upon the top thereof: 3 And two olive trees by it, one upon the right side of the bowl, and the other upon the left side thereof."

(See) Exodus 25:31-40; Jeremiah 1:11, 13; Amos 8:2; Revelation 4:5; 11:4

We should all be familiar with the seven-armed candelabrum, as mentioned in Exodus 25. Moses received instruction from the Lord relating to the manufacturing of the tabernacle and all the utensils. What was the purpose? To segregate the holy from the unholy; to prophetically show God's intention to redeem mankind.

Here a rather complicated contraption is revealed. The candelabrum is attached to pipes that come out of a bowl, which in turn are connected to two olive trees.

Again, I would like to admonish the reader not to picture this contraption in your mind, because we can only think in earthly dimensions; here, a spiritual truth is revealed from heavenly perspectives. Thus, it can only be fully grasped through the Spirit of God.

God could have caused the angel of the Lord to give Zechariah a simple statement regarding His intention and how He would accomplish it. But that is not what God does; instead, He shows him this golden candlestick with the attached pipes to the olive oil tank and to the olive trees. Zechariah's reaction is quite natural:

Zechariah 4:4: "So I answered and spake to the angel that talked with me, saying, What are these, my lord?"

He needs an explanation; he wants to know what he sees.

First, we see that the angel expected the question:

Zechariah 4:5: "Then the angel that talked with me answered and said unto me, Knowest thou not what these be? And I said, No, my lord."

Now Zechariah was prepared for the explanation of this unusual vision he had received.

Zechariah 4:6: "Then he answered and spake unto me, saying, This is the word of the LORD unto Zerubbabel, saying, Not by might, nor by power, but by my spirit, saith the LORD of hosts."

(See) Ezra 5:2; Isaiah 11:2-4; Hosea 1:7; Haggai 2:4-5

It is the Word of God that gives light and power. The Word of God is identified in John 1:1-3 as the Lord Jesus Christ: "In the beginning was the Word, and the Word was with God, and the Word was God. The same was in the beginning with God. All things were made by him; and without him was not any thing made that was made." Later, we hear Jesus state, "I am the light of the world." Only through and by the power of the Holy Spirit, pictured in the oil, can the candlestick burn and give light.

Zerubbabel

Who is this Zerubbabel? He is a descendant of David; we may call him the king of Jerusalem, or at least, the political and military leader of the people of Israel.

This message, "Not by might, nor by power, but by my spirit, saith the Lord of hosts," was of utmost importance to Zechariah, but more so to Zerubbabel. God is saying in plain terms: this is a spiritual matter and has no direct relationship to the circumstances and difficulties the Jews experienced while in the process of rebuilding the house of God in Jerusalem. As we will see later, this prophecy is not limited to the time of the rebuilding of the temple.

In the book of Ezra, we read that the king of Persia, Cyrus, gave an order to the Jewish people to return to the city of Jerusalem in the land of Israel, "and build the house of the Lord God of Israel." That is what they did, and we read in chapter 3, verse 11b: "And all the people shouted with a great shout, when they praised the Lord, because the foundation of the house of the Lord was laid."

The Church's Foundation

This is very important for us today. We do not need to build the foundation of the Church; it is already done: "For other foundation can no man lay than that is laid, which is Jesus Christ" (1 Corinthians 3:11).

We must build upon this existing foundation. Ephesians 2:20-22 gives us the answer: "And are built upon the foundation of the apostles and prophets, Jesus Christ himself being the chief corner stone; In whom all the building fitly framed together groweth unto an holy temple in the Lord: In whom ye also are builded together for an habitation of God through the Spirit." The Church is to be "an habitation of God through the Spirit."

But, we must admit, that is easier said than done. Why? Because of the adversary. Peter writes in 1 Peter 5:8-9: "Be sober, be vigilant; because your adversary the devil, as a roaring lion, walketh about, seeking whom he may devour: Whom resist stedfast in the faith, knowing that the same afflictions are accomplished in your brethren that are in the world."

The Adversary

Such was also the case during the rebuilding of the temple in Jerusalem. Ezra 4:1 reports: "Now when the adversaries of Judah and Benjamin heard that the children of the captivity builded the temple unto the LORD God of Israel..."

Further, in answer to Zechariah's question, "What are these, my lord?" the angel of the Lord gives a direct reference to Zerubbabel:

Zechariah 4:7: "Who art thou, O great mountain? before Zerubbabel thou shalt become a plain: and he shall bring forth the headstone thereof with shoutings, crying, Grace, grace unto it."

(See) Ezra 3:11; Psalm 84:11; 118:22; Isaiah 40:3-4; Jeremiah 51:25; Nahum 1:5; Matthew 21:21

Indeed, Zerubbabel was standing before a seemingly insurmountable "mountain" of opposition. The enemies did not rest; they tried everything to hinder the building of the house of God in Jerusalem.

Our Great Mountain

What a tremendous prophetic picture for the Church today. How often we have experienced this "great mountain," which attempts to annihilate our entire work. How many men of God, ministries and churches have simply folded because of this seemingly insurmountable mountain of opposition?

However, as we have seen in verse 7, the opposition, this "great mountain," should not concern us because the building of the spiritual house of God will not be done with weapons of war, of the flesh, "but by my spirit, saith the Lord of hosts."

Built Because of Grace

Under the leadership of Zerubbabel, the temple would be built. He would put in the headstone; that is, the keystone to the building. In that moment of final construction, voices are heard saying, "Grace, grace unto it." This reveals the spiritual quality of the house. It didn't come into being because of the energetic creativeness of the people; not because of their expertise, or the leadership of Zerubbabel, but by grace. For us this applies too: it is grace that will lead us home.

This issue is so important that for a second time it is confirmed that Zerubbabel would finish his task:

Zechariah 4:8-9: "Moreover the word of the LORD came unto me, saying, 9 The hands of Zerubbabel have laid the foundation of this house; his hands shall also finish it; and thou shalt know that the LORD of hosts hath sent me unto you."

(See) Ezra 3:8; 6:14-16; Haggai 2:18; 1 Corinthians 2:4

These words were most comforting to Israel; they would see the temple completed during the time of Zerubbabel. For us, it reveals that the foundation is built; Jesus Christ is the head cornerstone, and He will see to its completion because He said, "I will build my church."

Zechariah 4:10: "For who hath despised the day of small things? for they shall rejoice, and shall see the plummet in the hand of Zerubbabel with those seven; they are the eyes of the LORD, which run to and fro through the whole earth."

(See) 2 Chronicles 16:9; Nehemiah 4:2-4; Haggai 2:3; Zechariah 1:10; Revelation 5:6

Apparently, during the construction of the temple in Jerusalem, it seemed like they were only accomplishing "small things" due to the many adversaries, but that did not change God's resolution. Zerubbabel will finish the temple. He has "the plummet in [his] hand"; that means the authority of guiding the construction of the temple. A plummet is a tool by which one can measure the vertical plumb line (straightness) of a building. It was not in Zerubbabel's power, rather under the "eyes of the Lord." He will not only see to it that it is built properly, but also the eyes of the Lord will watch over it. Again, we must emphasize that this is not limited to Jerusalem, but extends to "the whole earth."

The Two Olive Trees

Zechariah 4:11-12: "Then answered I, and said unto him, What are these two olive trees upon the right side of the candlestick and upon the left side thereof? 12 And I answered again, and said unto him, What be these two olive branches which through the two golden pipes empty the golden oil out of themselves?"

This is quite mysterious. The olive trees and olive branches are the actual supplier of oil for the seven lamps! Most certainly we can say Zechariah had never seen such a thing. This is a very unusual picture: two olive trees, with two branches pouring out the golden oil for the menorah.

Who are these two? Revelation 11:3-4 reads: "And I will give power unto my two witnesses, and they shall prophesy a thousand two hundred and threescore days, clothed in sackcloth. These are the two olive trees, and the two candlesticks standing before the God of the earth." They are not identified by name in Holy Scripture. I am inclined to be in the camp of those who think they are Moses and Elijah. Why Moses and Elijah? For one thing, both did not die in Jerusalem. Remember, Jesus said, "...for it cannot be that a prophet perish out of Jerusalem" (Luke 13:33).

Actually, Elijah didn't die an earthly death at all; he was raptured into heaven. Moses did not die naturally, but God took his life while he was still functioning at 100%. Also, Moses was buried outside the land of Israel. Furthermore, both of these prophets wanted to die. That means, spiritually speaking, they had become a burnt offering. They were totally consumed by the work of the Lord; thus, they symbolized absolute dedication to the Lord.

Verse 6 gives us an additional clue to the identity of the two witnesses: "These have power to shut heaven, that it rain not in the days of their prophecy: and have power over waters to turn them to blood, and to smite the earth with all plagues, as often as they will" (Revelation 11:6). Elijah was the one whom the Lord used to shut up the heavens. To Moses, God gave the power to turn water into blood.

Moses and Elijah on the Mount

It was Moses and Elijah who appeared with Jesus on the Mount of Transfiguration: "And as he prayed, the fashion of his countenance was altered, and his raiment was white and glistering. And, behold, there talked with him two men, which were Moses and Elias: Who appeared in glory, and spake of his decease which he should accomplish at Jerusalem" (Luke 9:29-31). Jesus spoke several times about His death while alive. Moses, who represents God's law, prayed to God to end his life: "Yet now, if thou wilt forgive their sin; and if not, blot me, I pray thee, out of thy book which thou hast written" (Exodus 32:32). Moses is willing to die for his people. We can certainly say that Moses' life was put on the altar of sacrifice; there was nothing left of self—he was consumed with servitude to God.

Elijah too prayed to God to end his life after he had fled from Jezebel out of fear: "But he himself went a day's journey into the wilderness, and came and sat down under a juniper tree: and he requested for himself that he might die; and said, It is enough; now, O LORD, take away my life; for I am not better than my fathers" (1 Kings 19:4).

I cannot think of any other people who qualify as being these two olive trees, who "[emptied] the golden oil out of themselves."

Now the angel asks the question to Zechariah:

Zechariah 4:13: "And he answered me and said, Knowest thou not what these be? And I said, No, my lord."

The angel then gives him a very definite answer:

Zechariah 4:14: "Then said he, These are the two anointed ones, that stand by the Lord of the whole earth."

(See) Exodus 29:7; 40:15; 1 Samuel 16:12-13; Micah 4:13; Revelation 11:4

As evident from the last three words, "the whole earth," the issue is no longer limited to the rebuilding of the temple of the Lord by Zerubbabel, or to Israel's future, but extends to salvation for the whole world. Here we recognize the prophetic Word foreshadowing John 3:16: "For God so loved the world, that he gave his only begotten Son, that whosoever believeth in him should not perish, but have everlasting life."

Two important objects are revealed in this fifth night vision of Zechariah. The golden candlestick and the two olive trees, supplying the fuel for the light. These are the instruments by which God caused the temple to be rebuilt at that time. But prophetically, it reaches into the whole world, as the last verse indicates, "stand by the Lord of the whole earth."

Chapter 5

Introduction

The sixth and seventh visions of Zechariah are quite different from the previous five. These two visions reveal relentless destruction. No grace is shown whatsoever. First, he sees a flying scroll, which he identifies, but then he sees something that he does not recognize, so the angel has to give the answer: "This is an ephah that goeth forth."

Obviously, these visions were connected to the previous one, where Zechariah had to be awakened, "as a man that is awaken out of his sleep." Now he introduces this vision with the following words.

The Sixth Night Vision: The Flying Scroll

Zechariah 5:1: "Then I turned, and lifted up mine eyes, and looked, and behold a flying roll."

(See) Jeremiah 36:2; Ezekiel 2:9

He turned from what he had previously seen, the two olive trees, the two anointed ones that stand by the Lord of the whole earth, and now he sees a "flying roll." Zechariah identifies it plainly, without asking the angel what it is. But the angel wants confirmation and asks the question:

Zechariah 5:2: "And he said unto me, What seest thou? And I answered, I see a flying roll; the length thereof is twenty cubits, and the breadth thereof ten cubits."

Zechariah identifies this as a flying scroll or letter, and the dimensions thereof: 20 x 10 cubits.

Measurements of the Scroll

The number 20, according to Ed Vallowe's book *Biblical Mathematics*, stands for redemption. He writes: "The males of the children of Israel had to offer a ransom for their souls at the age of twenty. In connection with this ransom, twenty gerahs are mentioned (See Exodus 30:12-14). The money that was given for their ransom was silver money. Silver is a symbol of redemption."

What is the significance of ten? Dr. Vallowe writes: "As the basis of the decimal system, ten has been a significant number in all historical ages. This is a number of testimony...God gave the Ten Commandments to man for him to bear testimony before God and man. There were ten plagues upon Egypt and Pharaoh during the days of Moses...Abraham prayed for ten righteous people within the wicked city of Sodom."

If we are to take notice of the measurements—and we should because it's mentioned here—then we may say that this flying scroll demonstrates the testimony of redemption.

Redemption or Curse?

However, the angel gives quite a different meaning to this flying scroll:

Zechariah 5:3-4: "Then said he unto me, This is the curse that goeth forth over the face of the whole earth: for every one that stealeth shall be cut off as on this side according to it; and every one that sweareth shall be cut off as on that side according to it. 4 I will bring it forth, saith the LORD of hosts, and it shall enter into the house of the thief, and into the house of him that sweareth falsely by my name: and it shall remain in the midst of his house, and shall consume it with the timber thereof and the stones thereof."

(See) Leviticus 14:45; Proverbs 3:33; Isaiah 24:6; Jeremiah 26:6; Hosea 4:2-3; Malachi 3:5, 8-9; 4:6; Matthew 5:33-36; Hebrews 6:8

There is no redemption, no salvation, no grace, but utter destruction.

How are we to understand this seeming contradiction? This is the testimony of redemption that was rejected and became judgment unto destruction. The intended blessing is now turned into a curse.

We read, for example, how the intended curse of Balaam against Israel turned into a blessing: "Nevertheless the LORD thy God would not hearken unto Balaam; but the LORD thy God turned the curse into a blessing unto thee, because the LORD thy God loved thee" (Deuteronomy 23:5).

The law of God, the testimony of redemption, is a two-edged sword—it is a blessing and a curse. This is detailed in Deuteronomy chapter 29.

Salvation or Wrath?

Another example is found in the New Testament. This

189

occurs during the time when the sixth seal is opened. We read in Revelation 6:15-16: "And the kings of the earth, and the great men, and the rich men, and the chief captains, and the mighty men, and every bondman, and every free man, hid themselves in the dens and in the rocks of the mountains; And said to the mountains and rocks, Fall on us, and hide us from the face of him that sitteth on the throne, and from the wrath of the Lamb." The Lamb of God stands for salvation. He takes away the sins of the world, but in this case, it's the other side of the story. Those who could have been saved by the blood of the Lamb are experiencing the most horrible thing anyone can possibly experience: the realization that the Lamb of God they rejected could have saved them. Now the Lamb of God rejects them.

Stealing

The two-sided message of the scroll is a testimony against those who steal, lie and swear falsely in His name. Stealing is wanting something that does not belong to me.

Just think for a moment what our modern financial and economic system is built upon. A popular quote from a movie hit the nail on the head: "Greed is good." Our modern society is built on the precepts of covetousness: wanting that which does not belong to me; earning money without working.

We can trace this evil desire back to our first mother, Eve. She desired that which was not hers: "And when the woman saw that the tree was good for food, and that it was pleasant to the eyes, and a tree to be desired to make one wise, she took of the fruit thereof, and did eat, and gave also unto her husband with her; and he did eat" (Genesis 3:6).

We must also note that this is not directed against Israel only, but "the whole earth" (Zechariah 5:3).

When we begin to realize the seriousness of this message, I think we will be extremely cautious in using the name of God in connection with Lucifer's territory.

This twofold message exposes the content of the life of modern man. What is the fuel and the driving force in modern society? We can summarize it with just one phrase: "the love of money." It is the hoarding of possessions, whether I have earned them or not; it's wanting more things, desiring what others have.

Moreover, dishonesty is committed under religious pretenses, "sweareth falsely by my name." James speaks to the Church when he writes in James 5:3: "Your gold and silver is cankered; and the rust of them shall be a witness against you, and shall eat your flesh as it were fire. Ye have heaped treasure together for the last days." This verse must be uncomfortable for those who follow the false gospel of prosperity. Note that it targets our time: "for the last days."

The Seventh Night Vision: An Ephah

Now we come to the seventh vision. This time, the angel invites Zechariah to see:

Zechariah 5:5: "Then the angel that talked with me went forth, and said unto me, Lift up now thine eyes, and see what is this that goeth forth."

Zechariah does not know what it is. He could not identify it as he did the flying scroll.

Zechariah 5:6: "And I said, What is it? And he said, This is an ephah that goeth forth. He said moreover, This is their resemblance through all the earth."

(See) Leviticus 19:36; Micah 6:10

What is an ephah? Based on *Unger's Bible Dictionary*, an ephah is "a measure of Egyptian origin and in very common use among the Hebrews. It contains 10 omers. It can also mean in Hebrew 'gloom' or 'darkness.'" We do know it is a container for measuring dry goods. Measuring is also related to judgment. We have an example in the book of Daniel, where Belshazzar, King of the Chaldeans, saw the handwriting on the wall, "TEKEL; Thou art weighed in the balances, and art found wanting" (Daniel 5:27).

We emphasize again that this is directed toward the Jewish people in the first place, but it also includes "all the earth."

The Ephah and a Woman

This ephah relates to a woman, as is described in the next two verses:

Zechariah 5:7-8: "And, behold, there was lifted up a talent of lead: and this is a woman that sitteth in the midst of the ephah. 8 And he said, This is wickedness. And he cast it into the midst of the ephah; and he cast the weight of lead upon the mouth thereof."

(See) Hosea 12:7; Amos 8:5; Micah 6:11

This is the epitome of evil and wickedness. I take the liberty to identify this woman with Revelation 17:5: "And upon her forehead was a name written, MYSTERY, BABYLON THE GREAT, THE MOTHER OF HARLOTS AND ABOMINATIONS OF THE EARTH."

The manifestation of wickedness is contained in the ephah and sealed with a talent of lead. We know that lead is a very heavy substance. In olden times, lead was used for a plumb line, because the weight of it would not easily sway in the wind; therefore, it gave precise judgment of location. The lead, therefore, signifies total judgment.

Two Women

But then something strange happened:

Zechariah 5:9: "Then lifted I up mine eyes, and looked, and, behold, there came out two women, and the wind was in their wings; for they had wings like the wings of a stork: and they lifted up the ephah between the earth and the heaven."

(See) Leviticus 11:13, 19; Psalm 104:17; Jeremiah 8:7

The two unidentified women must be of demonic origin, because they had "wings like the wings of a stork"—a stork is an unclean animal. These two flying women car-

193

ried away the ephah with the woman inside, sealed with a lead lid. That indicates the fullness of wickedness—there is apparently no point of return.

Land of Shinar: Babylon

Next comes a natural question and answer:

Zechariah 5:10-11: "Then said I to the angel that talked with me, Whither do these bear the ephah? 11 And he said unto me, To build it an house in the land of Shinar: and it shall be established, and set there upon her own base."

(See) Genesis 10:10; 11:2; 14:1; Isaiah 11:11; Jeremiah 29:5; Daniel 1:2

The land of Shinar is the land of Babylon, the embodiment of ultimate evil. The very name Babylon means "gate of God." Here we see the imitation of the great deceiver: it is no longer the one way, one person, who said, "I am the way, the truth, and the life: no man cometh unto the Father, but by me" (John 14:6), but a substitute: Babylon—*gate of God*. Babylon represents the entire world, particularly the religious world.

Although the kingdom of Babylon is described as the best of the four Gentile superpowers, it is also identified as the last kingdom, the worst. Daniel reveals the king of Babylon as the head of gold, and Nebuchadnezzar himself is called "a king of kings" (Daniel 2:37). This reminds us of the real King of kings in Revelation 19:16: "And he hath on his vesture and on his thigh a name written, KING OF KINGS, AND LORD OF LORDS." But the kingdom that was considered the best and closest to God becomes the epitome and manifestation of ultimate evil.

Does it mean the physical, literal Babylon? No: it's the whole world. We remember this from verse 3, "This is the curse that goeth forth over the face of the whole earth"; and verse 6, "This is their resemblance through all the earth." Shinar-Babylon is not local but global—the whole world.

No Future for Planet Earth

In summary, this twofold vision with its twofold message, simply declares to Israel and the rest of the world: there is no future for planet Earth. Judgment unto destruction is determined by God and clearly proclaimed by His prophets: "For, behold, the LORD cometh forth out of his place, and will come down, and tread upon the high places of the earth. And the mountains shall be molten under him, and the valleys shall be cleft, as wax before the fire, and as the waters that are poured down a steep place" (Micah 1:3-4).

There is only one escape: Jesus Christ, who invites everyone, "Whosoever will" to come, and guarantees, "Him that cometh to me, I will in no wise cast out."

Chapter 6

Introduction

This is the eighth and last night vision Zechariah passes on to us. He clearly sees something with his eyes and describes what he sees—four chariots or wagons coming out from between two mountains, and those mountains are made of brass or copper.

Before we go into details of this vision, let us first reaffirm that Zechariah is addressing the Jewish people in Jerusalem. Here we must recall the words of our Lord: "Salvation is of the Jews." When we read of Judah, Jerusalem or Zion, it is connected to God's eternal plan of salvation, which was accomplished through Jesus Christ our Lord, when He poured out His life in His blood on Calvary's Cross.

Quite naturally, the entire world, under the leadership of the devil, stands in opposition to Judah and Jerusalem. The devil has no intention to surrender his own to God. Who are "his own"? Answer: "He who sins is of the devil." He tries everything in his power to distract the people of the world from knowing that salvation has been accomplished through Jesus Christ and is freely offered to "whosoever will." That leads us again to the conclusion: prophecy is not limited to Israel but includes the whole world.

The Eighth Night Vision: Four Chariots and Two Mountains

Zechariah 6:1: "And I turned, and lifted up mine eyes, and looked, and, behold, there came four chariots out from between two mountains; and the mountains were mountains of brass."

(See) Daniel 7:3; 8:22; Zechariah 1:18

Zechariah describes what he sees. There is apparently no need to explain the two mountains and the four chariots. He also recognizes that these mountains are of metal, translated in the KJV as brass, which in the Hebrew is called copper.

What are we to understand about these two mountains? Mountains symbolize power and strength. When a mountain is in your path of travel, then you are faced with great difficulties. Travel in ancient times was limited, either by animal or by foot. Worse yet, these mountains are of brass. That means no rest, no shade, no digging for water.

Jeremiah speaks against Babylon: "...I am against thee, O destroying mountain, saith the Lord..." (Jeremiah 51:25). We read in Zechariah 4:7: "Who are thou, O great mountain? Before Zerubbabel thou shalt become a plain...."

Next he describes the chariots and the color of the horses:

Zechariah 6:2-3: "In the first chariot were red horses; and in the second chariot black horses; 3 And in the third chariot white horses; and in the fourth chariot grisled and bay horses."

(See) Revelation 6:2-8

This vision is not understandable for Zechariah, thus the question:

Zechariah 6:4: "Then I answered and said unto the angel that talked with me, What are these, my lord?"

(See) Zechariah 1:9

Zechariah had seen in his first vision a rider that sat upon a red horse, followed by red horses, speckled and white; but here he sees the chariots with the horses: red, black, white and "grisled," or speckled.

Four Horses of the Apocalypse

Our mind directs us to Revelation 6, when the seals are being opened and, as a result, John saw a white, a red, a black, and a pale horse. Are we to assume there is a relationship between these two visions? Not likely. The Revelation horses reveal judgment unto destruction. In Revelation 6:8 it says: "And I looked, and behold a pale horse: and his name that sat on him was Death, and Hell followed with him. And power was given unto them over the fourth part of the earth, to kill with sword, and with hunger, and with death, and with the beasts of the earth." Such is not the case in Zechariah's vision.

Spirit Horses

The angel's answer reveals a totally different function of

these chariots and horses:

Zechariah 6:5: "And the angel answered and said unto me, These are the four spirits of the heavens, which go forth from standing before the Lord of all the earth."

(See) 1 Kings 22:19; Job 1:6; Psalm 68:17; Jeremiah 49:36; Ezekiel 37:9; Daniel 7:2, 10; 11:4; Zechariah 4:14; Matthew 24:31; Luke 1:19; Hebrews 1:7; Revelation 7:1

The chariots and the horses are identified as "the four spirits of the heavens." Most translations use the word "wind." Thus, we can say with assurance that these are heavenly identities; their task is to inspect planet earth.

Zechariah asked about the horses in chapter 1, and the angel said, "These are they whom the Lord hath sent to walk to and fro through the earth" (Zechariah 1:10). Here we see that these four chariots with the horses have a related task: to observe the people on the earth.

Next, the angel gives further explanation about the horses:

Zechariah 6:6-7: "The black horses which are therein go forth into the north country; and the white go forth after them; and the grisled go forth toward the south country. 7 And the bay went forth, and sought to go that they might walk to and fro through the earth: and he said, Get you hence, walk to and fro through the earth. So they walked to and fro through the earth."

(See) Genesis 13:1; Jeremiah 1:14-15; Ezekiel 1:4; Zechariah 1:10

Checking Planet Earth

He first identifies the black and the white horses; they go to the north. I don't think we should attempt to identify countries that lay to the north of Israel, because this is a vision that reveals something literally out of this world. Their activity is clear: they are checking out planet Earth, the northern and the southern hemisphere.

Verse 8 presents another mystery:

Zechariah 6:8: "Then cried he upon me, and spake unto me, saying, Behold, these that go toward the north country have quieted my spirit in the north country."

(See) Ezekiel 5:13

In this case, he speaks again of the "north country." It seems like a proclamation of peace, "All is quiet on the front." This again corresponds with the first vision, "...behold, all the earth sitteth still, and is at rest" (Zechariah 1:11).

We must look back at the first vision, where the Lord makes the distinct difference between Jerusalem and the heathen; that is, the whole world: "...I am jealous for Jerusalem and for Zion with a great jealousy. And I am very sore displeased with the heathen that are at ease: for I was but a little displeased, and they helped forward the affliction" (Zechariah 1:14-15).

Note the words, "that are at ease." When it comes to Jerusalem, Zionism and the Jewish people, the world really does not care; they are "at ease." There are innumerable opinions on how to deal with Jerusalem and Israel, but one thing on which all nations agree:

Jerusalem should not be the capital city of the Jewish state of Israel. With that, the nations are helping the enemies of the Jews, "they helped forward the affliction."

Northern Hemisphere

If we speculate that "the north country" represents the northern hemisphere, then we are to understand it to be the Roman world; that is, Europe and all the colonial countries, along with Russia. Today, they have achieved a certain level of peace. Such is not the case in the south. However, since we don't read any further information, we simply have to leave it as written. Those four chariots and horses are the reporters to "the Lord of all the earth."

Back to Judah

With verse 9, something new is revealed:

Zechariah 6:9: "And the word of the LORD came unto me, saying,"

Nothing more is said about those two mountains, the four chariots, and the horses. Zechariah receives a command to do something very specific:

Zechariah 6:10: "Take of them of the captivity, even of Heldai, of Tobijah, and of Jedaiah, which are come from Babylon, and come thou the same day, and go into the house of Josiah the son of Zephaniah;"

(See) Ezra 8:1; Jeremiah 28:6

He is to take these three men to the house of Josiah.
What next?

Zechariah 6:11: "Then take silver and gold, and make
crowns, and set them upon the head of Joshua the son
of Josedech, the high priest;"

(See) Exodus 28:36; 2 Samuel 12:30; Ezra 3:2; Psalm 21:3;
Song of Solomon 3:11; Haggai 1:1

This is doubtless a prophetic demonstration of the future.

A crown is a symbol of political authority and does
not belong on the head of a priest. This most certainly
does not indicate that Joshua, the son of Josedech, is the
Messiah, or the priest king. It is a prophetic demonstration of no one other than the One who is to come, as we
will learn in the next few verses.

The Branch

Zechariah 6:12-13: "And speak unto him, saying, Thus
speaketh the LORD of hosts, saying, Behold the man
whose name is The BRANCH; and he shall grow up out
of his place, and he shall build the temple of the LORD:
13 Even he shall build the temple of the LORD; and he
shall bear the glory, and shall sit and rule upon his
throne; and he shall be a priest upon his throne: and the
counsel of peace shall be between them both."

(See) Psalm 21:5; 80:15-17; 110:4; Isaiah 4:2; 9:6-7; 11:1, 10; 22:24;
Micah 5:5; Zechariah 3:8; Malachi 3:1; Hebrews 3:1

Doubtless, this is speaking of the Lord Himself, "The BRANCH." He is the *tsemach*. The prophet Isaiah heralded His coming over 700 years before his birth: "And there shall come forth a rod out of the stem of Jesse, and a Branch shall grow out of his roots" (Isaiah 11:1).

We read of this Branch in Zechariah 3:8:"Hear now, O Joshua the high priest, thou, and thy fellows that sit before thee: for they are men wondered at: for, behold, I will bring forth my servant the BRANCH." Thus, we learn that Joshua, the high priest, is not the branch; however, he is the servant of the BRANCH; he was cleansed by God Himself, as revealed in Zechariah 3:4: "Take away the filthy garments from him." After Joshua is cleansed and purified, prophecy is revealed pointing to the Lord Jesus Christ.

While this speaks of the temple that was rebuilt by the Jews who returned from Babylon, it also demonstrates prophetically the coming of the *tsemach*, the BRANCH.

More Crowns

But there is more: Other crowns are being given.

Zechariah 6:14: "And the crowns shall be to Helem, and to Tobijah, and to Jedaiah, and to Hen the son of Zephaniah, for a memorial in the temple of the LORD."

(See) Mark 14:9

These crowns are God-given authority for the building of the visible temple in Jerusalem, but this prophecy also extends to the spiritual temple. Jesus made that distinction when He spoke of the destruction of the temple made of stone and the spiritual temple He will raise up: "Destroy this temple, and in three days I will raise it up...But he spake of the temple of his body" (John 2:19, 21).

The Spiritual Temple

Zechariah 6:15: "And they that are far off shall come and build in the temple of the LORD, and ye shall know that the LORD of hosts hath sent me unto you. And this shall come to pass, if ye will diligently obey the voice of the LORD your God."

(See) Isaiah 56:6-8; 60:10; Ephesians 2:13

Doubtless, this speaks first of all members of the Church which have come from "far off"; from all over the world. The Apostle Peter speaks of this temple: "Ye also, as lively stones, are built up a spiritual house, an holy priesthood, to offer up spiritual sacrifices, acceptable to God by Jesus Christ" (1 Peter 2:5). The Apostle Paul confirms in Ephesians 2:21 this spiritual temple, the habitation of God, "In whom all the building fitly framed together groweth unto an holy temple in the Lord."

Prefabricated Temple

The first temple, built in Jerusalem under King Solomon, was actually a prefabricated construction by foreigners. This is evidenced in 2 Chronicles 2:17: "And Solomon numbered all the strangers that were in the land of Israel, after the numbering wherewith David his father had numbered them; and they were found an hundred and fifty thousand and three thousand and six hundred."

This temple was not built on site but somewhere else, and then assembled in Jerusalem. Surely this is a picture of the Church of Jesus Christ, which is made up of believers from all over the world. When the spiritual house is finished, then there is no more construction; our work will be done. Nothing can be added, altered, or repaired on that temple. This was also demonstrated during the building of the first temple: "And the house, when it was in building, was built of stone made ready before it was brought thither: so that there was neither hammer nor axe nor any tool of iron heard in the house, while it was in building" (1 Kings 6:7).

Chapter 7

Introduction

After Zechariah had received eight prophetic visions, primarily of spiritual and heavenly substance relating to his people Israel, he now finds himself back in Jerusalem, confronted with earthly realities.

This is down-to-earth information. Zechariah is now dealing with physical realities—the preparation of the people for the building of the temple.

Back to Jerusalem

Zechariah 7:1: "And it came to pass in the fourth year of king Darius, that the word of the LORD came unto Zechariah in the fourth day of the ninth month, even in Chisleu;"

(See) Nehemiah 1:1

Mentioning King Darius points to the fact that the political authority of a foreign king was accepted. Most commentaries agree that this was in the second year of the rebuilding of the temple, which lasted a total of four years. The month Chisleu is equivalent to November/December. The year is 518 BC.

Bethel Asks for Prayer

The next verse needs some explanation to grasp the meaning:

Zechariah 7:2: "When they had sent unto the house of God Sherezer and Regemmelech, and their men, to pray before the LORD,"

(See) 1 Kings 13:6; Jeremiah 26:19; Zechariah 8:21

We are not clearly told who "they" are. So, let's read the NIV translation: "The people of Bethel had sent Sharezer and Regem-Melek, together with their men, to entreat the LORD." The people are from Bethel, which means "house of God." This is the place where Jacob had his dream and said, "...How dreadful is this place! this is none other but the house of God, and this is the gate of heaven" (Genesis 28:17).

The inhabitants of Bethel were not of the tribe of Judah, but they recognized the God who brought Judah back from captivity after 70 years. They also knew that the temple in Jerusalem was under construction. They came to ask a specific question regarding their religious activity:

Zechariah 7:3: "And to speak unto the priests which were in the house of the LORD of hosts, and to the prophets, saying, Should I weep in the fifth month, separating myself, as I have done these so many years?"

(See) Deuteronomy 17:9; Ezra 3:10-12; Jeremiah 52:12; Zechariah 8:19;
Malachi 2:7

Religious Activity

The fifth month is Av (July/August). *Unger's Bible Dictionary*, page 164, names three reasons for fasting:

1) New moon; fast for death of Aaron, commemorated by children of Jethuel, who furnished wood to temple [construction] after the captivity.

2) Fast in memory of God's declaration against murmurers entering Canaan (Num. 14:29-31).

3) Fast, because in the time of Ahaz the evening lamp went out.

These people were religiously active. They did what they were supposed to do.

But there is no reaction from the priests or the prophets. The next verse reads:

Zechariah 7:4: "Then came the word of the LORD of hosts unto me, saying,"

Apparently, the men of Bethel did not need additional instruction from the priests or prophets; they needed to hear directly from the Lord, and that's what transpired:

Zechariah 7:5-7: "Speak unto all the people of the land, and to the priests, saying, When ye fasted and mourned in the fifth and seventh month, even those seventy years, did ye at all fast unto me, even to me? 6 And when ye did eat, and when ye did drink, did not ye eat for yourselves, and drink for yourselves? 7 Should ye not hear the words which the LORD hath cried by the former prophets, when Jerusalem was inhabited and in prosper-

ity, and the cities thereof round about her, when men inhabited the south and the plain?"

(See) Isaiah 1:11-12; 58:4-5; Jeremiah 17:26; 22:21; Zechariah 1:12;
Matthew 6:16; Romans 14:6

We note that this is addressed "unto all the people":
those who came from Bethel and those who had returned
from the Babylonian captivity. In other words, it was addressed to all of Israel.

The Lord asked three significant questions:

1) Did you fast because of Me?
2) Did you feast for yourselves?
3) Why did you not listen to the prophets?

While they fasted in the fifth month, they also had reasons to feast. Here again, *Unger's Bible Dictionary* (p.
164):

1) Feast, when wood was stored in temple.
2) Feast in memory of law providing for sons and
daughters alike inheriting estate of parents.

Fasting and Feasting

They fasted and were feasting as well. In plain words,
they did their religious duty for the sake of their own
selves. Now they inquire if they did enough.

The Lord reminds them of Jerusalem's former glory,
the times under David and Solomon, when peace and
prosperity reigned. This included Bethel, the place located about 20 kilometers north of Jerusalem. Interestingly, it also mentions the south and the plain, which
includes part of today's Negev. That was the time when

God looked upon the people and the land favorably.

It stands to reason therefore that the Israelites were in dire need during those days; they were hoping for the "good ole days" to return. They knew that the God of Israel was the source of all blessing; subsequently, they practiced their religious duty for the purpose of obtaining favor from God.

Next comes the Lord's thundering accusations against His people:

> **Zechariah 7:8-10:** "And the word of the LORD came unto Zechariah, saying, 9 Thus speaketh the LORD of hosts, saying, Execute true judgment, and show mercy and compassions every man to his brother: 10 And oppress not the widow, nor the fatherless, the stranger, nor the poor; and let none of you imagine evil against his brother in your heart."

(See) Exodus 22:21-22; Ezekiel 18:8; 45:9; Micah 6:8; Zechariah 8:16-17

They faithfully practiced their religious feasts, but apparently in a shallow manner; not in truth or compassion. They failed to practice the most essential thing, which can be summarized with the words of our Lord: "Thou shalt love thy neighbor as thyself" (Matthew 19:19). Their personal well-being, the accumulation of possessions, was how they defined the blessings of the Lord.

Blessings or Success?

What a message for the Church! In reading Christian literature today and listening to the voices over the air, it becomes crystal clear that we confuse blessing with success, possessions with compassion. When it comes to the poor of the land in this nation, they are either totally ignored or brushed off with the words, "They are too lazy to work." Often, Scripture is used to support such heartlessness, "...If any would not work, neither should he eat" (2 Thessalonians 3:10). But this Scripture is not applicable to a nation; it is addressed to the Church. Would you let a member of your church die of starvation because he or she does not work?

Diabolical Self-centeredness

Regarding immigrants—legal or illegal—allow for the possibility that the Lord brings these people to us, because we were too lazy to go to them and present the Gospel.

We too often think about ourselves, our family, our people. Self-centeredness is probably more evident today than ever before. What happened to "love thy neighbor as thyself"?

We are reminded of the words found in 2 Timothy 3, which specifically emphasizes the last days: "For men shall be lovers of their own selves, covetous, boasters, proud, blasphemers, disobedient to parents, unthankful, unholy, Without natural affection, trucebreakers, false accusers, incontinent, fierce, despisers of those that are good, Traitors, heady, highminded, lovers of pleasures more than lovers of God" (verses 2-4).

Israel did "imagine evil against his brother in [his] heart." That was the accusation of God against His people.

211

Hear the Word of God

Not heeding the Word of God and its warning of righteous judgment; not practicing mercy and compassion, leads to the hardening of the spiritual ear:

Zechariah 7:11: "But they refused to hearken, and pulled away the shoulder, and stopped their ears, that they should not hear."

(See) Psalm 58:4; Jeremiah 5:3, 21; 7:26; 8:5; 17:23

Throughout the Bible, over and again, man is invited, admonished, even urged to hear what the Lord has to say. In the last book of the Bible, we read of the exalted Lord urging the church seven times: "He that hath an ear, let him hear what the Spirit sayeth unto the churches."

Israel was chosen by God to be the nation above all other nations on the face of the earth, yet they stubbornly refused to listen to the prophetic Word of God. This is a deliberate act of rebellion. It reminds us of disobedient children: when faced with the truth, they will shrug their shoulders and act like they don't know what is being said; thus, deliberately refusing to acknowledge their wrongdoing.

Hear the Prophets

Zechariah 7:12: "Yea, they made their hearts as an adamant stone, lest they should hear the law, and the words which the LORD of hosts hath sent in his spirit by the former prophets: therefore came a great wrath from the LORD

212

of hosts."

(See) 2 Chronicles 36:13, 16; Nehemiah 9:30; Isaiah 48:4; Ezekiel 3:7-9

These accusations were directed "unto all the people" in the first place, but include the entire world.

Do we find many righteous people, upright in heart and full of compassion? The brutality and hatred against our fellow man is the very nature of our being; it is the old Adamic flesh with a heart of stone. It needs to come to the cross and remain there until the death of the old nature.

Unconditional Waiting

Israel refused to listen to the prophets. Today, Churchianity has excluded the prophetic Word from the proclamation of the Gospel. Worse yet, Bible-believing Christianity increasingly refuses to heed the prophetic Word: "waiting for the coming of our Lord Jesus Christ." This plain and simple admonition to wait is being changed. Many teach that we must first wait for the tribulation, or the middle of the tribulation. That is a false hope.

Prophets Killed

It is not just a matter of ignoring the prophetic Word or of shutting one's ear to the warning of God, but the very messengers proclaiming the warning are attacked.

Some 500 years after Zechariah, it was the Lord Jesus Christ Himself who stated, "…If we had been in the days of our fathers, we would not have been partakers with them in the blood of the prophets. Wherefore ye be witnesses unto yourselves, that ye are the children of them which killed the prophets" (Matthew 23:30-31).

We know what happened in 70 A.D. The Romans came, destroyed Jerusalem and burned the temple, not leaving one stone upon another. Hence, the Jewish people were dispersed all over planet Earth. Why? Because they refused to hear the Word of God.

When God Refuses to Hear

Zechariah 7:13: "Therefore it is come to pass, that as he cried, and they would not hear; so they cried, and I would not hear, saith the LORD of hosts:"

(See) Proverbs 1:24-28; Isaiah 1:15; Jeremiah 11:10, 14; 14:12

This too was literally fulfilled. There was no prophet in Israel for about 500 years. Finally, John the Baptist appeared on the scene with a very simple message: "...Repent ye: for the kingdom of heaven is at hand" (Matthew 3:2).

For about 500 years, they practiced their religion, read the Torah, but there was no answer from heaven; there was no prophet who said, "Thus saith the Lord God of Israel."

When we refuse to hear the words of the Lord, it will not only result in the hardening of the heart and the closing of the ear, but also something much worse: "I would not hear." He, the Lord God of Israel, would shut off His ear to the cry of His people.

214

The Land Suffers

With the rejection of the nation of Israel, the land suffered as well:

Zechariah 7:14: "But I scattered them with a whirlwind among all the nations whom they knew not. Thus the land was desolate after them, that no man passed through nor returned: for they laid the pleasant land desolate."

(See) Deuteronomy 4:27; 28:64; Jeremiah 23:19; 44:6

The fulfillment is evident from a number of historical documents. The land of Israel became a desert, virtually void of vegetation. It could no longer be defined as a pleasant land; the land was stripped of its fertile soil and exposed to the burning heat of the Middle Eastern sun.

Restoration Promise

We cannot conclude the study of this chapter without again showing God's mercy, His long-suffering and grace. His intention is to return His people to their land: "And I will bring them out from the people, and gather them from the countries, and will bring them to their own land, and feed them upon the mountains of Israel by the rivers, and in all the inhabited places of the country...And the tree of the field shall yield her fruit, and the earth shall yield her increase, and they shall be safe in their land, and shall know that I am the LORD, when I have broken the bands of their yoke, and delivered them out of the hand of those that served themselves of them" (Ezekiel 34:13, 27).

Chapter 8

Introduction

Beginning with chapter 8, the prophet Zechariah passes on the direct words of God. Only in verses 1 and 18 does Zechariah mention himself receiving the Word of God. The rest is the direct speaking of the Lord of hosts.

Zechariah is no longer involved in a dialogue, nor does he see visions that need to be explained, but he receives the words of God and passes them on.

It seems significant that the words "Lord of hosts" appear 18 times in this chapter. The word "Lord" is understood in Hebrew to be Jehovah, identifying the national name of the God of Israel. The word "hosts," according to *Strong's Hebrew Dictionary*, could be translated "a mass of persons." Thus, we recognize that God is speaking as the Almighty, the all-powerful, supreme authority over His people Israel, the city of Jerusalem, and the rest of the world. The issue here is the LORD's jealousy for Zion.

Return to Zion

Zechariah 8:1-2: "Again the word of the LORD of hosts came to me, saying, 2 Thus saith the LORD of hosts; I was jealous for Zion with great jealousy, and I was jealous for her with great fury."

(See) Nahum 1:2; Zechariah 1:14

Here it may be helpful to reread chapter 1:14: "...I am jealous for Jerusalem and for Zion with a great jealousy." Why? We dealt with the question previously, but to refresh our mind, let us also read verse 15: "And I am very sore displeased with the heathen that are at ease: for I was but a little displeased, and they helped forward the affliction." This is quite revealing: the LORD of hosts is "sore displeased" with the heathen, but only "a little displeased" with His people. Why was God—and is today—so displeased with the nations? Answer: "they helped forward the affliction."

Luciferian Pride

It seems necessary to explain this once again to better relate it to our times.

We are always in danger of the Luciferian opinion that all nations are somehow wrong and our nation is right. That seems quite natural, because we love ourselves. The Bible says, "...No man ever yet hated his own flesh" (Ephesians 5:29). For that reason, the Bible gives us the great commandment to love our neighbor as ourselves. Who is our neighbor? The ones we dislike, despise, and quite often hate. Would we all practice this commandment, there would be peace on earth.

Jesus said the following in Matthew 22:37-39: "Thou shalt love the Lord thy God with all thy heart, and with all thy soul, and with all thy mind. This is the first and great commandment. And the second is like unto it, Thou shalt love thy neighbour as thyself." Anyone who speaks about peace and freedom is instantly exposed by these precise words of our Lord, "Love they neighbour as thyself."

Love or Hate?

When we keep this biblical fact in mind, while reading and hearing the news media, even from Christian sources, we notice quickly the unbridled hatred expressed against our neighbors. Today, the often hidden hate is mainly directed against the poor, foreigners, illegal immigrants, and lately against the Muslims. In other words, we oppose anyone who is not like us. This tendency of the world, which unfortunately includes much of Christianity, stands in direct opposition to the commandment of Jesus Christ our Lord, "Love thy neighbour as thyself."

All Nations against Israel

Take Jerusalem and Israel for example. There is an abundance of Christian literature highlighting our friendship with Jews, our love for Israel and Jerusalem. Yet in reality, most contain half-truths. Joel 3:2 reads: "I will also gather all nations, and will bring them down into the valley of Jehoshaphat, and will plead with them there for my people and for my heritage Israel, whom they have scattered among the nations, and parted my land." Note carefully the words "all nations."

Is any nation really pro-Israel, or pro-Jerusalem? According to Holy Scripture, there is none! Is there any nation on the face of the earth that agrees with Israel's boundaries, according to God's covenant? There is none!

No nation takes God's Word seriously: "In the same day the LORD made a covenant with Abram, saying, Unto thy seed have I given this land, from the river of Egypt unto the great river, the river Euphrates" (Genesis 15:18).

Is there any nation that agrees with Israel regarding Jerusalem being the undivided capital city of the Jewish state? There is none!

Now we should understand why the word "jealous" appears three times in verse 2. It is directed against the nations of the world. Therefore, don't permit the diabolical thought to enter your mind that your nation is somehow different. It is NOT!

God's Return to Zion

Next comes the glorious promise of Zion's restoration:

Zechariah 8:3: "Thus saith the LORD; I am returned unto Zion, and will dwell in the midst of Jerusalem: and Jerusalem shall be called a city of truth; and the mountain of the LORD of hosts the holy mountain."

(See) Psalm 48:1-2; Isaiah 2:2-3; Jeremiah 31:23; Zechariah 1:16

It's not Rome, Moscow, Washington, London, or any other city, but Jerusalem. Truth was, is, and will be revealed in and through Jerusalem.

Zechariah 8:4-5: "Thus saith the LORD of hosts; There shall yet old men and old women dwell in the streets of Jerusalem, and every man with his staff in his hand for very age. 5 And the streets of the city shall be full of boys and girls playing in the streets thereof."

219

(See) 1 Samuel 2:31; Isaiah 65:20; Jeremiah 31:12-13

When it comes to Zion's restoration, the Lord prepares the city and the land first; then comes the people, the aged and the young.

Preparation for Restoration

In a very remarkable way, chapter 36 of the book of Ezekiel shows the succession. First, God prepares the land, and then He brings the people. Verse 8, "But ye, O mountains of Israel, ye shall shoot forth your branches, and yield your fruit to my people of Israel; for they are at hand to come."

We must keep in mind that this is the doing of "the LORD of hosts." It is the God of Israel who reveals Himself with irresistible force, "The LORD of hosts."

Often, it seems quite surprising that the Lord would concern Himself with a people who are stubborn, rebellious, and disobedient. Yet the Lord does.

Zechariah 8:6: "Thus saith the LORD of hosts; If it be marvellous in the eyes of the remnant of this people in these days, should it also be marvellous in mine eyes? saith the LORD of hosts."

(See) Numbers 11:23; Job 42:2; Psalm 118:23; 126:1-3; Jeremiah 32:17, 27; Luke 1:37; Romans 4:21

Next comes the regathering of the Jewish people:

Zechariah 8:7: "Thus saith the LORD of hosts; Behold, I will save my people from the east country, and from the west country;"

(See) Psalm 107:3; Isaiah 43:5

Note that this prophetic Word was not limited to the return of the Jewish people from Babylonian captivity. It says from the east and from the west: that means from around the world. That is actually happening in our generation. Millions upon millions of Jews have returned to the land of their fathers, but many more millions have yet to come home.

Nations Hindering Israel's Return

Immediately, we recognize why the nations, dominated by the god of this world, try so desperately to hinder the return of the Jewish people to the land of Israel. They are dividing the Promised Land into sections of Israeli and Arab territory. Israel is forced by the nations of the world to limit their territory to the geographical area before the Six-Day War. Why? So there will not be enough room to receive the remnant of about eight million Jews who are still in the Diaspora into the land of Israel.

Never must we be so naive as to think that certain political realities make it necessary to negotiate in order to accommodate the will of both the Arabs and the Jews. The real reason behind the opposition to Zionism is simply the attempted hindrance of the fulfillment of God's Word. If the land is taken away from the Jews, then they cannot return. That is the plan of the god of this world, and unanimously agreed to by all the nations of the world.

221

God's Intention for Israel

God ignores the opposition and simply states:

Zechariah 8:8: "And I will bring them, and they shall dwell in the midst of Jerusalem: and they shall be my people, and I will be their God, in truth and in righteousness."

(See) Ezekiel 11:20; 36:28; Zephaniah 3:20; Zechariah 2:11; 10:10

We notice that Israel's hope is not dependent on their ability to negotiate with the nations or with their Arab neighbors; nor can they accomplish it through weapons of war. There is only one way, and that is the way of grace. God Himself will be their truth and righteousness. This indeed is God's marvelous doing. When the LORD of hosts does something, it is absolute and final; all opposition is silenced.

Build the Temple

After revealing the prophetic Word about the Jewish people, the Lord turns to the building of the temple during those days:

Zechariah 8:9: "Thus saith the LORD of hosts; Let your hands be strong, ye that hear in these days these words by the mouth of the prophets, which were in the day that the foundation of the house of the LORD of hosts was laid, that the temple might be built."

(See) 1 Chronicles 22:13; Ezra 5:1-2; 6:14; Isaiah 35:3-4; Haggai 2:4, 18

The people are encouraged to heed the words of the

prophets.

What was the message? "Thus saith the LORD of hosts; Consider your ways. Go up to the mountain, and bring wood, and build the house; and I will take pleasure in it, and I will be glorified, saith the LORD" (Haggai 1:7-8). The Jews who had returned from Babylonian captivity were instructed to build the temple of the Lord in Jerusalem. But, as we know, they built their houses and the wall around Jerusalem instead.

Zechariah 8:10: "For before these days there was no hire for man, nor any hire for beast; neither was there any peace to him that went out or came in because of the affliction: for I set all men every one against his neighbor."

During those days, the people were working in vain. There was no gain; even the animals, the beasts of burden, brought no prosperity. Worse yet, there was no peace, but continuous war, conflict and fighting. They achieved nothing; everyone was against his neighbor.

Promise of Peace

Something new was going to happen:

Zechariah 8:11-12: "But now I will not be unto the residue of this people as in the former days, saith the LORD of hosts. 12 For the seed shall be prosperous; the vine shall give her fruit, and the ground shall give her increase, and the heavens shall give their dew; and I will cause the remnant of this people to possess all these things."

(See) Genesis 27:28; Leviticus 26:3-6; Deuteronomy 33:13, 28; Psalm 103:9; Isaiah 12:1; 61:7; Obadiah 17; Haggai 2:19; Matthew 6:33; 1 Timothy 4:8

Luther translates the words, "seed shall be prosperous" with, "they shall be seeds of peace."

This is definitely a prophecy of the coming Prince of Peace.

Later, when Jesus came, He made this promise: "Peace I leave with you, my peace I give unto you: not as the world giveth, give I unto you. Let not your heart be troubled, neither let it be afraid" (John 14:27). This is a totally different peace from anything that was ever offered in the world. Jesus actually emphasizes this fact when He says, "...not as the world giveth." In other words, the peace of the world is not real peace. His peace is so different that it passes all understanding. This type of peace is identical with the person, Jesus Christ our Lord. He is our peace, the Bible says.

As a result of their personal change, nature responds; the harvest increases. The Lord God will even moisten the ground with the dew of heaven.

"A Curse among the Heathen"

Zechariah 8:13: "And it shall come to pass, that as ye were a curse among the heathen, O house of Judah, and house of Israel; so will I save you, and ye shall be a blessing: fear not, but let your hands be strong."

(See) Genesis 12:2; Deuteronomy 20:3-4; Isaiah 19:24-25; Jeremiah 42:18; Ezekiel 34:26; Zechariah 14:11; Ephesians 6:10

The fact that the Jews were accursed among the heathen is well documented in the annals of history. For millennia they were chased from one place to another, trying desperately to be accepted by the Gentile host nations, but all in vain.

Just before their return to the land of Israel in modern times, over six million Jews were systematically and deliberately murdered under the auspices of Germany's Nazi regime.

Now all that is going to change. Israel is admonished again, "Fear not, but let your hands be strong." They now have the promise of God; they will be "seeds of peace." This is very important to understand, for only when we come in contact with the Prince of Peace can we harvest true peace. All other peace is an imitation: it will not last because it is the peace which "the world giveth."

Israel's Future

Although there are a number of nations that seem to be Israel-friendly, when we investigate it thoroughly, we note that it's only shallow. The whole world, without exception, is, must, and will be anti-Israel.

I realize that this is a hard saying, but I am convinced it is biblically-based. We must always keep in mind that this world is evil through and through: it is corrupt and hopelessly lost. Planet earth is ruled by the god of this world; all of humanity obeys the dictates of Satan. Anyone who commits sin is Satan's servant: "He who sins is of the devil." When we realize this truth, we immediately recognize our hopeless situation: not only hopeless, but also helpless. We cannot save ourselves; we cannot help ourselves. We need the interference of the supernatural, the God of heaven. We are subject to His grace; such was and always is the case.

Amazing Grace

Zechariah 8:14-15: "For thus saith the LORD of hosts; As I thought to punish you, when your fathers provoked me to wrath, saith the LORD of hosts, and I repented not: 15 So again have I thought in these days to do well unto Jerusalem and to the house of Judah: fear ye not."

(See) 2 Chronicles 36:16; Jeremiah 29:11; 31:28; Micah 7:18-20

Here we recognize God's intentions. He proclaimed severe judgment to the fathers who provoked Him, but His thoughts also turned to the well-being of Jerusalem and Judah. Grace breaks through and, praise God, not only for Israel but also for all the earth, "For God so loved the world."

Unchanging Promises

Does God change? In verse 14, He has thoughts of punishment, and in verse 15, He has thoughts of well-doing. On the surface, this may seem to be a contradiction, but it is not. All the punishments the Lord pronounced by His prophets were fully executed, but those punishments never invalidated the promises to the father of Israel— Abraham. God does not change; He continues to fulfill every single promise He has ever made. For example, Genesis 12:2: "And I will make of thee a great nation, and I will bless thee, and make thy name great; and thou shalt be a blessing." The fulfillment continues until our days.

Love Your Neighbor

Once again, the LORD of hosts pinpoints the people's responsibility toward each other:

> **Zechariah 8:16-17:** "These are the things that ye shall do; Speak ye every man the truth to his neighbour; execute the judgment of truth and peace in your gates: 17 And let none of you imagine evil in your hearts against his neighbour; and love no false oath: for all these are things that I hate, saith the LORD."

(See) Psalm 15:2; Proverbs 3:29; 6:16-19; 12:17-19; Zechariah 7:10; Ephesians 4:25

Commandment of Love

Can you imagine what would happen if all members of the Church would cease to imagine evil against one another? Quite simply, the Church would fulfill her task— hatred would be absent, and love would prevail. That is the new commandment of the Lord: "A new commandment I give unto you, That ye love one another; as I have loved you, that ye also love one another" (John 13:34).

In the midst of the world of chaos, hatred, war, controversies, and bloodshed, we are admonished to "love one another." This small group of people, the Church of Jesus Christ, would prove to be witnesses of Him; they would exhibit themselves to be true disciples: "By this shall all men know that ye are my disciples, if ye have love one to another" (John 13:35).

Joy of Fasting

Zechariah 8:18: "And the word of the LORD of hosts came unto me, saying,"

These are the same words as in the beginning, but now something glorious is being spoken by the LORD of hosts:

Zechariah 8:19: "Thus saith the LORD of hosts; The fast of the fourth month, and the fast of the fifth, and the fast of the seventh, and the fast of the tenth, shall be to the house of Judah joy and gladness, and cheerful feasts; therefore love the truth and peace."

(See) Psalm 30:11; Isaiah 12:1; 35:10; Jeremiah 52:6, 12; Zechariah 7:3, 5;
Luke 1:74-75

Fasting is not something that is joyful. A person who is fasting segregates himself from the pleasures of life, of which one is the indulgence of food. But here, the Lord specifically says that these fasts will be turned into *feasting*; there will be gladness and joy based upon "... [loving] the truth and peace." Israel is to demonstrate this through joyful feasts. They no longer have to strive toward the Lord's truth and peace, but they themselves have been translated into *love, truth* and *peace*.

Do We Really Love Truth?

We may be reluctant to admit it, but by nature we do not love truth and peace. We may affirm that we do with an oath a thousand times, but in reality, we would rather not be confronted with truth and with peace. Let us be honest in this matter. Would I really want to have my inner being, the very thoughts of my mind, exposed before the world? Am I willing to have truth revealed about the very secrets of my thought-life? Job was a person whom God could say was "perfect and upright." Yet when he was confronted with the God of truth, he had to confess: "I have heard of thee by the hearing of the ear: but now mine eye seeth thee. Wherefore I abhor myself, and repent in dust and ashes" (Job 42:5-6).

What is truth and peace? It is a person. Jesus said, "I am the truth"; He is our peace in person. We can only vaguely imagine what would happen if each of us began to walk in the light of His truth and peace.

Missionaries in Reverse

Zechariah 8:20-21: "Thus saith the LORD of hosts; It shall yet come to pass, that there shall come people, and the inhabitants of many cities: 21 And the inhabitants of one city shall go to another, saying, Let us go speedily to pray before the LORD, and to seek the LORD of hosts: I will go also."

(See) Psalm 117:1; Jeremiah 16:9; Micah 4:2-3; Zechariah 2:11

The word "people" can be translated "nations." This is

the reverse course of missionary activity; not to go out into all the world, but all the world is now coming to Israel. Why? For the sake of truth and peace.

Real Church Growth

Acts 2 confirms this divine principle: "And they, continuing daily with one accord in the temple, and breaking bread from house to house, did eat their meat with gladness and singleness of heart, Praising God, and having favour with all the people. And the Lord added to the church daily such as should be saved" (Acts 2:46-47). The words "with one accord" are the foundation of church growth.

Often we "put the cart before the horse": we try all kinds of methods to encourage people to come to church, but without making sure that we love truth and peace. That means practicing perfect unity with our brethren in the Lord in all things. That is when the Lord will add to His Church "such as should be saved."

Look at the chain reaction instituted by the practice of love, truth and peace:

Zechariah 8:22: "Yea, many people and strong nations shall come to seek the LORD of hosts in Jerusalem, and to pray before the LORD."

(See) Isaiah 2:2-3; 60:3-12

That is the true light, the beacon of freedom, peace and love, attracting the nations of the world.

Love, Truth, and Peace

Looking at Jerusalem today, the reality is certainly different. There are divisions between virtually all who are involved: between the Jews and the Arabs, the Muslims and the Christians. Every nation on the face of the earth has an opinion on how to solve the conflict. The majority agrees with the Vatican's philosophy: internationalize Jerusalem. That incorporates some truth, but in the reverse direction. The Gentiles, with force—political, financial or military—are attempting to solve the Jerusalem conflict in order to produce peace. That's not the way God intends to do it. The first requirement is to practice love, truth and peace; the rest God will do.

God Is with You

Only then will we see how Jesus' statement, "Salvation is of the Jews," is demonstrated for the entire world:

Zechariah 8:23: "Thus saith the LORD of hosts; In those days it shall come to pass, that ten men shall take hold out of all languages of the nations, even shall take hold of the skirt of him that is a Jew, saying, We will go with you: for we have heard that God is with you."

(See) Isaiah 45:14, 24; 60:14

That promise has not been fulfilled yet. Several organizations that monitor anti-Semitism tell us that there is an increase. Here, however, we see the opposite takes place. People the world over will recognize that God is with the Jews; subsequently, they want to be part of it. That is yet to be fulfilled!

231

Chapter 9

Introduction

Chapter 9 consists exclusively of the speaking of God. The message is primarily directed against Israel's enemies: from the north, along the coast, and down to Gaza. Intermingled are comforting words for Jerusalem. But the promise of the Messiah, the Lord's salvation for Israel, is the target of this chapter.

Israel's Enemies

Zechariah 9:1-2: "The burden of the word of the LORD in the land of Hadrach, and Damascus shall be the rest thereof: when the eyes of man, as of all the tribes of Israel, shall be toward the LORD. 2 And Hamath also shall border thereby; Tyrus, and Zidon, though it be very wise."

(See) Isaiah 17:1; Jeremiah 47:4; 49:23; Ezekiel 28:2-5; Amos 1:3-5

In the first two verses, six names are listed. "Hadrach," according to *Strong's Hebrew Dictionary*, was a Syrian deity. Damascus today is the capital of Syria. "Hamath" is mentioned in Numbers 34:8 as being on the border of the Promised Land. "Tyrus" and "Zidon" are located in today's Lebanon. God sees all of them in relationship to Israel.

232

Demonic Powers?

"The burden of the word of the Lord" reveals names of places but not people; thus, we must assume that this is directed against the demonic power structures of these places. It concerns the enemy of God. Important to realize is that the archenemy of God, Satan, is the same all over planet Earth.

It may be necessary to explain this issue a little further. Based on Daniel 10:13, the words "prince" and "kings" are of demonic origin: "But the prince of the kingdom of Persia withstood me one and twenty days: but, lo, Michael, one of the chief princes, came to help me; and I remained there with the kings of Persia." The Contemporary English Version translates this, "...to rescue me from the kings of Persia" (see Ephesians 3:10; 6:12; Revelation 12:7). Daniel was praying for the fulfillment of prophecy for the liberation of his people from Persia. But something was hindering the answer: it was "the prince of the kingdom of Persia" and "the kings of Persia." We know that these are demonic forces, because literal, physical people do not have the capacity to withstand spiritual entities.

Only after Michael, the archangel, assists the heavenly messenger, does the prophetic message breaks through. The next verse reads: "Now I am come to make thee understand what shall befall thy people in the latter days: for yet the vision is for many days" (Daniel 10:14). Interestingly, little is said about the Jews, while the bulk of the information is about the Gentiles. That means Gentile history reveals the future about the Jews' redemption.

The God of the Nations

Considering Daniel, we must come to the conclusion that all nations, groups of peoples, even cities and villages, are subject to demonic *princes* and *kings* who rule them. This may shock some of us, but it should not because the Bible says, "He who sins is of the devil..." (1 John 3:8, NKJV). And since all have sinned and come short of the glory of God, we are subject to the god of this world. This is confirmed in Galatians 4:3: "Even so we, when we were children, were in bondage under the elements of the world."

The exception is those who have been translated into another kingdom; they have received a new citizenship, a heavenly one. Ephesians 2:19 confirms this: "Now therefore ye are no more strangers and foreigners, but fellow citizens with the saints, and of the household of God." Yet in the flesh we retain our national citizenship for the rest of our lives.

God, the Ultimate Authority

We must add that despite all the powers of Satan and his innumerable hosts, God has the absolute and ultimate authority: "For all men's eyes will turn to the Lord—like all the tribes of Israel," says the *Tenakh* (Zechariah 9:1). The Menge translation makes it even clearer: "For to the Lord belonged the eyes of Aram (East Syria) just like all the tribes of Israel." He, the God of heaven, the God of Israel, always stands infinitely higher than any other power there is in heaven and on earth.

Tyrus Destroyed

In the next verse, Tyrus is specifically mentioned, but his riches will come to naught:

Zechariah 9:3-4: "And Tyrus did build herself a strong hold, and heaped up silver as the dust, and fine gold as the mire of the streets. 4 Behold, the Lord will cast her out, and he will smite her power in the sea; and she shall be devoured with fire."

(See) Joshua 19:29; 2 Samuel 24:7; Job 27:16;
Ezekiel 26:17; 27:33; 28:4-5, 18

Ashkelon, Gaza and Ekron

Next in line comes the southern coast of Israel: Ashkelon, Gaza, and the city of Ekron.

Zechariah 9:5-6: "Ashkelon shall see it, and fear; Gaza also shall see it, and be very sorrowful, and Ekron; for her expectation shall be ashamed; and the king shall perish from Gaza, and Ashkelon shall not be inhabited. 6 And a bastard shall dwell in Ashdod, and I will cut off the pride of the Philistines."

(See) Jeremiah 40:7; Amos 1:8; Zephaniah 2:4; Acts 8:26

This is the territory of the Philistines. Ekron is located about 70 km (around 43 mi.) northeast of Ashkelon in Judah. First Samuel 5:10 identifies this town as the place where the Philistines sent the Ark of the Covenant.

Again, we do not read any names of people. We only

have Ashkelon, Gaza, Ekron, the king of Gaza, and the Philistines. We know that the Philistines were the bitterest enemies of Israel. The strength of the Philistines was manifested in their giant Goliath, but this very powerful Goliath became the stepping-stone for David, who later became king of Israel.

These prophecies clearly proclaim one thing: there is no hope, no future, only shame for the enemies of the Lord. It seems that Ekron had hoped for some turn of good fortune because the Ark of the Covenant rested there, but that too did not help.

Judgment and Grace

The city of Ashdod today is made up of modern Israeli subdivisions and is rather prosperous. Yet verse 6 specifically says, "A bastard shall dwell in Ashdod." Most translations use the word "strangers" or "foreigners." That means the people who dwelled there had no national identity. They did not belong to the people of Israel or the Philistines.

Next God pronounces judgment, but also grace.

Zechariah 9:7: "And I will take away his blood out of his mouth, and his abominations from between his teeth: but he that remaineth, even he, shall be for our God, and he shall be as a governor in Judah, and Ekron as a Jebusite."

Again, this seems to identify demonic activity. It presents to us a picture of one devouring blood and flesh, obviously sacrificed to the idols of the Philistines.

It is God Himself who takes away these abominations,

and then likens them to the house of Judah. That's amazing grace. For better understanding, let us read from the *Tenakh*: "They shall become like a clan of Judah, and Ekron shall be like the Jebusites" (verse 7b).

We note here the mention of the Jebusites. These people were one of the original nations in the land of Canaan. The Jebusites were mentioned last in the enumeration of the ten clans residing in the Promised Land. This is documented in Genesis 15:18-21: "In the same day the LORD made a covenant with Abram, saying, Unto thy seed have I given this land, from the river of Egypt unto the great river, the river Euphrates: The Kenites, and the Kenizzites, and the Kadmonites, And the Hittites, and the Perizzites, and the Rephaims, And the Amorites, and the Canaanites, and the Girgashites, and the Jebusites."

The Jebusites were the inhabitants of the city of Jerusalem. Actually, the city was called "Jebus" first: "And David and all Israel went to Jerusalem, which is Jebus; where the Jebusites were, the inhabitants of the land" (1 Chronicles 11:4). Thus, we see that even the bitterest enemies of Israel will experience the grace of God.

The House of God

We note that these verses are not based on a vision or the Word of God that came to the prophet, but they are the direct words of God: "the burden of the word of the Lord."

Now comes the identification of the burden in verse 8:

237

Zechariah 9:8: "And I will encamp about mine house because of the army, because of him that passeth by, and because of him that returneth: and no oppressor shall pass through them any more: for now have I seen with mine eyes."

(See) Exodus 3:7; Deuteronomy 33:7; Psalm 34:7; Isaiah 52:1; 54:14; 60:18; Zechariah 2:9

The name of the city is not mentioned, but we know it is Jerusalem because of the words "mine house." Later in the New Testament, we read the words of the Lord in Mark 11:17: "...Is it not written, My house shall be called of all nations the house of prayer? but ye have made it a den of thieves."

Future Prophecy

Quite naturally, God is not just speaking about the physical Jerusalem or the temple on Mt. Moriah, built with man's hand. There is more: God is revealing to us the spiritual substance—His eternal resolutions. How do we know? Because the city of Jerusalem has been destroyed many times since the writing of the book of Zechariah, approximately 2,500 years ago. Yet we just read, "and no oppressor shall pass through them anymore." Actually, many oppressors are passing through that city even today.

Jerusalem is the only city in the world whose status is dictated by the nations of the world, obviously under the dominance of Lucifer, the god of this world.

Jerusalem Unique

If Israel were a nation like all others on planet Earth, Jerusalem would be the capital city of the sovereign state of Israel. Actually, Israel did declare Jerusalem their capital city in 1980, but the whole world rejects it with the word *illegal*. The nations decide which city should be the Jews' capital city. From the approximately 200 nations of the world, not one agrees with Israel that Jerusalem is Israel's sovereign capital city.

We must never be so naïve as to think that if the United States would move its embassy to the city of Jerusalem, that this conflict would be solved. Actually, it would agitate it even more. No political solution can solve the Jerusalem issue. We are dealing with the eternal God. It is His city, His land, and the Jews are His people.

Jerusalem is not free today and has not been free for the last 2,500 years. Jerusalem will not be free until the Prince of Peace comes. Jesus Himself prophesied: "And they shall fall by the edge of the sword, and shall be led away captive into all nations: and Jerusalem shall be trodden down of the Gentiles, until the times of the Gentiles be fulfilled" (Luke 21:24). This plainly tells us that we are still living in the times of the Gentiles, who still have power over Jerusalem. All of them—the UN, the EU, the USA and the rest of the world—are deciding what Israel can and cannot do.

Jerusalem Rejoices

In spite of seemingly insurmountable difficulties and horrendous judgments, the Lord proclaims His saving intention nevertheless:

Zechariah 9:9: "Rejoice greatly, O daughter of Zion; shout, O daughter of Jerusalem: behold, thy King cometh unto thee: he is just, and having salvation; lowly, and riding upon an ass, and upon a colt the foal of an ass."

(See) Psalm 2:6; Isaiah 45:21; Zephaniah 2:10; 3:14; Matthew 21:5; Luke 19:38; John 1:49; 12:15; Acts 22:14; 1 Peter 3:18

The Two Daughters

We may consider this verse the highlight of chapter 9, because it brings heaven down to earth. God is revealed in the flesh, but no names are mentioned. We only read, "daughter of Zion...daughter of Jerusalem." Who are they? They present to us an allegorical picture of their identity relating to the coming Savior.

The prophet Isaiah proclaimed the birth of the Messiah: "Therefore the Lord himself shall give you a sign; Behold, a virgin shall conceive, and bear a son, and shall call his name Immanuel" (Isaiah 7:14). And Micah speaks of the daughter of Zion and the daughter of Jerusalem: "And thou, O tower of the flock, the strong hold of the daughter of Zion, unto thee shall it come, even the first dominion; the kingdom shall come to the daughter of Jerusalem. Now why dost thou cry out aloud? Is there no king in thee? is thy counsellor perished? for pangs have taken thee as a woman in travail" (Micah 4:8-9).

The King of Meekness

It is quite humbling and contrary to our perception and imagination that the King of kings and Lord of lords will come to Jerusalem, "lowly, and riding upon an ass, and upon a colt the foal of an ass." Luther translates this, "poor, riding upon a donkey, a foal of a donkey." That is the epitome of poverty and extremely humiliating. The King of kings comes as a poor fellow, humble, lowly, not regarded. He is not even riding upon a donkey, but a little foal of a donkey.

Unbroken Pride of the Gentiles

Imagine the Lord of lords and King of kings, sitting on this donkey. This animal is considered to be one of the most unintelligent ones. It is destined to carry burdens all of its life. This picture indeed is embarrassing; it illustrates contempt and rejection. But it is a true picture of our Lord and Savior.

Mark and Luke specifically emphasize, "whereon never man sat." That is an unbroken animal; obviously, a picture of the Gentiles. In the process of history, God broke the pride of Judah and Israel, but not the pride of the Gentiles yet.

The Gentiles, in their diabolical pride, use lions, tigers, eagles, elephants, and other powerful animals to propagate their national identity. I have searched but have not found a nation that uses a flea, a cockroach, a maggot or a worm as a national symbol of identity. But our God is so different. He uses that which is despised and rejected to show His glory.

Jacob the Worm

Jacob, the great hero of Israel, of whom we read in Genesis 32:28: "...Thy name shall be called no more Jacob, but Israel: for as a prince hast thou power with God and with men, and hast prevailed," is pictured in Isaiah 41:14: "Fear not, thou worm Jacob, and ye men of Israel; I will help thee, saith the LORD, and thy redeemer, the Holy One of Israel." Jacob, the father of the greatest nation on planet earth, is pictured here as a rather insignificant and unimpressive animal—a worm.

Peace without Weapons?

This King, who is just and has salvation, appears in utter humility to the people of Israel, in order to execute righteous judgment and to prepare for peace:

Zechariah 9:10: "And I will cut off the chariot from Ephraim, and the horse from Jerusalem, and the battle bow shall be cut off: and he shall speak peace unto the heathen: and his dominion shall be from sea even to sea, and from the river even to the ends of the earth."

(See) Psalm 2:8; 72:3, 7-8; Isaiah 9:6-7; 11:10; 57:19; 60:12; Hosea 1:7; 2:18; Micah 5:4, 10

The chariot and the horse are symbols of military power. But they are no longer needed: "Not by might, nor by power, but by my spirit." All Israel is meant here. The name Ephraim is used collectively for the rebellious ten tribes, and Jerusalem for the tribes of Judah.

Here we learn an important lesson which, in reality, most of us refuse to accept; namely, that peace and true freedom will never be accomplished with weapons of war, by "chariot, horse, and bow." True freedom will only come about when the Prince of Peace arrives and abolishes all militaries with their equipment of destruction. It is the Lord Himself who will bring about total elimination of all weapons. That will result in the implementation of the 1,000-year Kingdom of Peace. Our perception of peace and freedom is so twisted that we are often incapable of recognizing what real, true peace is.

An Unknown Peace

Interestingly, the King does not proclaim freedom and peace to His people—Ephraim and Jerusalem—but "he shall speak peace unto the heathen." This most certainly is a prophecy identifying the Church of Jesus Christ on earth. How do we know? Because Christ gave His peace to His Church.

But that's not all. This is also a prophecy revealing the Church of Jesus Christ on earth during the 1,000-year Kingdom of Peace. That's the time when the Lord will implement His dominion over all the earth.

Of course, the peace Jesus speaks about to the Church must not be confused with the peace of the world. "Peace I leave with you, my peace I give unto you: not as the world giveth, give I unto you. Let not your heart be troubled, neither let it be afraid" (John 14:27). Thus, we have two types of peace: the peace of the world and *His* peace. One is real, the other fake.

The Blood Covenant

After He speaks to the Gentiles, He addresses His people again:

Zechariah 9:11: "As for thee also, by the blood of thy covenant I have sent forth thy prisoners out of the pit wherein is no water."

(See) Exodus 24:8; Isaiah 51:14; 61:1; Hebrews 10:2

This speaks of "the blood of *thy* covenant." It is the blood we read of in Exodus 24:8: "And Moses took the blood, and sprinkled it on the people, and said, Behold the blood of the covenant, which the LORD hath made with you concerning all these words."

The Pit with No Water

The children of Israel who are in captivity are meant here. They are in a "pit wherein is no water." That signifies hopelessness. Where there is no water, there is no cleansing, and no life. Israel, for over 2,000 years, was dispersed throughout the world. Only occasionally in some places did the Jews have limited freedom; but in the long run, it turned out that they were in "the pit wherein is no water."

Double Reward

So the Lord admonishes them:

Zechariah 9:12: "Turn you to the strong hold, ye prisoners of hope: even to day do I declare that I will render double unto thee;"

244

(See) Isaiah 61:7; Jeremiah 16:19; Joel 3:16

The English Standard Version reads, "Return to your stronghold, O prisoners of hope; today I declare that I will restore to you double."

This is God's encouragement to the Jews to return to their homeland; in doing so, the Lord will reward them double.

It corresponds to a prophecy of Ezekiel: "And I will multiply upon you man and beast; and they shall increase and bring fruit: and I will settle you after your old estates, and will do better unto you than at your beginnings: and ye shall know that I am the LORD" (Ezekiel 36:11).

Although the land of Israel has been a semi-desert for over 2,000 years and was considered agriculturally unproductive, we can with assurance declare that today a reversal is taking place. Each time we travel to the land of Israel, we read the Scripture found in Ezekiel 36:34-35: "And the desolate land shall be tilled, whereas it lay desolate in the sight of all that passed by. And they shall say, This land that was desolate is become like the garden of Eden; and the waste and desolate and ruined cities are become fenced, and are inhabited."

Israel's Fight for Survival
This process of taking possession of the Promised Land is accomplished with weapons of war:

Zechariah 9:13: "When I have bent Judah for me, filled the

> bow with Ephraim, and raised up thy sons, O Zion, against thy sons, O Greece, and made thee as the sword of a mighty man."

(See) Psalm 45:3; Jeremiah 51:20; Daniel 8:21-22; Joel 3:6

During the time of writing, Greece was the power to be reckoned with. Then it was followed by Rome. But no power structure was concerned with the well being of the people of Judah and Ephraim. They had to fight for themselves. They became "mighty men" with weapons.

This fact was especially evident just before the founding of the State of Israel in May 1948. Britain was in control of the territory of Israel (mostly called Palestine). At that time, an arms embargo was enacted for the Middle East region, although plainly intended only against the Jews. Britain, France and the U.S.A. had the freedom to sell arms to the established nations such as Egypt, Saudi Arabia, Jordan, Iraq, Syria and Lebanon. But the Jews were literally cut off with virtually no hope. This is expressed in the prophecy of Ezekiel 37:11: "...Behold, they [Israel] say, our bones are dried, and our hope is lost: and we are cut off for our parts."

USSR to the Rescue

It is ironic that the only power that gave and sold weapons of war to the Jews in Israel was the communist Soviet Union. Doubtless, they too, as all others, did it for political opportunity. But the whole world was witness to the miracle of Israel. These "mighty men"—virtually untrained with remnants of World War II weaponry—victoriously fought against well-equipped Arab armies and won. It was the Spirit of the Lord who caused Israel to be victorious.

The Lord of Hosts Shall Defend

Verses 14-15 confirm the Lord's interference on behalf of Israel:

Zechariah 9:14-15: "And the LORD shall be seen over them, and his arrow shall go forth as the lightning: and the Lord GOD shall blow the trumpet, and shall go with whirlwinds of the south. 15 The LORD of hosts shall defend them; and they shall devour, and subdue with sling stones; and they shall drink, and make a noise as through wine; and they shall be filled like bowls, and as the corners of the altar."

(See) Exodus 27:2; Leviticus 4:25; Job 41:28; Psalm 18:14; 78:65; Isaiah 27:13; 37:35; 66:15; Habakkuk 3:11; Zechariah 12:8

This seems to speak of military victory. But when we read it carefully, we note that something unusual happened. It is revealed in the words, "shall drink, and make a noise as through wine." That describes the Jews' transformation—but not the rebirth.

Here we must recall Acts 2, where we read, "These men are full of new wine." That was in the past, and will be in the future regarding Israel's salvation. While it definitely speaks of physical, earthly victory, it is the Lord God who blows the trumpet. He is the unseen and mostly unrecognized cause of Israel's problems and success.

No Spiritual Fruit

Reading the last two verses of this chapter, we notice that it does not reveal spiritual fruit. God is dealing with Israel in an earthly manner.

Zechariah 9:16-17: "And the LORD their God shall save them in that day as the flock of his people: for they shall be as the stones of a crown, lifted up as an ensign upon his land. 17 For how great is his goodness, and how great is his beauty! corn shall make the young men cheerful, and new wine the maids."

(See) Psalm 27:4; Isaiah 11:12; 33:17; 62:3; Jeremiah 31:10-14; Ezekiel 37:23; Malachi 3:17

Rebirth of the Land

The Jews who returned to the land of Israel, continue to strive for three reasons: 1) identity, 2) security and 3) possession. We need to read the last few verses in the *Tenakh* to make this more obvious: "The Lord their God shall prosper them on that day; [He shall pasture] His people like sheep. [They shall be] like crown jewels glittering on His soil. How lovely, how beautiful they shall be, producing young men like new grain, young women like new wine." Plainly, this does not speak of the spiritual rebirth of the people, but the rebirth of the land. It is producing; it has changed from being barren to fruitful.

Chapter 10

Introduction

What we read in chapter 10 is not based on a vision, but contains the direct words of God.

The restoration of Judah in particular is the issue. The first verse speaks of rain; that means life. When rain ceases, crops, animals and man will cease also. Yet this is not the end, because God's plan calls for the restoration of those who were oppressed; a new door of blessing is opened for the people.

The Latter Rain

Zechariah 10:1: "Ask ye of the LORD rain in the time of the latter rain; so the LORD shall make bright clouds, and give them showers of rain, to every one grass in the field."

(See) Isaiah 30:23; Jeremiah 14:22; Joel 2:23

While addressed to Israel, this also has spiritual significance, for rain is refreshing to the land; it makes things grow. But, spiritually speaking, we need this "latter day rain" continuously so we are refreshed, grounded deeply in our faith in Jesus, which causes joy, the fruit of the spirit, to spring forth.

The Environmental Issue

There is much talk about the environment in our days. Leaders of the nations are coming together to decide what to do regarding planet earth and the apparent climate change known as global warming. They argue, debate, hold meetings and conferences, and use the most sophisticated technological data to prove that man somehow interferes with the earth's climate. Thus, the nations are forced, based on their available science, to take action to prevent a global catastrophe. Yet from biblical perspectives, we know that man is totally dependent on God's grace; in this case, for rain.

Environment in God's Hand

We must realize that this world is created by God; even though it sometimes seems like the world is getting out of control, we can with full assurance say it will not. Why? Because the Bible says: "While the earth remaineth, seedtime and harvest, and cold and heat, and summer and winter, and day and night shall not cease" (Genesis 8:22). That is the final authoritative answer to the concern about our environment.

Pray for Rain

Here in verse 1, man is asked not only to acknowledge God's authority over the weather, but also to pray for rain. This is especially applicable to the land of Israel today: it has thirsted for two millennia, and as result, the country became a semi-desert. With the return of the Jews to Israel, a reversal is slowly taking place; not by increased rainfall, but by technology. Yet technology is

not the final answer: for the land of Israel to accommodate all the Jews of the world, it needs to be more pro-
ductive agriculturally, and that can only happen when
Israel asks the Lord for the latter rain.

False Prophets

Zechariah 10:2: "For the idols have spoken vanity, and the
diviners have seen a lie, and have told false dreams; they
comfort in vain: therefore they went their way as a flock,
they were troubled, because there was no shepherd."

(See) Jeremiah 23:32; Ezekiel 34:5, 8; Matthew 9:36

In verse 1, God invites the people to rely on Him. Here
we see how they relied on idols, vanity, diviners and
dreams.

Idol of Technology
This fits our modern, sophisticated, technology-based society. We seem to know everything, and can explain the
world topographically and biologically. We know how
the earth functions. Scientists continue to make amazing
discoveries deep in the earth and the oceans, even in
space. But in the end, it changes nothing; the world continues just the way God created it.

No Shepherd
The people of Israel were in dispersion for two millennia;
they had no real shepherd. Those who seemed to be
shepherds of the Jewish people often led them in the
wrong direction:

251

Zechariah 10:3: "Mine anger was kindled against the shepherds, and I punished the goats: for the LORD of hosts hath visited his flock the house of Judah, and hath made them as his goodly horse in the battle."

(See) Exodus 4:31; Ruth 1:6; Jeremiah 25:34-36; Ezekiel 34:12;
Zephaniah 2:7; Zechariah 11:5; Luke 1:68; 1 Peter 2:12

"Goats," according to *Strong's Hebrew Dictionary*, could be translated "leaders of the people." Instead of being led toward God, the people were led away from God to all sorts of prognosticators, who in the end did no good, but caused Israel to enter into even more trouble.

Judah the Shepherd

Now the Lord God begins to pronounce some mighty promises to the Jewish people:

Zechariah 10:4: "Out of him came forth the corner, out of him the nail, out of him the battle bow, out of him every oppressor together."

(See) Isaiah 22:23; Jeremiah 30:21; 51:20; Luke 20:17;
Ephesians 2:20; 1 Peter 2:6

Here the tribe of Judah is identified, but represents all of Israel. To understand this better, let us go back to the father of Israel, Jacob, who uttered a specific prophecy about Judah: "Judah, thou art he whom thy brethren shall praise: thy hand shall be in the neck of thine enemies; thy father's children shall bow down before thee.

Judah is a lion's whelp: from the prey, my son, thou art gone up: he stooped down, he couched as a lion, and as an old lion; who shall rouse him up? The sceptre shall not depart from Judah, nor a lawgiver from between his feet, until Shiloh come; and unto him shall the gathering of the people be" (Genesis 49:8-10). These are mighty words: salvation will come from Judah.

Who is this Shiloh? It is the Messiah. This is confirmed in the last book of the Bible: "And one of the elders saith unto me, Weep not: behold, the Lion of the tribe of Judah, the Root of David, hath prevailed to open the book, and to loose the seven seals thereof" (Revelation 5:5). Jacob prophesied that Judah would lead, "Unto him shall the gathering of the people be."

Gathering of the Tribes of Israel

This is a two-fold promise: 1. The eleven tribes of the children of Israel would be identified by the name of Judah, i.e. Jews. This is clearly evident in the New Testament; for example, in the book of Acts. The Apostle Peter is addressing the Jews in Jerusalem. He does not say, "Let the house of Judah know," but rather, "...let all the house of Israel know assuredly" (Acts 2:36).

We know that the tribe of Judah included the tribes of Benjamin and Levi; they became part of Judah. Later, remnants of the ten rebellious tribes joined themselves to Judah as well. This is documented in 2 Chronicles 11:16: "And after them out of all the tribes of Israel such as set their hearts to seek the LORD God of Israel came to Jerusalem, to sacrifice unto the LORD God of their fathers." Furthermore, 2 Chronicles 15:9 reads: "And he

253

gathered all Judah and Benjamin, and the strangers with them out of Ephraim and Manasseh, and out of Simeon: for they fell to him out of Israel in abundance, when they saw that the LORD his God was with him." Therefore, the gathering of the people means that all the tribes of Israel became Jews, and so it is today.

Gathering the Nations

Furthermore, the "gathering of the people" includes the nations. We read in Matthew 28:19: "Go ye therefore, and teach all nations, baptizing them in the name of the Father, and of the Son, and of the Holy Ghost." The Gentiles will be "gathered" to Israel, according to Amos 9:12: "That they may possess the remnant of Edom, and of all the heathen, which are called by my name, saith the LORD that doeth this."

The "Corner, Nail, and Battle Bow"

In verse 4, we find the words, "the corner." This is the Cornerstone—Jesus Christ the Lord. The American Standard Version reads: "From Him shall come forth the cornerstone, from Him the nail, from Him the battle bow, from Him every ruler together." He, the Lord, is the source of all things.

The "nail" is also translated "tent peg." That symbolizes Israel's habitation, a place of security. Isaiah 22:23 reads: "And I will fasten him as a nail in a sure place; and he shall be for a glorious throne to his father's house."

The "battle bow" is a demonstration of His invincibility; He is the Victor today and for all eternity. He is even in charge of "every oppressor"; that means all political authority. All this will be visibly implemented when Jesus Christ establishes His dominion over the earth.

This is confirmed by Jesus, who said: "All power is given unto me in heaven and in earth." His Church is included: "And hast made us unto our God kings and priests: and we shall reign on the earth" (Revelation 5:10).

Jewish Victory

There will be no opposition. Judah will dominate:

Zechariah 10:5-6: "And they shall be as mighty men, which tread down their enemies in the mire of the streets in the battle: and they shall fight, because the LORD is with them, and the riders on horses shall be confounded. 6 And I will strengthen the house of Judah, and I will save the house of Joseph, and I will bring them again to place them; for I have mercy upon them: and they shall be as though I had not cast them off: for I am the Lord their God, and will hear them."

(See) 2 Samuel 22:45; Isaiah 54:4, 8; Amos 2:15; Haggai 2:22; Zechariah 13:9

From history we know that the Jews were dispersed all over the world; they were rejected, despised, mistreated, and quite often killed. Yet this Scripture says they will be "mighty men, which tread down their enemies." The "riders on horses" are the enemies; they will be put to shame.

Past or Future Victory?

Many scholars apply this to the time when Israel shall be saved and the Jews will have a preeminent position among the people of the world. Such spiritual application can be accepted. However, if we take this chapter and try to understand it in the full context, then we must see it from the perspective of Israel's existence in the face of insurmountable difficulties throughout the centuries.

For all practical purposes, the Jews should not exist. The fact that they have been so severely persecuted should have guaranteed their demise. Even before the State of Israel was resurrected, over six million Jews were deliberately and systematically murdered during the reign of Hitler's Nazi Germany.

Who would want to be a Jew after being so severely oppressed?

The Jewish Contribution

There is another victory of the Jews that goes mostly unnoticed. Jews have left a tremendous mark on the development of Europe and the world. Whether it's the arts, music, science, medicine, or politics, a rather lopsided number of Jews stand at the top. The contribution of the Jewish people toward the establishment of the civilized world is supported by history and is undeniable.

We must come to the conclusion that when it speaks of what seems to be a military victory, it is equally referring to the very survival and existence of the Jewish people throughout history. That in itself is a Jewish victory.

It was accomplished by the "I will" of the eternal God. He will strengthen, He will save, He will bring again, and

He will hear them. This is not limited to the *house of Judah*, but also includes the *house of Joseph*, a term often used to define the ten tribes of Israel.

Return by Action, Not by Faith

What is so remarkable is the fact that God is bringing the Jews back to their land; not because of their faith in the God of the Bible, but by action. From the original 37 signers of the Declaration of Independence, the overwhelming majority were communist-educated. They came from Russia, Ukraine, Belarus, Poland, etc. Three came from Germany, one from Denmark, one from Yemen, and one from Israel. The actions they initiated were not based on religion at all.

Godless Declaration of Independence

One of the major issues relating to the Declaration of Independence was the objection to the word "God" in the document.

Wikipedia details this under the "Declaration of Independence of Israel":

> The second major issue was over the inclusion of God in the last section of the document, with the draft using the phrase, 'and placing our trust in the Almighty.' The two rabbis, Shapira and Yehuda Leib Maimon, argued for its inclusion, saying that it could not be omitted, with Shapira supporting the wording 'God of Israel' or 'the Almighty and Redeemer Israel.' It was strongly opposed by Zisling, a member of the secularist Mapam. In the end the phrase 'Rock of Israel' was used, which could be interpreted as either referring to God, or the land of Eretz

Israel, Ben-Gurion saying, "Each of us, in his own way, be-lieves in the 'Rock of Israel' as he conceives it. I should like to make one request: Don't let me put this phrase to a vote." Although its use was still opposed by Zisling, the phrase was accepted without a vote.

Theodor Herzl an Atheist?

The driving force to return the Jewish people to the land of Israel was Zionism, not religion. The modern move-ment of Zionism was articulated by Theodor Herzl, who considered himself an atheist.

God works so differently than we think or imagine. No wonder He tells us in Isaiah 55:8-9: "For my thoughts are not your thoughts, neither are your ways my ways, saith the LORD. For as the heavens are higher than the earth, so are my ways higher than your ways, and my thoughts than your thoughts."

Restoration of the Land

Reading chapter 36 in the book of Ezekiel, one notices that God first speaks to the land, the topographical area of Israel: "But ye, O mountains of Israel, ye shall shoot forth your branches, and yield your fruit to my people of Israel; for they are at hand to come" (Ezekiel 36:8). In verse 11 we read: "And I will multiply upon you man and beast; and they shall increase and bring fruit: and I will settle you after your old estates, and will do better unto you than at your beginnings: and ye shall know that I am the LORD." That surely reminds us of the words we read in verse 6: "....they shall be as though I have not cast them off." God's immeasurable grace is self-evident in the process of bringing the Jews back to the land of their fathers, and the founding of the state of Israel in 1948.

Israel Shall Rejoice

Zechariah 10:7: "And they of Ephraim shall be like a mighty man, and their heart shall rejoice as through wine: yea, their children shall see it, and be glad; their heart shall rejoice in the LORD."

(See) Isaiah 54:13; Ezekiel 37:25

Ephraim is also a collective name for the ten rebellious tribes of Israel. Both Judah and Israel receive the promise of full restoration. But the fulfillment will take place in the 1,000-year Kingdom of Peace.

It will be fulfilled after the Church has been taken out of the world. Then, seven years later, Jesus will literally and physically return to Israel, and from there make an end of all the nations of the world, and rule in truth and righteousness.

2,500 Year Old Prophecy

The Lord's love for His people continues to be exemplified in verses 8-9:

Zechariah 10:8-9: "I will hiss for them, and gather them; for I have redeemed them: and they shall increase as they have increased. 9 And I will sow them among the people: and they shall remember me in far countries; and they shall live with their children, and turn again."

259

(See) Isaiah 5:26; 7:18-19; 66:19; Jeremiah 30:20; 33:22; Ezekiel 36:11;
Revelation 7:9

Again, we must keep in mind that these prophecies were written about 2,500 years ago, but are not limited exclusively to a certain time period. While He speaks of salvation in verse 8, He proclaims Israel's dispersion in verse 9.

Remembering God in the Diaspora

There is one specific item we must highlight, "they shall remember me in far countries." That is the key to the keeping of the identity of the Jewish people throughout the millennia: whether servant or rich, whether communist, socialist, or atheist, the Jew would always remember his special relationship to the God of Israel. That was something no one could take away from the Jew.

Not Enough Room for Returnees

The "I will" of God is the power behind the return of the Jewish people from specific countries:

Zechariah 10:10: "I will bring them again also out of the land of Egypt, and gather them out of Assyria; and I will bring them into the land of Gilead and Lebanon; and place shall not be found for them."

(See) Exodus 14:26-27; Isaiah 11:11; 49:20; Jeremiah 50:19

The last sentence in particular highlights today's developments. A relatively small group of Israelis insist on taking possession of all of the Promised Land, including Judea and Samaria. The reason is simple: if all Jews from all countries return to Israel, there will indeed not be enough room to accommodate them. Thus, a change will and must take place.

Nations Deny Promised Land

Today, ALL nations of the world are united in denying the Jews the right to take possession of the Promised Land. No nation agrees to the clearly defined borders as given in Genesis 15:18: "In the same day the LORD made a covenant with Abram, saying, Unto thy seed have I given this land, from the river of Egypt unto the great river, the river Euphrates." The nations, under the dominance of the god of this world, Satan, vehemently oppose Israel's taking possession of the Promised Land. That, in brief, is the center of the conflict in the Middle East. The whole world says NO to Israel.

Never must we allow the thought to enter our mind that the territorial conflict is due to the opposition by the Arabs and the Islamic world. That in fact is very naïve, because it is the entire world that opposes Israel's possession of the entire Promised Land. That is the cornerstone of Israel's conflict. Nevertheless, the "I will" of God is irrevocable. The nations will be put to shame in their opposition to Israel.

Syria and Egypt Judged

Israel has in the past, is today, and will in the future experience affliction, as evident from verse 11. But we must note that this is accompanied by severe judgment upon

261

two named countries: Syria and Egypt.

Zechariah 10:11: "And he shall pass through the sea with affliction, and shall smite the waves in the sea, and all the deeps of the river shall dry up: and the pride of Assyria shall be brought down, and the sceptre of Egypt shall depart away."

(See) Exodus 14:16; Isaiah 11:15; 19:5-7; 51:9-10; Ezekiel 30:13; Zephaniah 2:13

In the end, Israel will experience the fulfillment of the prophecy Moses uttered before he died: "Happy art thou, O Israel: who is like unto thee, O people saved by the LORD, the shield of thy help, and who is the sword of thy excellency! and thine enemies shall be found liars unto thee; and thou shalt tread upon their high places" (Deuteronomy 33:29). Never must we allow ourselves to think that our nation or any other nation is capable of helping Israel effectively, or opposing them decisively. God's eternal "I will" is the only decisive word that will remain for all eternity:

Zechariah 10:12: "And I will strengthen them in the LORD; and they shall walk up and down in his name, saith the LORD."

(See) Micah 4:5

This has not happened yet, but in due time God will cause Israel to walk in His name.

Chapter 11

Introduction

We may title this chapter "The Evil Shepherd." Israel rejected the Good Shepherd who layed down His life for the sheep, instead accepting the evil shepherd who destroys, the father of lies, the murderer from the beginning.

Jesus revealed Israel's choice when He said, "I am come in my Father's name, and ye receive me not: if another shall come in his own name, him ye will receive" (John 5:43).

We are reminded of the great imitation within the Church. The apostle Paul warned of the end times in Acts 20:29-30, "For I know this, that after my departing shall grievous wolves enter in among you, not sparing the flock. Also of your own selves shall men arise, speaking perverse things, to draw away disciples after them." The danger is that the imitation often looks real. Those who do not have the ability to distinguish between the real and the fake, between truth and lies are living in extreme peril.

The imitation for the Church is exposed in 2 Corinthians 11:4, "For if he that cometh preacheth another Jesus, whom we have not preached, or if ye receive another spirit, which ye have not received, or another gospel, which ye have not accepted, ye might well bear with him." This clearly speaks of another Jesus, another spirit and another gospel. This is the work of the deceiver, who

263

looks real by appearing as apostles, even an angel of light: "For such are false apostles, deceitful workers, transforming themselves into the apostles of Christ. And no marvel; for Satan himself is transformed into an angel of light. Therefore it is no great thing if his ministers also be transformed as the ministers of righteousness; whose end shall be according to their works" (verses 13-15).

How are we to recognize these false messengers? There are two important marks:

1. The imitation messengers will never proclaim the whole truth of the Bible. The horrendous judgment that is prophesied to come upon planet Earth, as revealed through the prophetic Word, is conveniently left out in the proclamation of their gospel.

2. The messengers of the evil shepherds will always proclaim the positive aspects of being a Christian: a better life, more possessions, greater success on all levels of life and society.

The apostle Paul was a well-to-do, highly educated and respected member of society. He had significant power over other people before he became a believer in Jesus Christ. Here is his testimony: "Are they ministers of Christ? (I speak as a fool) I am more; in labours more abundant, in stripes above measure, in prisons more frequent, in deaths oft. Of the Jews five times received I forty stripes save one. Thrice was I beaten with rods, once was I stoned, thrice I suffered shipwreck, a night and a day I have been in the deep; In journeyings often, in perils of waters, in perils of robbers, in perils by mine own countrymen, in perils by the heathen, in perils in the city, in perils in the wilderness, in perils in the sea, in perils among false brethren; In weariness and painfulness, in watchings often, in hunger and thirst, in fastings often, in cold and nakedness" (2 Corinthians 11:23-27). The apostle Paul clearly testifies that he had no advantage by becoming a Christian.

Lebanon and Bashan

Again, we note that the words of this chapter are the direct words of God. Zechariah is not passing on a vision.

Zechariah 11:1-2: "Open thy doors, O Lebanon, that the fire may devour thy cedars. 2 Howl, fir tree; for the cedar is fallen; because the mighty are spoiled: howl, O ye oaks of Bashan; for the forest of the vintage is come down."

(See) Jeremiah 22:6-7; Ezekiel 31:3

Lebanon is praised for its abundance of timber. The cedars are famous. Solomon imported them for the building of the temple in Jerusalem.

Bashan is the territory that Moses gave to the half tribe of Manasseh, according to Deuteronomy 3:13, "And the rest of Gilead, and all Bashan, being the kingdom of Og, gave I unto the half tribe of Manasseh; all the region of Argob, with all Bashan, which was called the land of giants."

This is quite noteworthy: the two and a half tribes of Israel asked Moses to have as their inheritance, the land that was on the east side of the Jordan, although this was not originally called the Promised Land, the land flowing with milk and honey. This is the work of man, for it was not in the original promise.

265

We note the destructive connotation in the words, "fire may devour...Howl, fir tree...the cedar is fallen... mighty are spoiled...howl, O ye oaks...the vintage is come down." This is most certainly a description of judgment upon the physical territory of the land of Lebanon and Bashan.

Shepherds Spoiled

Zechariah 11:3: "There is a voice of the howling of the shepherds; for their glory is spoiled: a voice of the roaring of young lions; for the pride of Jordan is spoiled."

(See) Jeremiah 2:15; 25:34-36; 50:44

Not only does the vegetation of the land come under judgment, but also the shepherds and the animals (as well as the Jordan River) are placed under the judgment of God.

Zechariah 11:4-5: "Thus saith the LORD my God; Feed the flock of the slaughter; 5 Whose possessors slay them, and hold themselves not guilty: and they that sell them say, Blessed be the LORD; for I am rich: and their own shepherds pity them not."

(See) Deuteronomy 29:19; Psalm 44:22; Jeremiah 2:3; 50:7; Ezekiel 34:2-3; Hosea 12:8; John 16:2; 1 Timothy 6:9; 2 Peter 2:3

Doubtless, this is a picture of the people of Israel. They had appropriated the blessings and prosperity God had given them for their own selfish purposes. God does not just say, "Feed the flock," but, "Feed the flock of the slaughter." The *Tanakh* reads, "Tend the sheep meant for slaughter." This is nothing other than the slaughter of the flock for the gain of the rich and powerful individuals.

Those who are in charge, who have the power and take advantage of the flock, are so hardened in their hearts that they are incapable of recognizing their evildoing. They say, "Blessed be the LORD; for I am rich." This confirms that prosperity was prevalent during those days, and religion was highly esteemed. Things were going rather well for these "possessors"; they had it all. Everything was going splendidly, and they gave their religion credit for their success.

Idols of Possession

What a picture of our days. Possessions have become one of the idols of the endtimes. People work longer hours to earn more money, primarily for the purpose of having things, being possessors, totally disregarding God's ordinances to take care of the flock.

This reminds us of the words found in James 5:1, which are addressed to the rich, "Go to now, ye rich men, weep and howl for your miseries that shall come upon you." Then in verse 3 it speaks of the last days, "Ye have heaped treasure together for the last days." Verse 5 speaks of the slaughter, "Ye have lived in pleasure on the earth, and been wanton; ye have nourished your hearts, as in a day of slaughter."

No Deliverance

Because of this diabolically merciless behavior, we read in verse 6:

Zechariah 11:6: "For I will no more pity the inhabitants of the land, saith the LORD: but, lo, I will deliver the men every one into his neighbour's hand, and into the hand of his king: and they shall smite the land, and out of their hand I will not deliver them."

(See) Psalm 50:22; Jeremiah 13:14; Micah 5:8

There is no more grace, but utter destruction; this is expressed with the words, "I will not deliver."

"Beauty and the Bands"

Next, we come to a peculiar action:

Zechariah 11:7: "And I will feed the flock of slaughter, even you, O poor of the flock. And I took unto me two staves; the one I called Beauty, and the other I called Bands; and I fed the flock."

(See) Ezekiel 37:16; Zephaniah 3:12; Matthew 11:5

For the sake of the poor, He uses two staffs: one "Beauty" and the other "Bands." "Beauty" represents the covenant God made with His people. "Bands" represents the unity between Judah and Israel. We must take note of the word "poor." They too come under the judgment, but there is a distinct difference, as we will see later.

268

Three Shepherds

With verse 8, something new and different is revealed:

Zechariah 11:8: "Three shepherds also I cut off in one month; and my soul lothed them, and their soul also abhorred me."

(See) Hosea 5:7

Who are the three shepherds? We propose: 1. the king; 2. the priests; and 3. the prophets. All three failed miserably.

Therefore, a new King, Priest and Prophet had to come. Hebrews 8:13 speaks of that one: "...A new covenant, he hath made the first old. Now that which decayeth and waxeth old is ready to vanish away." Quite obviously, this also points prophetically to Jesus. He is the King, Priest, and Prophet. But within the infrastructure of the people of Israel under the Old Covenant, those three failed miserably. As a result, God withdrew His provision for His people and literally left them alone.

Zechariah 11:9: "Then said I, I will not feed you: that that dieth, let it die; and that that is to be cut off, let it be cut off; and let the rest eat every one the flesh of another."

(See) Jeremiah 15:2

That meant total rejection of the King, Priest, and Prophet.

Covenant with All Nations

Zechariah 11:10: "And I took my staff, even Beauty, and cut it asunder, that I might break my covenant which I had made with all the people."

(See) Psalm 89:39; Jeremiah 14:21

This is not the unconditional covenant made with Abraham, but the covenant He made with "all the people." Luther translates this, "with all the nations." What covenant is that? It is a covenant of grace. We read of it in Genesis 8:22, "While the earth remaineth, seedtime and harvest, and cold and heat, and summer and winter, and day and night shall not cease." This is for all people at all times, anywhere on planet Earth.

Furthermore, it is pointing to God's new covenant of grace that He would offer to all people of the world, "For God so loved the world, that he gave his only begotten Son, that whosoever believeth in him should not perish, but have everlasting life" (John 3:16).

The Poor

The breaking of this covenant was a sign recognized by those who were waiting for the Lord:

Zechariah 11:11: "And it was broken in that day: and so the poor of the flock that waited upon me knew that it was the word of the LORD."

(See) Zephaniah 3:12

"The poor of the flock" can also be translated "oppressed" or "despised." Here we are immediately reminded of our Lord in Matthew 5:3, "Blessed are the poor in spirit: for theirs is the kingdom of heaven." This poor flock was waiting upon the Lord, and they recognized it to be the Word of the Lord.

Thirty Pieces of Silver

Next, another amazing prophecy is made.

Zechariah 11:12: "And I said unto them, If ye think good, give me my price; and if not, forbear. So they weighed for my price thirty pieces of silver."

(See) Genesis 37:28; Exodus 21:32; Matthew 26:15

The Lord is asking the price of His worth; the answer: "thirty pieces of silver." This points to Judas Iscariot, "And [Judas] said unto them, What will ye give me, and I will deliver him unto you? And they covenanted with him for thirty pieces of silver" (Matthew 26:15). So our Lord was sold for thirty pieces of silver.

What happened with that money?

Zechariah 11:13: "And the LORD said unto me, Cast it unto the potter: a goodly price that I was prised at of them. And I took the thirty pieces of silver, and cast them to the potter in the house of the LORD."

(See) Matthew 27:9-10

The price was determined by the enemy. In the New Testament, the enemies of Jesus agreed on 30 pieces of silver. What a precise prophecy almost 500 years before the birth of Christ!

Blood Money

Judas, who betrayed Jesus, later confessed that he had sinned, "Saying, I have sinned in that I have betrayed the innocent blood..." (Matthew 27:4). His action fulfilled prophecy, "And he cast down the pieces of silver in the temple, and departed, and went and hanged himself" (verse 5).

The priests recognized that the blood money should not be used for the temple service, "It is not lawful for to put them into the treasury, because it is the price of blood" (Matthew 27:6). Instead, "And they took counsel, and bought with them the potter's field, to bury strangers in" (Matthew 27:7).

The "Other Staff"

Next comes the "other staff," which is translated in the KJV as "Bands" and in the *Tanakh* with the word "Unity."

Zechariah 11:14: "Then I cut asunder mine other staff, even Bands, that I might break the brotherhood between Judah and Israel."

(See) Ezekiel 37:22

We see the reaffirmation over and again that the ten-tribe Israel ceased to be a separate identity from the tribe of Judah. However, those who were waiting for the Lord

272

joined the tribe of Judah and became Jews. Hence today, no one really knows precisely from which tribe they descend, but they all know that they are Jews.

The Foolish Shepherd

Zechariah 11:15: "And the LORD said unto me, Take unto thee yet the instruments of a foolish shepherd."

(See) Ezekiel 34:2

We are not informed as to what these instruments are that belong to a foolish shepherd, but quite obviously, they were things that were not needed to lead the sheep to the green pasture.

Feed My Sheep

This contains an important admonition for the Church. We are instructed by the Lord to "feed my sheep," which means: lead my sheep to the pasture. We read the instruction in John 21. Jesus asked Peter three times, "lovest thou me?" After each affirmative answer, Jesus said, "Feed my lambs," and twice, "Feed my sheep." Why three times? Peter had denied the Lord three times.

The words, "Feed my sheep" are rather limited in translation. "Lead my sheep to the pasture" seems to be more accurate. We don't feed sheep; we lead them to the pasture, to the precious Word of God. They may eat anywhere on the green pastures "from Genesis to Revelation."

The famous 23rd Psalm expresses this leading to the pasture very fittingly, "The LORD is my shepherd; I shall

273

not want. He maketh me to lie down in green pastures: he leadeth me beside the still waters...Yea, though I walk through the valley of the shadow of death, I will fear no evil: for thou art with me; thy rod and thy staff they comfort me" (verses 1-2, 4). In this case too the rod and the staff—the irrevocable, eternal law of God, "the rod," and the guiding "staff"—comfort and protect the sheep.

The "Idol Shepherd"

Zechariah 11 ends with the revelation of the "idol shepherd," the Antichrist:

Zechariah 11:16-17: "For, lo, I will raise up a shepherd in the land, which shall not visit those that be cut off, neither shall seek the young one, nor heal that that is broken, nor feed that that standeth still: but he shall eat the flesh of the fat, and tear their claws in pieces. 17 Woe to the idol shepherd that leaveth the flock! the sword shall be upon his arm, and upon his right eye: his arm shall be clean dried up, and his right eye shall be utterly darkened."

(See) Jeremiah 23:1; Micah 3:6; John 10:12

The sword is the Word of God, and will render the idol shepherd's political and military capacity useless. He will be totally separated from his "flock." His "right eye" will become useless, and he will not see nor recognize the flock.

He will not visit those in prison, protect the little ones, heal the brokenhearted, or feed the hungry. The idol shepherd fulfills the measure of evil by doing the opposite of good.

The Good Shepherd lays down his life for his sheep. It was Isaiah who proclaimed, "The Spirit of the Lord GOD is upon me; because the LORD hath anointed me to preach good tidings unto the meek; he hath sent me to bind up the brokenhearted, to proclaim liberty to the captives, and the opening of the prison to them that are bound; To proclaim the acceptable year of the LORD, and the day of vengeance of our God; to comfort all that mourn" (Isaiah 61:1-2). That is the Good Shepherd.

Chapter 12

Introduction

Except for verse 1, the entire chapter, including the next two, consists exclusively of the words of the Lord. God is speaking directly.

This chapter can be titled the "Jerusalem Chapter." It identifies Jerusalem as God's point of contact with planet earth. While Judah, along with the rest of the world, is included in this address, Jerusalem is the target.

We do well to note the two phrases, "I will" and "will I." God is dealing directly with Jerusalem, Judah and the world.

Jerusalem's Burden

Zechariah 12:1: "The burden of the word of the LORD for Israel, saith the LORD, which stretcheth forth the heavens, and layeth the foundation of the earth, and formeth the spirit of man within him."

(See) Job 26:7; Psalm 102:25-26; Isaiah 42:5; 44:24; Jeremiah 51:15;
Hebrews 1:10-12; 12:9

Here the word of the God of creation is being introduced with "the burden...for Israel." That simply means the target of the message is directed to the people of Israel.

We know that the center of Israel is Jerusalem; the center of Jerusalem is the holy temple of God; and in the center of the temple is the Holy of Holies, the visible manifestation of the place where the name of God dwelt.

The importance and significance of the name of God, in relationship to the temple in Jerusalem, is recorded in Solomon's prayer at the dedication of the temple in 2 Chronicles 6:5: "Since the day that I brought forth my people out of the land of Egypt I chose no city among all the tribes of Israel to build an house in, that my name might be there; neither chose I any man to be a ruler over my people Israel."

The Lord God, who is burdened for Israel, includes the entire universe, "which stretcheth forth the heavens." How far and how large are the heavens? Immeasurable!

Largest Space Telescope

Lately, several nations are claiming to have built or are planning to build the largest telescope the world has ever known. The purpose? To see deeper into space. We have to admit that modern astronomy has discovered mind-boggling things, yet we cannot grasp the distance of space. It cannot be measured in any way, shape or form. This reinforces the fact that the heavens are unimaginably infinite. What the astronomers have found and established as scientific fact about the universe, is but a drop in the ocean.

Man's Dominion Over Earth

He "layeth the foundation of the earth." That is our place. Man has taken charge of the earth, at least to a certain degree. The circumference of the earth has been

measured. The world has been divided into seven continents. Maps show the depths of the ocean and the
heights of the mountains. Man knows that water runs
down the mountains into creeks, forming rivers, empty-
ing into the oceans. So, we may say man has dominion
over all the earth.

Nevertheless, when it comes to the elements of the
earth—fire, water and air—man is totally powerless.
This is evident during so-called natural catastrophes.
When volcanoes spew out fire and ash thousands of me-
ters into the air, or discharge massive volumes of lava
into the oceans or down mountains, man is exposed as
being utterly helpless.

Furthermore, He "formed the spirit of man within
him." Man's spirit comes from God. God gives life and
God takes life. He is the absolute Almighty, the all-know-
ing and the eternal One.

Jerusalem, the Cup of Trembling

Zechariah 12:2: "Behold, I will make Jerusalem a cup of
trembling unto all the people round about, when they
shall be in the siege both against Judah and against
Jerusalem."

(See) Psalm 75:8; Isaiah 51:17, 22-23

Clearly, Jerusalem is the center of the world. If we ask
why, we find several answers in Scripture.

First of all, God's name dwelled in Jerusalem.

Secondly, God became man in Jesus Christ, came to
Jerusalem and did the unimaginable: "...God was in

Christ, reconciling the world unto himself" (2 Corinthians 5:19).

Thirdly, He left planet earth from Jerusalem, from the Mount of Olives, and will return there. That message was proclaimed by angels: "...this same Jesus, which is taken up from you into heaven, shall so come in like manner as ye have seen him go into heaven" (Acts 1:11).

Now we should better understand the significance of Jerusalem: "I will make Jerusalem a cup of trembling unto all the people round about." Luther translates this "unto all nations." In plain words, to the entire world.

Before we occupy ourselves more with the Jerusalem issue, let us first determine if this is speaking about the *future*, *past* or *present*. The assumption that everything prophetic applies only to the future is shortsighted.

Jerusalem was very important to God even before the name Jerusalem appears in Holy Scripture.

King of Salem

We read of a certain mysterious king of Salem, Melchizedek, who offered bread and wine to Abraham. Who was this king? The Psalmist speaks of him as a priest: "The LORD hath sworn, and will not repent, Thou art a priest for ever after the order of Melchizedek" (Psalm 110:4). Salem stands for Jerusalem, as documented in Psalm 76:1-2: "In Judah is God known: his name is great in Israel. In Salem also is his tabernacle, and his dwelling place in Zion."

Furthermore, we read in Hebrews 5:6-7 about Jesus: "...Thou art a priest for ever after the order of Melchizedec. Who in the days of his flesh, when he had offered up prayers and supplications with strong crying and tears unto him that was able to save him from death, and was heard in that he feared." This is the only time Jesus asked for His life to be spared. When did that happen? In the Garden of Gethsemane. Jesus was not praying to be spared death on the cross, but death here and now in the garden of Gethsemane. This twofold death is documented in Philippians 2:8, "And being found in fashion as a man, he humbled himself, and became obedient unto death, even the death of the cross."

Thus we see: Jerusalem is much more than a city in the land of Israel. Jerusalem has eternal spiritual significance.

2,600 Year History

See another example where events transcend time by thousands of years. Daniel 2:44 reads: "And in the days of these kings shall the God of heaven set up a kingdom, which shall never be destroyed: and the kingdom shall not be left to other people, but it shall break in pieces and consume all these kingdoms, and it shall stand for ever." That was written about 2,600 years ago. His prophecy includes all four Gentile superpowers: Babylon, Persia, Greece and Rome. The Bible simply says, "in the days of these kings." Thus, the prophetic Word totally ignores the gap of these 2,600 years, from the king of Babylon to the last king—the Antichrist—whose empire is now in the process of being finalized.

Therefore, to allocate this event to some future time may be correct from earthly perspectives, but definitely not from the spiritual level. God has established and continues to establish His kingdom until all is finalized.

History or Future?

Does the prophecy in chapter 12:2, "shall be in the siege both against Judah and against Jerusalem," apply to the future? We answer both yes and no. Yes, because we know that according to Revelation 16:14, "...the kings of the earth and of the whole world...gather them to the battle of that great day of God Almighty." That is part of the Battle of Armageddon. Also, Jesus prophesies of it in Luke 21:24: "And they shall fall by the edge of the sword, and shall be led away captive into all nations: and Jerusalem shall be trodden down of the Gentiles, until the times of the Gentiles be fulfilled." Yet this belongs to the past, the present, *and* the future. Today, Jerusalem is not recognized as the capital city of Israel by the nations, thus still "trodden down of the Gentiles."

However, when we answer the question with "no," then we must take into consideration the historical fact that Jerusalem has been destroyed at least 14 times. Therefore, when we read that all nations "shall be in siege...against Jerusalem," it is applicable to the past, the present and the future.

Jerusalem, the Burdensome Stone

Verse 3 gives additional details:

Zechariah 12:3: "And in that day will I make Jerusalem a burdensome stone for all people: all that burden themselves with it shall be cut in pieces, though all the people of the earth be gathered together against it."

(See) Daniel 2:34-35, 44-45; Matthew 21:44

281

PROPHECY FOR JUDAH

We take note that this is the result of the Lord, who says, "will I." Again, is this future? The answer is yes and no.

Looking at the Old City, we see it is surrounded by a wall built by the Muslims about 500 years ago. It is a relatively small area, approximately one square kilometer. Although not divided by actual borders, when one enters into the Jewish section, one must pass through security. Thus, the city is divided into a Muslim, Jewish, Christian and Armenian section. This is based on the various religions. One thing is clear: Jerusalem is not a united Jewish city. It is still trodden down of the Gentiles. The nations still "burden themselves" with Jerusalem.

World against Jerusalem

While there is law and order prevailing throughout the Old City on the day-to-day basis, such is definitely not the case from political perspectives. The city is actually divided into two: Israel and the world. The whole world, under the leadership of the god of this world, is "in siege...against Jerusalem." Therefore, we arrive at the understanding that this does not exclusively apply to the future, but is a present day reality.

There is a great volume of material available in books, videos and the internet, clearly documenting that all nations of the world—regardless of their political preference, or their religion or non-religion—have one thing in common: namely, they do not accept Jerusalem as the sovereign capital city of the State of Israel!

282

Building the Spiritual Temple

There is an assumption by well-meaning evangelical Christians, that one must use political means to help Israel take total possession of the city of Jerusalem. They are fervently supporting various Jewish religious groups, which are attempting to build the Jewish temple on Mount Moriah. What's wrong with that? They are ignoring the clear task given to the Church; namely, the building of the spiritual temple of God as outlined in Ephesians 2:20-22: "And are built upon the foundation of the apostles and prophets, Jesus Christ himself being the chief corner stone; In whom all the building fitly framed together groweth unto an holy temple in the Lord: In whom ye also are builded together for an habitation of God through the Spirit." Christians should be concerned with only one temple, and that is the spiritual one.

Nations Oppose Judah

Zechariah 12:4: "In that day, saith the LORD, I will smite every horse with astonishment, and his rider with madness: and I will open mine eyes upon the house of Judah, and will smite every horse of the people with blindness."

Verse 4 begins with, "In that day." Again, we reiterate that this day belongs to the collective judgment of the nations, and includes the past, present and future. Nevertheless, there will be a direct confrontation between the Prince of Peace and the Prince of Darkness, and that is the Battle of Armageddon.

283

During Zechariah's days, military power was exhibited by horse and rider. Israel's enemies will act with madness, yet their weapons of wars will not work toward the intended purpose.

In contrast, God says: "I will open mine eyes upon the house of Judah." In the midst of the commotion, God's eye will watch over Judah. God "will smite every horse of the people with blindness." Luther translates this, "All horses of the nations will I smite with blindness."

The Strength of Judah

Zechariah 12:5: "And the governors of Judah shall say in their heart, The inhabitants of Jerusalem shall be my strength in the LORD of hosts their God."

When we think of the enemies of the Jewish people, whether Pharaoh, Haman or Hitler, they all acted with great madness; they were blind to God's plan and intention with His people Israel.

Judah to Be Victorious

The Lord continues to emphasize the difference between His people Judah and the nations of the world, and highlights His plan for the city Jerusalem:

Zechariah 12:6: "In that day will I make the governors of Judah like an hearth of fire among the wood, and like a torch of fire in a sheaf; and they shall devour all the people round about, on the right hand and on the left: and Jerusalem shall be inhabited again in her own place, even in Jerusalem."

(See) Isaiah 10:17-18; Obadiah 18

Surely, "the people round about" (the Arab nations) have experienced how Judah (the Jews) was like "fire" when they encountered the Israeli army.

Israel's Future Guaranteed

The Jewish people have not ceased to exist in spite of the threat of annihilation from the nations of the world. Some time ago, the president of Persia (Iran) proclaimed publicly that the nation of Israel would be wiped off the map. But no such thing will happen. Why not? Because Israel has eternal promises. Their existence is based on the existence of our solar system. This is what the prophet Jeremiah proclaims: "Thus saith the LORD, which giveth the sun for a light by day, and the ordinances of the moon and of the stars for a light by night, which divideth the sea when the waves thereof roar; The LORD of hosts is his name: If those ordinances depart from before me, saith the LORD, then the seed of Israel also shall cease from being a nation before me for ever" (Jeremiah 31:35-36).

We all know that Israel did cease to be a nation in their own country for a time span of approximately 2,000 years. But from God's perspective, Israel never ceased to be a nation. This helps us realize that we should not place certain verses only in the context of certain time periods. God is eternal, and so is Israel.

The nations of the world may burden themselves with Jerusalem, allocating certain parts of the city to the Muslims, other parts to the Christians, and a portion for the Jews. But the Bible says, "Jerusalem shall be inhabited again in her own place, even in Jerusalem." There will be no division in Jerusalem. It is, it was, and always will be the capital city of the Jewish state and God's residence on earth.

The Tents of Judah

Something peculiar is revealed in the next verse:

Zechariah 12:7: "The LORD also shall save the tents of Judah first, that the glory of the house of David and the glory of the inhabitants of Jerusalem do not magnify themselves against Judah."

(See) Jeremiah 30:18; Amos 9:11; 1 Corinthians 1:27, 29, 31

The "tents of Judah" signify the geopolitical identity of the Jewish people. A date can be named, 14 May 1948, when the Jews proclaimed the State of Israel. With that declaration, the Jews were telling the world, we are here; we are a nation; we are an identity; we will fight for our place among the nations.

Only three days after Israel's declaration as a State, the first nation to recognize the Jewish State was the Soviet Union, followed by Poland, Czechoslovakia, Yugoslavia, Ireland and South Africa. The United States officially recognized Israel on 31 January 1949.

Judah, David, and Jerusalem

Judah is the geopolitical identity of Israel, while "David" and "Jerusalem" signify the spiritual identity. We need to recall the words of Revelation 5:5: "Behold, the lion of the tribe of Juda, the Root of David, hath prevailed...."

Thus, the succession becomes clear: the Jews will return to the land of Israel in unbelief. They had to have an address; there was no such thing as "the tents of Judah." Then, in 1967 they captured Jerusalem, and from that point on, the nations of the world have been in an uproar against the Jews for claiming sovereignty over Jerusalem.

The New Heart and Spirit

How was the establishment of Israel accomplished? Something incredible had to happen. Let us first read Ezekiel 36:26: "A new heart also will I give you, and a new spirit will I put within you: and I will take away the stony heart out of your flesh, and I will give you an heart of flesh." Note the succession: a *new heart*, and then a *new spirit*. What does it mean? The moment the Jew returned to the land of Israel, he experienced a transformation; he changed from being the whipping boy of the nations, to having the most effective military in the world. The Jew was transformed from a defender to an attacker.

But that's not all. Verse 27 continues with God's action, "...I will put *my spirit* within you, and cause you to walk in my statutes, and ye shall keep my judgments, and do them." We should note the difference between a *new spirit* and *my spirit*. Israel's collective salvation is caused by His Spirit.

Here is the process:

Zechariah 12:8: "In that day shall the LORD defend the inhabitants of Jerusalem; and he that is feeble among them at that day shall be as David; and the house of David shall be as God, as the angel of the LORD before them."

(See) Exodus 14:19; 33:2; Psalm 82:6; Isaiah 33:24; Joel 3:10, 16

The Jews had been known as bad soldiers. Why? Because they never fully integrated with the host nation. Although there are many exceptions, Jews were always waiting for something else; namely, the fulfillment of their ancient prayer, "Next year in Jerusalem." Coming back to the land of their fathers, the Jews experienced a change: "a new heart...and a new spirit."

Miraculous War of 1967

There is an abundance of documentation available relating to Israel's establishment in 1948. That was the War of Liberation. Eight years later, it was followed by the Suez Canal War in 1956. But the most spectacular military event was the Six-Day War. Israel surprised the nations of the world. Something definitely went wrong for the Arabs, and something definitely went right for the Jews in their fight for survival.

During these short six days, Israel was not cast into the Mediterranean, as the Arabs had promised, but expanded its territory at least threefold.

Below are some figures listed by Wikipedia:

Total Troops
Israel: 264,000
Arab: 547,000

Combat Aircraft
Israel: 300
Arab: 957
Tanks
Israel 800
Arab: 2,504

Israel's victory was the result of God giving Israel "a new heart...and a new spirit."

Gathering against Jerusalem

Zechariah 12:9: "And it shall come to pass in that day, that I will seek to destroy all the nations that come against Jerusalem."

All nations, all people, all that dwell upon the earth are destined to express their decided "no" to a Jewish Jerusalem. But God says YES.

If anything is to be identified with the words "fulfillment of prophecy," it would be the opposition against Jerusalem by the entire world.

Of course, there are no armies gathered today with the intent to physically destroy Jerusalem. I doubt that strategies exist detailing their intended attack on Jerusalem in the European Union, the Asian nations or the United States. However, their combined and unanimous decision to allocate the city of Jerusalem to various religious groups, most certainly qualifies as fulfillment of "all the nations that come against Jerusalem."

The Day of Bitterness

Finally, we see God's "I will" in relationship to Israel's collective salvation:

Zechariah 12:10: "And I will pour upon the house of David, and upon the inhabitants of Jerusalem, the spirit of grace and of supplications: and they shall look upon me whom they have pierced, and they shall mourn for him, as one mourneth for his only son, and shall be in bitterness for him, as one that is in bitterness for his firstborn."

(See) Psalm 22:16; Isaiah 44:3; Jeremiah 6:26; Ezekiel 39:29; Joel 2:28; 3:1; Amos 8:10; Luke 2:35; John 19:34, 37; Revelation 1:7

Note, it does not say "in that day," but simply that Israel will experience the act of the grace of God. Their eyes will be opened to see and recognize Him whom they have pierced. Thus, the revelation of *that day* remains hidden.

The World Crucified Christ

Mind you, it wasn't Israel alone who pierced Jesus Christ while He was hanging on the cross; it was a Roman soldier. Yet the Bible specifically emphasizes this act as if done by Israel. Peter proclaimed in Acts 4:10: "Be it known unto you all, and to all the people of Israel, that by the name of Jesus Christ of Nazareth, whom ye crucified...." Israel collectively was responsible for the execution of the Prince of Life.

But there is more: the whole world is co-responsible for the crucifixion of Jesus. This fact is so clearly documented in Acts 4:27: "For of a truth against thy holy child Jesus, whom thou hast anointed, both Herod, and

Pontius Pilate, with the Gentiles, and the people of Israel, were gathered together."

Note the succession: Herod (whom we can call a half-Jew); Pontius Pilate (the Roman representative); the Gentiles (the whole world); and lastly, the people of Israel. All are co-responsible for the unjust crucifixion of Jesus Christ, the Messiah of Israel and Savior of the world.

From Mourning to Salvation

When the Spirit of grace comes upon Israel, they will recognize that this Jew, Jesus, is the Prince of Peace; the One they rejected, mocked and ridiculed; the One who was led like a lamb to the slaughter, who opened not His mouth. That's the point where true, genuine, and bitter repentance will take place. But, as already mentioned, it is an act of the grace of God.

Zechariah 12:11: "In that day shall there be a great mourning in Jerusalem, as the mourning of Hadadrimmon in the valley of Megiddon."

(See) 2 Chronicles 35:24-25; Matthew 24:30; Acts 2:37

Second Kings 23 refers to King Josiah, a good king of Judah who walked in the ways of David his father. It was he who broke down the altars, destroyed the graven images, and cleansed Israel from its idols. But this king of Judah committed a fatal mistake. We read of it in 2 Chronicles 35:22: "Nevertheless Josiah would not turn his face from him, but disguised himself, that he might fight with him, and hearkened not unto the words of Necho from the mouth of God, and came to fight in the valley of Megiddo." That mistake cost him his life, "And all Judah and Jerusalem mourned for Josiah. And Jeremiah lamented for Josiah: and all the singing men and the singing women spake of Josiah in their lamentations to this day, and made them an ordinance in Israel: and, behold, they are written in the lamentations" (2 Chronicles 35:24-25).

The heartbreaking mourning in Judah was for a good king who made a terrible mistake. Yet the mourning for the Good Shepherd—who did not make a mistake, nor was sin found in Him; who laid down His life for the sins of Israel and all of mankind—will cause the entire nation to be in bitterness "as one that is in bitterness for his firstborn." That's the One who will appear and be seen and recognized by all of Israel. It will result in unprecedented mourning of the nation. However, it will end in the glorious salvation of Israel.

Personal Repentance

Zechariah 12:12-14: "And the land shall mourn, every family apart; the family of the house of David apart, and their wives apart; the family of the house of Nathan apart, and their wives apart; 13 The family of the house of Levi apart, and their wives apart; the family of Shimei apart, and their wives apart; 14 All the families that remain, every family apart, and their wives apart."

Although the Spirit of grace and supplication will be poured upon all of Israel, repentance will not be collective, but individual: the house of David (the royal family), the house of Nathan (the prophets), the house of Levi (the priesthood), and the family of Shimei, which is part of the house of Levi. But the rest of the families are not excluded; all, individually and privately, will repent.

We have a relating story in 1 Corinthians 7:29-30: "But this I say, brethren, the time is short: it remaineth, that both they that have wives be as though they had none; And they that weep, as though they wept not; and they that rejoice, as though they rejoiced not; and they that buy, as though they possessed not." The key here is, "the time is short." Our total and unconditional dedication to the Lord supersedes all that we have, including our possessions and our family. The difference between weeping and rejoicing dissolves into the reality of the issue, "the time is short."

Real Peace for Israel

In summary, the world will be judged. Israel will go through great tribulation, but it will end in salvation. Finally, peace will have arrived for the people of Israel, who so desperately needed peace, real peace. They do not need peace based on a piece of paper, but on the payment of the accomplished atonement of the Lamb of God. He alone laid down His life for each of us, so we may taste real peace and freedom. He is the One who accomplished all. Thus, it is the Lamb of God who receives the eternal, incomparable praise from the lips of the great unnumbered multitude: "Saying with a loud voice, Worthy is the Lamb that was slain to receive power, and riches, and wisdom, and strength, and honour, and glory, and blessing" (Revelation 5:12).

Chapter 13

Introduction

This chapter continues to record the direct words of God. These 9 verses are a powerful prophecy pointing to the New Covenant for the people of Israel, proclaiming the end of idolatry, the end of prophets, and the end of unclean spirits.

Verses 6-7 reveal Jesus the Crucified One, the Shepherd, who was taken and the sheep scattered. The chapter concludes with the remnant of Israel being refined and converted to the Lord, exclaiming, "The Lord is my God."

Sin Shall Be Taken Away

Zechariah 13:1: "In that day there shall be a fountain opened to the house of David and to the inhabitants of Jerusalem for sin and for uncleanness."

(See) Numbers 19:17; Psalm 51:2, 7; Isaiah 1:16-18; 4:4;
Jeremiah 2:13; 17:13; Ezekiel 36:25

What a tremendous promise—a remedy for sin. This is something most unusual. Why? Because the Old Testament proclaimed, "The soul that sinneth, it shall die." The cleansing of sin was not possible under the Old Covenant. God's calling of Abraham, Isaac, and Jacob served to bring forth a nation to whom God could present His intention—priests, temple, sacrifice. But the purpose was only to cover sin temporarily.

Moses the Lawgiver

Moses instructed his people what to do and what not to do. At certain times in specific places, they were to sacrifice animals, spill their blood in order to obtain God's grace and mercy. But, the New Covenant reveals, "For it is not possible that the blood of bulls and of goats should take away sins" (Hebrews 10:4).

The Sin Forgiver

Here in verse 1, we read of a fountain, actually an opened fountain, for the remission of sin. This could not be achieved through the sacrificing of animals, nor by the glorious worship service in the temple in Jerusalem. It could only be accomplished through the perfect sacrifice of the "Lamb of God, which taketh away the sin of the world."

We recall here an event where Jesus told the man "sick of the palsy; Son, be of good cheer; thy sins be forgiven thee" (Matthew 9:2). The Bible scholars who heard that statement protested, "This man blasphemeth." However, this man was Jesus, the sinless One. He not only spoke forgiveness, but also Himself became the cause of forgiveness, through His poured out blood on Calvary's Cross. The perfect Lamb of God, spotless and without sin, became sin for us. Eternal life had to die, which by definition is impossible.

He is the sinless One, and did not qualify to be judged under the law, "The soul that sinneth, it shall die." The devil did make a fatal mistake by inspiring evil man to crucify the Sinless One. Jesus' death on Calvary's Cross opened the door to eternal salvation. By faith in a lie, Adam lost paradise, but now by faith in Jesus, everlasting life is given to all who will accept the free gift of salvation.

To "the house of David," forgiveness of sin would become available by the "fountain opened." And from Jerusalem, the offer of salvation was sent to the entire world.

The Process of Fulfillment

Now we come to an important question: was this fulfilled, or will it be fulfilled in the future? We may safely say "yes" to both options, because Jesus of the house of David did come to Jerusalem to offer forgiveness of sin. But John 1:11 reads: "He came unto his own, and his own received him not." Therefore, the final offering of salvation to Israel is yet to come.

Many Did Receive Him

The Church was born in Jerusalem. Multitudes of His own accepted Him, believed in Him, and were born again of the Spirit of God and added to His Church.

When the Apostle Peter preached "the name of Jesus Christ for the remission of sins" in Jerusalem, Acts 2:41 reports: "Then they that gladly received his word were baptized: and the same day there were added unto them about three thousand souls." The last sentence of chapter 2 reads: "…And the Lord added to the church daily such as should be saved" (verse 47).

Moreover, in Acts 4, we read of another great multitude who received Jesus: "Howbeit many of them which heard the word believed; and the number of the men was about five thousand" (verse 4). Chapter 6 documents that even priests became obedient to the faith: "And the word of God increased; and the number of the disciples multiplied in Jerusalem greatly; and a great company of the priests were obedient to the faith" (verse 7).

We don't know what the population of Jerusalem was at that time, but it stands to reason that the city was saturated with Jewish believers in the Lord Jesus Christ. Therefore, when the Bible says, "He came unto his own, and his own received him not," it does not mean Israel collectively.

Separation from Idols

Zechariah 13:2: "And it shall come to pass in that day, saith the LORD of hosts, that I will cut off the names of the idols out of the land, and they shall no more be remembered: and also I will cause the prophets and the unclean spirit to pass out of the land."

(See) Exodus 23:13; Micah 5:12; 2 Peter 2:1

The words we read reveal God's intention regarding the house of David and the inhabitants of Jerusalem. A threefold cleansing is initiated by the Lord:
1. Cut off the names of the idols.
2. Get rid of the prophets.
3. Remove the unclean spirit.

Idols are a visible manifestation of the words of

prophets, inspired by unclean spirits. They will be done away with in the land of Israel.

Family Judgment

Now we come to verse 3, which reveals a horrendous tragedy: namely, a son who is a false prophet in the family of God, and the parents are the ones who will execute judgment:

Zechariah 13:3: "And it shall come to pass, that when any shall yet prophesy, then his father and his mother that begat him shall say unto him, Thou shalt not live; for thou speakest lies in the name of the LORD: and his father and his mother that begat him shall thrust him through when he prophesieth."

(See) Deuteronomy 13:6-11; Jeremiah 23:34; Matthew 10:37

Father and Mother Kill Son

Why do the parents have to kill the false prophet? After all, it is their flesh and blood; it is their precious son whom they nursed, brought up, and taught in the ways of the Lord. The reason is the law. Israel was redeemed from the slavery of Egypt by the substance of the blood of a lamb. If, therefore, the son prophesied in the name of the Lord, but in actual fact is prophesying in the name of an idol, he is polluting the substance of redemption—the blood of the Lamb. Israel was guided by the law they received from Moses, directing them to the coming Messiah, the Lord Jesus Christ, the Son of David, born in Bethlehem. Therefore, any prophecy contrary to redemption must be judged.

In Deuteronomy 18, Moses speaks of the two prophets: the real one and the fake one. In verse 15 we read: "The LORD thy God will raise up unto thee a Prophet from the midst of thee, of thy brethren, like unto me; unto him ye shall hearken." That's the real one. In verse 20, we see the false one, "But the prophet, which shall presume to speak a word in my name, which I have not commanded him to speak, or that shall speak in the name of other gods, even that prophet shall die" (verse 20).

Serving Other Gods Calls for Death

Here is what it says in the Law of God: "If thy brother, the son of thy mother, or thy son, or thy daughter, or the wife of thy bosom, or thy friend, which is as thine own soul, entice thee secretly, saying, Let us go and serve other gods, which thou hast not known, thou, nor thy fathers...But thou shalt surely kill him; thine hand shall be first upon him to put him to death..." (Deuteronomy 13:6-9).

False Prophet

Not only the false prophet, but also the entire religious infrastructure is exposed in verse 4:

Zechariah 13:4: "And it shall come to pass in that day, that the prophets shall be ashamed every one of his vision, when he hath prophesied; neither shall they wear a rough garment to deceive:"

(See) 2 Kings 1:8; Jeremiah 8:9; Micah 3:7

The pretension to be a prophet was exhibited by the wearing of "a rough garment." That, apparently, was the uniform of a prophet. Here we are reminded of Elijah the prophet in 2 Kings 1:8: "He was an hairy man, and girt with a girdle of leather about his loins. And he said, It is Elijah the Tishbite." We know that Elijah plays a significant role in the coming of the Messiah. In the second to last verse of the Old Testament, we read, "Behold, I will send you Elijah the prophet before the coming of the great and dreadful day of the Lord" (Malachi 4:5).

John the Baptist

Another important prophet was John the Baptist, the herald of the Lord's coming. The Gospel of Mark describes him with these words: "And John was clothed with camel's hair, and with a girdle of a skin about his loins; and he did eat locusts and wild honey" (Mark 1:6).

"I Am No Prophet"

Verse 5 introduces a different identity:

Zechariah 13:5: "But he shall say, I am no prophet, I am an husbandman; for man taught me to keep cattle from my youth."

(See) Amos 7:14

The translation of this verse varies widely. Menge reads, "I am not a prophet, no, I am a farmworker. I have been bought from my youth as a slave." The *Tenakh* says,

"I am not a 'prophet'; I am a tiller of the soil, you see, I was plied with the red stuff from my youth on." Reading the various translations, one senses the difficulty in finding the right combination of words to identify this person, who states that he is not a prophet.

Who Is It?

Who is this person who says, "I am not a prophet"? If we connect this statement to verse 4, he is identified as a false prophet who wants to get back to farming. But connecting this to verse 6 identifies none other than Jesus Christ, who indeed "was wounded in the house of my friends." We realize that this verse includes various identities: the Lord, the prophet, and the origin of the prophet. For example, "Then answered Amos, and said to Amaziah, I was no prophet, neither was I a prophet's son; but I was an herdman, and a gatherer of sycomore fruit" (Amos 7:14).

"Born Free"

While verse 5 identifies a prophet under bondage, verse 6 reveals one not under bondage but "born free." Jesus came from the line of the house of David. Based on the record we find in 1 Samuel 17, when David defeats Goliath, he receives the promise from the king that he will receive riches and becoming the king's son-in-law, "and make his father's house free in Israel" (verse 25).

Thus, we may allegorically interpret this verse to mean Israel. They lived off the land and from the land. But their entire religious infrastructure did not produce faith in the prophetic Word, which would cause them to recognize the Messiah.

Although they believed the Bible and quoted the prophets, they did not in reality react to the proclaimed message of God through the prophets.

Bible Scholars Disbelieved

The wise men from the east came to Jerusalem asking, "Where is he that is born King of the Jews?" (Matthew 2:2). The scribes, the priests, the Bible scholars of that day, answered correctly, "In Bethlehem of Judaea: for thus it is written by the prophet" (verse 5). They surely knew and believed Scripture, but definitely not with the heart, because there is no record of the priests and scribes going to Bethlehem to worship the newborn King of the Jews. Therefore, Israel as a nation, particularly the religious authority, had to confess, "I am no prophet."

The Rejected Prophet

Zechariah 13:6: "And one shall say unto him, What are these wounds in thine hands? Then he shall answer, Those with which I was wounded in the house of my friends."

Most scholars agree this is a clear revelation of the Son of God, Jesus Christ, the Messiah of Israel and Savior of the world: "...he was wounded for our transgressions, he was bruised for our iniquities: the chastisement of our peace was upon him; and with his stripes we are healed. All we like sheep have gone astray; we have turned every one to his own way; and the LORD hath laid on him the iniquity of us all. He was oppressed, and he was afflicted, yet he opened not his mouth: he is brought as a lamb to the slaughter, and as a sheep before her shearers is dumb, so he openeth not his mouth" (Isaiah 53:5-7).

The Genuine Shepherd

God in His infinite wisdom caused the "sword" to be turned against His beloved Son. That is the key point of the message of Holy Scripture. "For God so loved the world, that he gave his only begotten Son, that whosoever believeth in him should not perish, but have everlasting life" (John 3:16). The real Shepherd, the One who laid down His life for His sheep, was smitten. Jesus Himself, on the way to Gethsemane, quoted these words: "All ye shall be offended because of me this night: for it is written, I will smite the shepherd, and the sheep of the flock shall be scattered abroad" (Matthew 26:31).

"The Little Ones"

Zechariah 13:7: "Awake, O sword, against my shepherd, and against the man that is my fellow, saith the LORD of hosts: smite the shepherd, and the sheep shall be scattered: and I will turn mine hand upon the little ones."

(See) Isaiah 40:11; 53:4-6; Ezekiel 34:23-24; 37:24; Matthew 26:31; Mark 14:27; Hebrews 13:20

Who are "the little ones"? To begin with, these are the under-shepherds; in the first place, the apostles, of whom all were executed except John, who wrote the book of

Revelation. Church history documents the persecution of church leaders.

But we may also include the "little ones" of Bethlehem, "Then Herod, when he saw that he was mocked of the wise men, was exceeding wroth, and sent forth, and slew all the children that were in Bethlehem, and in all the coasts thereof, from two years old and under, according to the time which he had diligently enquired of the wise men" (Matthew 2:16).

Two-thirds Cut Off

Next, we come to prophecy that was fulfilled and will be fulfilled in the future:

Zechariah 13:8: "And it shall come to pass, that in all the land, saith the LORD, two parts therein shall be cut off and die; but the third shall be left therein."

(See) Isaiah 6:13; Ezekiel 5:2-4, 12; Romans 11:5

Various sources indicate that during the Great Tribulation, two-thirds of the Jews in Israel will be annihilated. The reason I am not in agreement with this interpretation is that we overlook the time span of judgment upon the people of Israel. If we place this event within the time period of the Great Tribulation, then indeed such an interpretation is correct. However, I venture to say that this verse and the next one must be applied for the entire time period of *the times of the Gentiles.* That means about 2,600 years.

Furthermore, innumerable Jews have been killed throughout the world, particularly during the Second

World War, when over 6 million Jews were systematically murdered under the Nazi regime in Europe. If we take these facts into consideration, then the Jews residing in the land of Israel and in the rest of the world represent only one-third of the Jewish race.

Time-span of Fulfilling Prophecy

How prophecy is fulfilled during a time-span of millennia is recorded in Acts 2. Here we have the record of the birth of the Church in Jerusalem, confirmed by the pouring out of the Holy Spirit and the subsequent signs. Verse 16 states: "But this is that which was spoken by the prophet Joel." Peter then enumerates the signs such as prophecy, visions and dreams. However, in one breath, this prophecy continues, "And I will show wonders in heaven above, and signs in the earth beneath; blood, and fire, and vapour of smoke: The sun shall be turned into darkness, and the moon into blood, before that great and notable day of the Lord come" (verses 19-20). That part is still waiting to be fulfilled. The sun shall be turned into darkness and the moon into blood. Therefore, I venture to say that the words, "two parts therein shall be cut off and die..." were fulfilled during the last 2,600 years.

The Refining Process

Zechariah 13:9: "And I will bring the third part through the fire, and will refine them as silver is refined, and will try them as gold is tried: they shall call on my name, and I will hear them: I will say, It is my people: and they shall say, The LORD is my God."

(See) Psalm 66:10; Isaiah 48:10; Hosea 2:23; Malachi 3:3; 1 Peter 1:6-7;
Revelation 2:10

The final refining of the Jewish people will ultimately lead to their confession: "The Lord is my God." We cannot fit this event in the short period of seven years, and ignore the previous 2,600 of the persecution of the Jewish people throughout the world.

Israel's Only Friend

There is a group of people scattered all over the world, those who have surrendered their lives and subsequently are born again of His Spirit. They are the only pro-Israel people on earth: they are the Body of Christ. We are admonished to be pro-Israel, pro-Jerusalem and pro-Jewish: "Comfort ye, comfort ye my people, saith your God. Speak ye comfortably to Jerusalem, and cry unto her, that her warfare is accomplished, that her iniquity is pardoned: for she hath received of the LORD'S hand double for all her sins" (Isaiah 40:1-2).

Double Punishment

Now comes the great question: when did Israel receive of the Lord's hand double for all her sins?

When they came out of Egypt? Not so, because they were richly rewarded by the Egyptians as they moved out. Exodus 12:36 records, "...And they spoiled the Egyptians."

Israel was totally enveloped in the provision and grace of God throughout their journey in the desert for 40 years. They came to the Promised Land and enjoyed the fruit of the land they had not planted, living in houses they had not built. God took care of His people in a marvelous way.

Did Israel receive of the Lord's hand double for all her sins when they came out of Babylon? We have the documentation in Ezra, Nehemiah, and Haggai. These prophets clearly reveal that King Cyrus of Persia supported the Jews generously on their return to Jerusalem. Money was not an object, neither was security. As a matter of fact, the prophet Ezra confesses, "And after all that is come upon us for our evil deeds, and for our great trespass, seeing that thou our God hast punished us less than our iniquities deserve, and hast given us such deliverance as this" (Ezra 9:13).

That is *less*, not *double punishment.*

Israel's Last Return

However, before Israel's last return, they experienced the double portion of punishment. The *Timeline of Jewish Persecution* gives details about their persecution, such as forced conversions, expulsion, enslavement, etc. In 1096, one-third of Jews were massacred as part of the First Crusade. When one adds the 6 million Jews murdered in the Holocaust, this certainly qualifies for the Bible's statement that only one-third will be left.

No Help in Sight

No one helped the Jews when they returned to the land of Israel in large numbers. These Jews that came back from the Diaspora found a land relatively desolate and empty. This is recorded in Ezekiel 36:4, where we read,

"Therefore, ye mountains of Israel, hear the word of the Lord GOD; Thus saith the Lord GOD to the mountains, and to the hills, to the rivers, and to the valleys, to the desolate wastes, and to the cities that are forsaken, which became a prey and derision to the residue of the heathen that are round about."

Having established an agriculture community in Israel, the Jews were placed under the dominion of Great Britain. But during that time too, the Jews experienced oppression from the Arabs and the British occupational forces.

The Holocaust

As if that wasn't enough, Hitler's war machine decimated the Jewish population in Europe by over 6 million. History records that on several occasions, the remnant, which tried to escape to Israel, were forced back to the land of their captivity by British soldiers.

US and UK Arms Embargo

Finally, in 1948, Israel was ready to declare to the world that the nation would be called into existence as a political identity. But once again, great disappointment awaited them. The United States placed an arms embargo on the Middle East, under the pretense of avoiding violent confrontation. Britain did likewise. Yet they generously supplied weapons and know-how to the surrounding Arab nations, which were considered legitimate sovereign states.

That was the time when the remnant, the third part of the Jewish nation, went through the fire. They were refined as silver and tried as gold. But, we must add, not spiritually. Today, Israel has become a vibrant nation, scoring incredible successes in science and technology. Yet, at this point, they are still in darkness spiritually.

The Church and Israel

Here is where the Church comes in, the true believers. Not Churchianity, but individuals who love the Lord with all of their heart, all of their mind, and all of their soul. They speak comfortably to Israel. They are the ones who are eagerly involved in the building of His Church on earth. They are the Christians who don't care about the cost, who surrender everything freely. Their calling is defined in 1 Peter 2:9: "But ye are a chosen generation, a royal priesthood, an holy nation, a peculiar people; that ye should show forth the praises of him who hath called you out of darkness into his marvellous light."

What will happen when the last one from among the Gentiles is added to the Church? The Church is the Bride of Christ, and will be raptured into His presence. Then Romans 11:25-26 will be fulfilled: "...Blindness in part is happened to Israel, until the fulness of the Gentiles be come in. And so all Israel shall be saved: as it is written, There shall come out of Sion the Deliverer, and shall turn away ungodliness from Jacob."

Chapter 14

Introduction

The last chapter of the book of Zechariah may be titled "Summary of Judgment and Salvation." This chapter too consists exclusively of the Lord speaking. At the beginning of the book of Zechariah, we read, "came the word of the Lord unto Zechariah." Then follows the eight night visions, which conclude with chapter 6. Beginning with chapter 7, verse 5, it's the Lord speaking all the way through the end of the book.

Summary of Judgment and Salvation

Zechariah 14:1: "Behold, the day of the LORD cometh, and thy spoil shall be divided in the midst of thee."

(See) Isaiah 13:6, 9; 39:6

What "spoil" is being divided, and to whom? Let's read the Menge translation: "Know assuredly a day of the Lord is to come when the spoil they took from you will be divided in your midst."

This is a very powerful statement. What is the "spoil?" It is the intellectual treasure of the Jew, which was stolen from them throughout the times of the Gentiles—for 2,600 years. That is fulfillment of Bible prophecy.

Prophetic Warning

Moses prophesied what would transpire if Israel was to disobey the commandment of the Lord: "Thou shalt plant vineyards, and dress them, but shalt neither drink of the wine, nor gather the grapes; for the worms shall eat them. Thou shalt have olive trees throughout all thy coasts, but thou shalt not anoint thyself with the oil; for thine olive shall cast his fruit. Thou shalt beget sons and daughters, but thou shalt not enjoy them; for they shall go into captivity. All thy trees and fruit of thy land shall the locust consume. The stranger that is within thee shall get up above thee very high; and thou shalt come down very low. He shall lend to thee, and thou shalt not lend to him: he shall be the head, and thou shalt be the tail" (Deuteronomy 28:39-44).

The blessings of the Lord consist in the abundance of harvest. That was the measurement of riches in olden days. Note verse 44: the heathen will lend to the Jew, and the heathen shall be the head and the Jew shall be the tail. That is the exact opposite of what God had promised through Moses earlier: "For the LORD thy God blesseth thee, as he promised thee: and thou shalt lend unto many nations, but thou shalt not borrow; and thou shalt reign over many nations, but they shall not reign over thee" (Deuteronomy 15:6).

Gentiles Rob the Jews

There is an abundance of documentation available, clearly showing that the Jews have been persecuted severely for over two and a half millennia.

Look at today's world. Who are the greatest contrib-

311

utors to the wellbeing of humanity? The answer is indisputable: the Jew. Take a glance at the recipients of the internationally recognized Nobel Prize, and you will find a lopsided number of Jews who have won that prestigious award.

Yet from Russia to Spain, from Britain to Italy, the Jews have been persecuted. Even in relatively recent times, during the Second World War, six million Jews were systematically murdered by the Nazi regime in Germany under Adolf Hitler. Study German history, and you will find that the Jews were one of the most significant contributors toward Germany's leading position in the world in the scientific field. But the Jews were robbed of their reward.

Even in the new colonial countries, Jews were blatantly discriminated against. In plain words, the nations robbed you: now it's payback time.

Future Punishment?

Zechariah 14:2: "For I will gather all nations against Jerusalem to battle; and the city shall be taken, and the houses rifled, and the women ravished; and half of the city shall go forth into captivity, and the residue of the people shall not be cut off from the city."

(See) Isaiah 13:16; Joel 3:2; Zechariah 12:2-3

Most Bible scholars place this event in the time period of the Great Tribulation. In doing so, we ignore history. The nations of the world, beginning with Babylon, have gathered against Jerusalem for the past 2,600 years. The nations did destroy Jerusalem, rifle the houses, ravish the women, and led the Jews captive. This can be documented from the beginning of the times of the Gentiles until our time.

History Documents Persecution of Jews

Here is an example: A respected historian, James Carroll, is quoted in *Jews and Judaism*, listed under "Anti-Semitism" in Wikipedia, "Jews accounted for 10% of the total population of the Roman Empire. By that ratio, if other factors such as pogroms and conversions had not intervened, there would be 200 million Jews in the world today, instead of something like 13 million."

When we read Scripture and compare it with historical facts, then we must come to the conclusion that Israel has received from the Lord's hand *double* punishment for their sins. That is why we, who believe in Jesus Christ as our Lord, are admonished to comfort Israel: "Comfort ye, comfort ye my people, saith your God. Speak ye comfortably to Jerusalem, and cry unto her, that her warfare is accomplished, that her iniquity is pardoned: for she hath received of the LORD'S hand double for all her sins" (Isaiah 40:1-2).

To reemphasize this fact, let's re-read verse 2: "For I will gather all nations against Jerusalem to battle; and the city shall be taken, and the houses rifled, and the women ravished; and half of the city shall go forth into captivity, and the residue of the people shall not be cut off from the city."

For the USA or any nation to fulfill this verse would violate the Geneva Convention and international law. It is forbidden to steal private property or to rape women during a military conflict. Although this does happen, it is the exception and not the rule of operation. Therefore, if we place this in the future, during the time of the Great Tribulation, then we must acknowledge such a scenario.

The Lord Fights against the Nations

Zechariah 14:3: "Then shall the LORD go forth, and fight against those nations, as when he fought in the day of battle."

(See) Zechariah 9:14-15; Revelation 19:19

Here we have the Lord intervening; He acts on behalf of Israel.

We are reminded here of the Exodus, when Israel moved out of Egypt toward the Promised Land. They stood before the Red Sea, and behind them came Pharaoh's chosen army to recapture Israel and lead them back into bondage. "And Moses said unto the people, Fear ye not, stand still, and see the salvation of the LORD, which he will show to you to day: for the Egyptians whom ye have seen to day, ye shall see them again no more for ever" (Exodus 14:13).

Over and again we read in Israel's history that it was God who fought on their behalf. He has done so in the past, He is doing it today, and that is exactly what God will do on that certain day. Therefore, we are convinced of God's supernatural intervention on behalf of Israel.

The Second Coming

Zechariah 14:4: "And his feet shall stand in that day upon the mount of Olives, which is before Jerusalem on the east, and the mount of Olives shall cleave in the midst thereof toward the east and toward the west, and there shall be a very great valley; and half of the mountain shall remove toward the north, and half of it toward the south."

(See) Isaiah 64:1-2; Ezekiel 11:23; Micah 1:3-4; Acts 1:11-12

We do know that His feet shall touch the Mount of Olives, resulting in topographical changes. The Mount of Olives will split from east to west, creating a large rift and causing a mountain in the north and the south.

What is the purpose?

Zechariah 14:5: "And ye shall flee to the valley of the mountains; for the valley of the mountains shall reach unto Azal: yea, ye shall flee, like as ye fled from before the earthquake in the days of Uzziah king of Judah: and the LORD my God shall come, and all the saints with thee."

(See) Psalm 96:13; Isaiah 29:6; 66:15-16; Joel 3:11; Amos 1:1; Matthew 16:27; 24:30; 25:31

This again is not listed chronologically. When the Lord comes and His feet shall stand on the Mount of Olives, Israel's salvation has come. So, why do they have to "flee"? The Jews do not need to flee when the Messiah comes. Here again, we must understand that this

315

prophecy is a picture of the Jews' dispersion throughout the times of the Gentiles, which is about 2,600 years.

We all know that the Lord's feet stood on the Mount of Olives when He ascended into heaven, and the message of the angel made it clear that He will return likewise. His feet shall stand on the Mount of Olives again. That has not taken place, nor has the Mount of Olives split in half yet; subsequently, the words, "...ye shall flee, like as ye fled from before the earthquake in the days of Uzziah king of Judah," have been in the process of fulfillment for several millennia.

Place of Refuge

Where will they flee? The Bible does not give us an answer; therefore, we should not speculate. However, based on Revelation chapter 11, we know that God will intervene supernaturally. This is recorded in Revelation 12:6 and 14: "And the woman fled into the wilderness, where she hath a place prepared of God, that they should feed her there a thousand two hundred and threescore days... And to the woman were given two wings of a great eagle, that she might fly into the wilderness, into her place, where she is nourished for a time, and times, and half a time, from the face of the serpent."

We know that this woman is Israel, for "she brought forth a man child, who was to rule all nations with a rod of iron." Unmistakably, this is Jesus returning to the Mount of Olives, making an end of the Antichrist system and establishing His 1,000 Year Kingdom of Peace. It will not be ruled by weapons of war, but by the Lord Himself, who will strictly implement His law "with a rod of iron."

The Most Unusual Day in History

This event—the return of Christ on the Mount of Olives—will be a very unique day:

Zechariah 14:6-7: "And it shall come to pass in that day, that the light shall not be clear, nor dark: 7 But it shall be one day which shall be known to the LORD, not day, nor night: but it shall come to pass, that at evening time it shall be light."

(See) Mark 13:32; Revelation 21:23; 22:5

Words apparently are not sufficient to describe what will happen, because suddenly light is no longer light, and dark is no longer dark. It is neither day nor night, but something we don't know. It is literally out of this world, but "shall be known to the Lord."

Jerusalem on the Seashore

Next, we come to the second important result caused by the Lord's appearance on the Mount of Olives. The first served as an escape, "ye shall flee." The second result will make Jerusalem a harbor city:

Zechariah 14:8: "And it shall be in that day, that living waters shall go out from Jerusalem; half of them toward the former sea, and half of them toward the hinder sea: in summer and in winter shall it be."

(See) Ezekiel 47:1-12; Joel 3:18; John 7:38; Revelation 22:1-2

317

For a better understanding, let's read the *Tenakh*: "In that day, fresh water shall flow from Jerusalem, part of it to the Eastern Sea and part to the Western Sea, throughout the summer and winter" (verse 8). Water from Jerusalem will flow to the Mediterranean and into the Dead Sea.

Healing of the Dead Sea

The prophet Ezekiel has more to say about this topographical change in chapter 47, verses 8-9: "...These waters issue out toward the east country, and go down into the desert, and go into the sea: which being brought forth into the sea, the waters shall be healed. And it shall come to pass, that every thing that liveth, which moveth, whithersoever the rivers shall come, shall live: and there shall be a very great multitude of fish, because these waters shall come thither: for they shall be healed; and every thing shall live whither the river cometh." In plain words, the Dead Sea will come to life.

The King of Kings

Zechariah 14:9: "And the LORD shall be king over all the earth: in that day shall there be one LORD, and his name one."

(See) Deuteronomy 6:4; Psalm 2:8; 97:1; Isaiah 2:2-4; 45:21-24; Ephesians 4:5-6; Revelation 11:15

This goes far beyond Israel, because it says, "over all the earth." Doubtless, that's the day when Jesus rules planet Earth.

Jerusalem Untouchable

Contrary to man's desire to destroy Jerusalem, as we have seen in verse 2, the Lord now declares Jerusalem untouchable:

Zechariah 14:10-11: "All the land shall be turned as a plain from Geba to Rimmon south of Jerusalem: and it shall be lifted up, and inhabited in her place, from Benjamin's gate unto the place of the first gate, unto the corner gate, and from the tower of Hananeel unto the king's winepresses. 11 And men shall dwell in it, and there shall be no more utter destruction; but Jerusalem shall be safely inhabited."

(See) Nehemiah 3:1; Isaiah 2:2; Jeremiah 30:18; 31:38; 33:16; Amos 9:11; Zechariah 12:6; Revelation 22:3

The Lord is in control. He is King over all the earth, and Jerusalem is now secure. We may safely say this is the beginning of the 1,000 Year Kingdom of Peace for Israel. Now, for the first time in history, the earth will be judged righteously.

Zechariah 14:12: "And this shall be the plague wherewith the LORD will smite all the people that have fought against Jerusalem; Their flesh shall consume away while they stand upon their feet, and their eyes shall consume away in their holes, and their tongue shall consume away in their mouth."

(See) Leviticus 26:16; Deuteronomy 28:21-22

God-made Judgment

There are several interpretations, one of which is a nuclear war. However, that does not stand because we are now dealing with the judgment of God. Here I would like to distinguish between two types of judgment. The first is during the Great Tribulation at the opening of the six seals, where it clearly states that this judgment is not manmade, but comes from heaven: "And the kings of the earth, and the great men, and the rich men, and the chief captains, and the mighty men, and every bondman, and every free man, hid themselves in the dens and in the rocks of the mountains; And said to the mountains and rocks, Fall on us, and hide us from the face of him that sitteth on the throne, and from the wrath of the Lamb" (Revelation 6:15-16). This reveals that the people of the world know where the judgment comes from because of the statement, "…hide us from the face of him that sitteth on the throne, and from the wrath of the Lamb." So, it's not manmade but God-made.

This is not the Battle of Armageddon, not some type of third, fourth, or fifth world war. Nor is it a nuclear explosion; this is direct judgment from God in heaven.

The second type of judgment upon Earth is specifically directed toward those who oppose Jerusalem. For the first time in history, we see all the nations of the world unitedly gathered against Jerusalem.

Enemies of Jerusalem

This needs explanation. Today, no nation, not even Iran, is gathering her military power with the intention to fight against Jerusalem; much less the nations of the European world (West). But we cannot deny that all nations, without exception, agree upon one thing: Jerusalem should not be the undivided capital of the State of Israel. That fact qualifies all nations of the world as enemies of Jerusalem; subsequently, the statement in verse 2, "I will gather all nations against Jerusalem to battle," is a very precise, up-to-date statement.

Based on these facts, we must come to the conclusion that when the Messiah comes to Israel, He will destroy the power of the enemy and sets up the millennial Kingdom of Peace. This peace will not automatically be transferred to the nations of the world. They will first have to be judged.

Egypt Example

We find an example in the book of Ezekiel: "Behold, therefore I am against thee, and against thy rivers, and I will make the land of Egypt utterly waste and desolate, from the tower of Syene even unto the border of Ethiopia. No foot of man shall pass through it, nor foot of beast shall pass through it, neither shall it be inhabited forty years. And I will make the land of Egypt desolate in the midst of the countries that are desolate, and her cities among the cities that are laid waste shall be desolate forty years: and I will scatter the Egyptians among the nations, and will disperse them through the countries. Yet thus saith the Lord GOD; At the end of forty years will I gather the Egyptians from the people whither they were scattered" (29:10-13). We know this has not happened yet. Egypt has not experienced the "desolate forty years." But at the end of the judgment, Egypt shall know the God of Israel and will enjoy the same peace with Israel.

Self-destruction of the Nations

During those days, there will be utter confusion among the nations of the world, caused by the Lord Himself, as revealed by Zechariah:

Zechariah 14:13: "And it shall come to pass in that day, that a great tumult from the LORD shall be among them; and they shall lay hold every one on the hand of his neighbour, and his hand shall rise up against the hand of his neighbour."

(See) 1 Samuel 14:15; Zechariah 11:6

End of Poverty

In the meantime, verse 1 will continue to be fulfilled, as we read in verse 14:

Zechariah 14:14: "And Judah also shall fight at Jerusalem; and the wealth of all the heathen round about shall be gathered together, gold, and silver, and apparel, in great abundance."

(See) Isaiah 23:18

Israel will then be the richest nation on the face of the earth. For the first time in history, a social system will be so perfected that poverty will be eliminated, as prophesied in Deuteronomy 15:4: "Save when there shall be no poor among you; for the LORD shall greatly bless thee in the land which the LORD thy God giveth thee for an inheritance to possess it."

Animals

The judgment we read of in verse 12 is now applied to the animals as well:

Zechariah 14:15: "And so shall be the plague of the horse, of the mule, of the camel, and of the ass, and of all the beasts that shall be in these tents, as this plague."

Worship or Else

Zechariah 14:16: "And it shall come to pass, that every one that is left of all the nations which came against Jerusalem shall even go up from year to year to worship the King, the Lord of hosts, and to keep the feast of tabernacles."

(See) Leviticus 23:34-44; Isaiah 60:6-9; 66:18-21, 23

This is the time when the Lord will enforce His law of righteousness. The Gentiles will have to acknowledge, "The Lord, he is the God" (1 Kings 18:39).

Zechariah 14:17: "And it shall be, that whoso will not come up of all the families of the earth unto Jerusalem to worship the King, the Lord of hosts, even upon them shall be no rain."

(See) Jeremiah 14:3-6; Amos 4:7

There are dire consequences when one does not obey the law of the Lord: no rain.

Zechariah 14:18: "And if the family of Egypt go not up, and come not, that have no rain; there shall be the plague, wherewith the Lord will smite the heathen that come not up to keep the feast of tabernacles."

Egypt will be forced to acknowledge the God of Israel; otherwise, in addition to "no rain," there will be a plague.

Zechariah 14:19: "This shall be the punishment of Egypt, and the punishment of all nations that come not up to keep the feast of tabernacles."

This punishment is not limited to Egypt, but is applicable to "all nations."

The Rod of Iron

After God's destructive judgment upon the nations, only a remnant will be left. Now these nations will live under the strict law of the Lord; they will be ruled with His rod of iron. One of the duties of the nations will be to participate in the feast of tabernacles in Jerusalem. If they neglect to do so, that nation will not receive rain.

Unfortunately, most modern people today do not realize that rain is the element absolutely essential to sustain life on earth. When there is no rain, there is no food;

life on earth ceases to exist.

Millennium Starts

The Lord's law will be enforced; this supports our conclusion that the people of the nations who enter the
1,000 Year Kingdom of Peace are not necessarily all
saints. They are not saved by the blood of the Lamb.
They are placed under a righteous law system, which
they cannot oppose. Those that do oppose will die. For
that reason, it is my personal understanding that at the
end of the 1,000 Year Kingdom of Peace, the world will
be populated by saints only.

Isaiah 65 speaks of the 1,000 Year Kingdom of Peace,
where we find the famous words: "The wolf and the lamb
shall feed together, and the lion shall eat straw like the bul-
lock: and dust shall be the serpent's meat. They shall not
hurt nor destroy in all my holy mountain, saith the
LORD" (verse 25). But it also speaks of judgment: "…for
the child shall die an hundred years old; but the sinner
being an hundred years old shall be accursed" (verse 20b).

Holiness unto the Lord

Now we come to the last two verses, which we must read
as one:

> **Zechariah 14:20-21:** "In that day shall there be upon the bells
> of the horses, HOLINESS UNTO THE LORD; and the
> pots in the LORD'S house shall be like the bowls before
> the altar. 21 Yea, every pot in Jerusalem and in Judah
> shall be holiness unto the LORD of hosts: and all they
> that sacrifice shall come and take of them, and seethe

therein: and in that day there shall be no more the Canaanite in the house of the LORD of hosts."

(See) Exodus 28:36; Nehemiah 8:10; Isaiah 35:8; Ezekiel 46:20; Zephaniah 1:11; Ephesians 2:19; Revelation 21:27

The words "HOLINESS UNTO THE LORD" were reserved for the high priest; it was part of his consecration to the Lord. It says in Exodus 28:36: "And thou shalt make a plate of pure gold, and grave upon it, like the engravings of a signet, HOLINESS TO THE LORD." Here in Zechariah, holiness unto the Lord is engraved "upon the bells of the horses." That means there will be a continuous ringing of the bells, reminding even the animal world, "HOLINESS UNTO THE LORD."

Even all the utensils in Jerusalem and Judah come under the banner of "HOLINESS UNTO THE LORD." For the first time, there will be perfect Old Testament sacrifice to the Lord God of heaven. Jerusalem will then exclude everything that is foreign; nothing that does not bear the words, "HOLINESS UNTO THE LORD" will enter therein.

This is confirmed in the New Testament: "And there shall in no wise enter into it any thing that defileth, neither whatsoever worketh abomination, or maketh a lie: but they which are written in the Lamb's book of life" (Revelation 21:27).

Holy People
Now for the first time in Israel's history, the words found in Deuteronomy 14:2 will be fulfilled: "For thou art an holy people unto the LORD thy God, and the LORD hath chosen thee to be a peculiar people unto himself,

above all the nations that are upon the earth."

During the times of the Gentiles, approximately 2,600 years, the world collectively failed to realize the blessings and the honor God gave to the Jews in His unconditional covenant. The Jews have been despised, rejected, persecuted, and too often killed. That is why at the beginning of the book of Zechariah, we read, "And I am very sore displeased with the heathen that are at ease: for I was but a little displeased, and they helped forward the affliction" (Zechariah 1:15).

The Gospel of Eternity

For the last 2,000 years, the gospel of salvation through Jesus Christ the Lord has been proclaimed all over the world, yet only a small remnant has accepted the message, the message of the cross: Jesus Christ crucified. The overwhelming majority within Churchianity continues to proclaim the gospel for the benefit to the flesh, but that is a partial gospel; it is definitely not the whole gospel: "For to me to live is Christ, and to die is gain" (Philippians 1:21).

The message of the gospel clearly declares that I cannot please God under any circumstances; I must die to self and be born again as a new creation. That new creation in Christ is to rule my old nature until the day I die. That is the only good news, the gospel of salvation, the gospel of eternity.

For Israel, as we have seen throughout this book, judgment is proclaimed. The reason? Because "The LORD hath been sore displeased with your fathers" (Zechariah 1:2). But Israel's 2,600 year period of judgment will end in absolute and unconditional "HOLINESS UNTO THE LORD."

MALACHI

Messenger of the Lord

MALACHI

Book of the Bible	God's Directly Spoken Words (%)	Prophecy %*	Significant Names Listed in Each Book						
			Judah	Israel	Ephraim	Jerusalem	Zion	Heathen	Samaria
Hosea	93.32	56	15	44	37	0	0	0	6
Joel	57.70	68	6	3	0	6	7	5	0
Amos	80.95	58	4	30	0	2	2	1	5
Obadiah	97.69	81	1	1	1	2	2	4	1
Jonah	7.39	10	0	0	0	0	0	0	0
Micah	44.88	70	4	12	0	8	9	1	3
Nahum	40.30	74	1	1	0	0	0	0	0
Habakkuk	47.84	41	0	0	0	0	0	2	0
Zephaniah	96.92	89	3	4	0	4	2	1	0
Haggai	67.61	39	4	0	0	0	0	1	0
Zechariah	77.38	69	22	5	3	41	8	5	0
Malachi	93.80	56	3	5	0	2	0	2	0

* Percentage of book as prophecy according to *Tim LaHaye Prophecy Study Bible*

Introduction to Malachi

Based on available research, the ministry of the prophet Malachi lies between 450 – 400 B.C. The fact that he is placed last in the Old Testament is not surprising for several reasons.

1. Malachi is the last of the 12 Minor Prophets to speak to Israel.

2. Although his message is similar to the preceding prophets, it is unique because of the absoluteness of his proclamation.

3. Malachi reveals Israel in its most horrendous apostasy. Israel actually dares to challenge God.

4. Fourteen times we read of God addressing a question to Israel, and ten times we read of Israel's rebellious answer.

5. While the prophet Zechariah only uses the word "curse" or "cursed" twice, Malachi uses the word seven times.

6. The last verse of the Old Testament is "curse." That means utter rejection. We read in Galatians 3:10, "For as many as are of the works of the law are under the curse: for it is written, Cursed is every one that continueth not in all things which are written in the book of the law to do them."

That does not mean that the law is cursed, but the person who claims to attain righteousness or salvation through the law is cursed.

The law exposes sin and, according to Scripture, the one that sins must die.

Malachi embodies the absoluteness of all the prophets. He shows in unmistakable terms that there is no other way, there is no escape. There is only one possibility to save Israel, and through Israel all of mankind. It is the Son of righteousness, the One who became a curse for all of humanity. Again, the Bible says, "Cursed is everyone that hangeth on a tree" (Galatians 3:13).

Rebellious Questions

1. "Wherein hast thou loved us?"
2. "Wherein have we despised thy name?"
3. "Wherein have we polluted thee?"
4. "Yet ye say, Wherefore?"
5. "Wherein have we wearied him?"
6. "Where is the God of judgment?"
7. "Wherein shall we return?"
8. "Wherein have we robbed thee?"
9. "What have we spoken so much against thee?"
10. "What profit is it that we have kept his ordinance, and that we have walked mournfully before the Lord of hosts?"

Ten times Israel opposed God in an arrogant manner. We are reminded here of the Ten Commandments. We also recall that there were ten patriarchs before the flood, and ten plagues upon Egypt. Abraham prayed for ten righteous people in Sodom, and Jesus gives us the parable of the ten virgins (*Biblical Mathematics* by Ed Vallowe, p. 91).

Malachi is a mystery when compared with all the other prophets. We only know his name. No father is mentioned, nor is the place of his birth listed.

Malachi can be translated "my messenger" or "messenger of the Lord." This fact signifies the importance of the message and the insignificance of the messenger.

Here we are reminded of the words of John the Baptist, who answered the question, "Who art thou?" with the words, "I am the voice of one crying in the wilderness." In plain words, don't worry about me; I am a nobody, but my message is what counts.

May our Lord yet awaken many preachers of the Word of God who have such a spirit, debasing themselves to nothingness for the exaltation and glory of the message.

Also, we are reminded of the words of our Lord Jesus in Luke 17:10, "...when ye shall have done all those things which are commanded you, say, We are unprofitable servants: we have done that which was our duty to do." This type of humility is for-eign to our culture. We would rather like to emphasize our ac-complishments.

Apparently, this kind of humility is the case with the prophet: He is simply the messenger of the Lord.

Chapter 1

Introduction

The words, "I loved Jacob, and I hated Esau" reveal the absoluteness of good and evil, of real and fake, of blessing and cursing. Chapter 1 ends with hope for the heathen, "My name is dreadful among the heathen." The *Tenakh* reads, "My name is revered among the nations."

The Burden

Malachi 1:1: "The burden of the word of the LORD to Israel by Malachi."

(See) Isaiah 13:1; Nahum 1:1; Habakkuk 1:1; Zechariah 9:1

This is a unique introduction. In most cases, the word of the Lord came to the prophet, but here it is the "burden of the word of the Lord to Israel," not Malachi's burden. That is an important issue to take note of, and that is what sets Malachi apart.

Esau Hated, Jacob Loved

Malachi 1:2-3: "I have loved you, saith the LORD. Yet ye say, Wherein hast thou loved us? Was not Esau Jacob's brother? saith the LORD: yet I loved Jacob, 3 And I hated Esau, and laid his mountains and his heritage waste for the dragons [jackals] of the wilderness."

(See) Deuteronomy 4:37; 7:8; 23:5; Isaiah 41:8-9;
Jeremiah 31:3; 49:10, 16-18; Ezekiel 35:3-4, 7-8, 15; Romans 9:13

Apparently, Israel had arrived at the ecumenical conclusion, "We are all God's children; God loves everyone." But that statement is only partial truth. While "God so loved the world" is perfectly true, it is conditional to the acceptance of His offer of salvation.

The people oppose with the words, "Wherein hast thou loved us?" What arrogance! God's Word reveals the clear distinction: He loved Jacob. Why? Because Jacob deep down in his heart loved God. He totally relied upon His blessing, "I will not let thee go, except thou bless me" (Genesis 32:26). What was the result? "Thy name shall be called no more Jacob, but Israel" (verse 28).

Esau, however, lived for himself. He wanted the blessings, but not the Blesser. He wanted the fruit of the land, the food his brother Jacob had prepared, more than the Lord who is the source of all sustenance.

Esau knew about the promise of God to give a double portion of blessing to the firstborn, but he rejected it. "Thus Esau despised his birthright," we read in Genesis 25:34.

Esau was a self-reliant man. We may rightly call him godless; thus, God rejected him.

Malachi 1:4: "Whereas Edom saith, We are impoverished, but we will return and build the desolate places; thus saith the LORD of hosts, They shall build, but I will throw down; and they shall call them, The border of wickedness, and, The people against whom the LORD hath indignation for ever."

337

(See) Isaiah 9:9-10; Ezekiel 35:9; Amos 3:15; 5:11; 6:11; Obadiah 10

With this statement, God makes the clear distinction between Jacob and Esau, Israel and Edom.

The Border of Israel

Now God turns to Israel with a significant statement:

Malachi 1:5: "And your eyes shall see, and ye shall say, The LORD will be magnified from the border of Israel."

(See) Psalm 35:27; Micah 5:4

Notice that it says "the border of Israel," not Palestine, Jordan, Egypt, Syria, or Lebanon. The borders of Israel are clearly declared in Genesis 15:18: "In the same day the LORD made a covenant with Abram, saying, Unto thy seed have I given this land, from the river of Egypt unto the great river, the river Euphrates."

Never should we be so naive as to think that the various political agreements between Israel and the Arab neighbors are final; they are just temporary. They serve a specific purpose; namely, the self-condemnation of the nations of the world. They all, without exception, interfere with the borders of the land of Israel.

Esau and Jacob, the twins, are a lesson for the entire world. Esau lost his heritage so that his borders were cursed, while Jacob's borders were magnified. In other words, there is no blessing or eternal inheritance outside God's clearly defined identity: the people and the land of Israel.

338

Despising God

Malachi 1:6: "A son honoureth his father, and a servant his master: if then I be a father, where is mine honour? and if I be a master, where is my fear? saith the LORD of hosts unto you, O priests, that despise my name. And ye say, Wherein have we despised thy name?"

(See) Exodus 20:12; Proverbs 30:11, 17; Isaiah 1:2; Zephaniah 3:4

The burden of the word of the Lord continues with a simple question: "Where is mine honor?" That is something very natural. A son honors his father; he respects him, just like a faithful employee respects his employer. That is a given; there should be no debate about it. Yet, the Lord complains to Israel, in particular to the priests: "where is mine honor...where is my fear?"

This does not mean that the priests and Israel outright rejected the Lord; they continued to sacrifice, keep the feasts, and did what they thought was right, but that was only on the surface.

One can faithfully go to church, even attend prayer meetings, donate generously, and serve on committees within the church, yet it does not prove that such a person actually fears the Lord and honors His name.

Polluted Sacrifice

In the next two verses, the condition of the priests in Israel is exposed:

Malachi 1:7-8: "Ye offer polluted bread upon mine altar; and ye say, Wherein have we polluted thee? In that ye

339

say, The table of the LORD is contemptible. 8 And if ye offer the blind for sacrifice, is it not evil? and if ye offer the lame and sick, is it not evil? offer it now unto thy governor; will he be pleased with thee, or accept thy person? saith the LORD of hosts."

(See) Leviticus 3:11; 21:6, 8; 22:22; Deuteronomy 15:21

Quite obviously, religious activity continued. They sacrificed in the temple, but only as a routine. Sacrificing an inferior animal is an abomination to the Lord, but apparently this was not recognized by the one making the offering. They ask arrogantly, "Wherein have we polluted thee?" They had become so dull spiritually that they were incapable of recognizing the truth about their relationship with God.

The Lord uses a very simple illustration with His question, "...offer it now unto thy governor; will he be pleased with thee, or accept thy person?"

To give someone a present is done out of love for that person. Something special is selected, and the giver carefully inspects the gift to see if it meets the standard that would be appreciated by the receiver.

The verdict is very plain: Israel has withdrawn herself from the Lord, in spirit and in truth. Religious activity was practiced only because of tradition.

Churchianity

What a picture of the Church today. Multiple millions attend church regularly, because that is the right thing to do. Others go only on special occasions, demonstrating that they are religious and identifying themselves with

340

Christianity. But their heart, mind and spirit are distant. They have little to no interest in spiritual things, like prayer and reading God's Word regularly. Church has become a convenient expression of religiosity. Many would wholeheartedly support, even fight for "In God we trust," the inscription on American currency. In other words, "yes" to religion, but "no" to the God of true religion, the Lord Jesus Christ.

Stubborn Pride

Malachi 1:9: "And now, I pray you, beseech God that he will be gracious unto us: this hath been by your means: will he regard your persons? saith the LORD of hosts."

(See) Jeremiah 27:18; Joel 2:12-14; Amos 5:22

Again, God's grace is extended, another opportunity to repent. The question, "Will he regard your persons?" targets those who pride themselves in the priest's office particularly.

Close the Doors

Malachi 1:10: "Who is there even among you that would shut the doors for nought? neither do ye kindle fire on mine altar for nought. I have no pleasure in you, saith the LORD of hosts, neither will I accept an offering at your hand."

(See) Isaiah 1:13; Jeremiah 14:10, 12; Hosea 5:6

This is most tragic. God is not looking for someone who will stand in the gap, who will serve as a true priest. He is looking for someone to close the door of the temple, not one who will kindle a fire on the altar and present an offering. The Lord is closing the door to the Old Testament.

"The Doors Were Shut"

Here we are reminded of the Apostle Paul, who testified that Jesus Christ is the Savior of the world. This resulted in protest, as we read in Acts 21:30, "And all the city was moved, and the people ran together: and they took Paul, and drew him out of the temple: and forthwith the doors were shut." The doors of the temple were shut. Why? Because a new temple had been built, that is the spiritual temple, the living Church of Jesus Christ on earth.

Malachi 1:11: "For from the rising of the sun even unto the going down of the same my name shall be great among the Gentiles; and in every place incense shall be offered unto my name, and a pure offering: for my name shall be great among the heathen, saith the LORD of hosts."

(See) Isaiah 12:4-5; 45:6; 60:6; 66:18-19; Jeremiah 10:6-7

Here we clearly see that after the doors of the temple are shut, the Lord turns to the Gentiles, the heathen, the people outside Israel. It is emphasized with the words, "from the rising of the sun even unto the going down of the same." That envelopes the entire globe—a rather profound statement revealing the essence of true globalism.

I am aware that this word has a negative connotation in the minds of many Christians, but please remember that God is speaking here. This is later confirmed with the words, "For God so loved the world." It is not surprising, therefore, that the god of this world, who rules all the nations, tries desperately to establish globalism. He is doing it successfully by the avenue of commercialism. Unfortunately, many Christians assume that commercial success equals spiritual blessing. That is far from the truth. Already, the prophet Jeremiah exclaimed that Israel "worshipped the works of their own hands" (Jeremiah 1:16). But spiritual globalism represents the body of Christ.

After the doors of the temple are shut, a new global identity is created: "in every place incense shall be offered unto my name, and a pure offering."

The Incense of Prayer

Psalm 141:2 reads, "Let my prayer be set forth before thee as incense; and the lifting up of my hands as the evening sacrifice." Prayer becomes the "sacrifice." In the last book of the Bible, we read about the pure offering, "And the smoke of the incense, which came with the prayers of the saints, ascended up before God out of the angel's hand" (Revelation 8:4).

"Profaned, Polluted and Contemptible"

The Lord turns again to Israel:

Malachi 1:12: "But ye have profaned it, in that ye say, The table of the LORD is polluted; and the fruit thereof, with these words, even his meat, is contemptible."

343

This is a strange statement, indicating that the people knew the table of the Lord was "profane, polluted and contemptible." This reveals the hardness of their heart. They continue to do their religious duty, all the while knowing it's worthless.

Malachi 1:13: "Ye said also, Behold, what a weariness is it! and ye have snuffed at it, saith the LORD of hosts; and ye brought that which was torn, and the lame, and the sick; thus ye brought an offering: should I accept this of your hand? saith the LORD."

(See) Isaiah 43:22; 61:8

In modern language, we may say, "What a waste of time and energy." They offer that which is inferior, even while realizing that their sacrifice is an abomination to the Lord.

Cursed Deceiver

Malachi 1:14: "But cursed be the deceiver, which hath in his flock a male, and voweth, and sacrificeth unto the Lord a corrupt thing: for I am a great King, saith the LORD of hosts, and my name is dreadful among the heathen."

(See) Leviticus 22:18-20; Zephaniah 2:11; Zechariah 14:9; Acts 5:1-4

This verse reveals the end of the Old Testament. Israel had invalidated the Holy Covenant; thus, it could not bring forth salvation.

The New Priesthood

Here we are reminded of Hebrews 8:13, "...A new covenant, he hath made the first old. Now that which decayeth and waxeth old is ready to vanish away." Something new had already been prepared, "For the priesthood being changed, there is made of necessity a change also of the law" (Hebrews 7:12).

The last sentence of chapter 1 reveals God's intention to include the heathen nations in His plan of salvation, "I am a great King, saith the LORD of hosts, and my name is dreadful among the heathen."

Chapter 2

Introduction

The priests are the target of God's accusation agaist Judah. The priests deliberately misuse their God-ordained office. The epitome of depravity is revealed in the last verse, "Every one that doeth evil is good."

Priests Targeted

While chapter 1 addresses the burden of the Lord to Israel, chapter 2 begins with giving a commandment to a very special group: the priests. What is the office of a priest? He is to speak to God on behalf of the people. His task is clearly defined in the book of Moses, as to what, how and when he was to sacrifice to make atonement for the people.

The Curse

Malachi 2:1-2: "And now, O ye priests, this commandment is for you. 2 If ye will not hear, and if ye will not lay it to heart, to give glory unto my name, saith the LORD of hosts, I will even send a curse upon you, and I will curse your blessings: yea, I have cursed them already, because ye do not lay it to heart."

(See) Leviticus 26:14-17; Deuteronomy 28:15-20

These are very strong words directed toward the priests, highlighted by the words, "I will curse your blessings." What an unspeakable tragedy. The people chosen of God, the tribe of Levi, the priests who were to instruct the people, to guide them toward God and bless them in the name of the Lord, have now become a cursed thing.

While this verse seems to indicate a spark of hope with the phrase, "If ye will not...," God already knows their reaction, expressed with the words, "I have cursed them already."

At that time, the office of the priest was still functioning. They performed the sacrifices, taught the people, and pronounced the blessings, but all in vain because they did it out of their own evil heart. Thus, their own words, their imagination and their blessing, in the end became a curse.

A Warning

This contains a serious warning to all believers. When we proclaim the Word of God, testify or even pray and our heart is not in it; when we are not totally consecrated, then our entire work not only becomes ineffective, but also may become an object of mockery.

We have many examples in recent years right here in our own country. Popular ministers of the gospel took it upon themselves to prophesy against certain segments of our society. When it did not come true, the world laughed and hell was celebrating.

The Dung Heap

Malachi 2:3: "Behold, I will corrupt your seed, and spread

dung upon your faces, even the dung of your solemn
feasts; and one shall take you away with it."

(See) Nahum 3:6

As if the curse is not enough, the Lord shows that their
entire service will become a dung heap: "spread dung
upon your faces." That is utter waste!

Those who have lived or worked on a farm, know
what a dung heap is. The manure, mixed with straw, is
carried out of the barn and piled in a heap. It becomes
an object of disgust, emanating a horrible smell.

A Glimmer of Hope

Then we read of a glimmer of hope in verse 4:

Malachi 2:4: "And ye shall know that I have sent this commandment unto you, that my covenant might be with
Levi, saith the LORD of hosts."

(See) Numbers 3:11-13, 45; 18:21; Nehemiah 13:29

After they have been cursed and discarded upon the dung
heap, the Levites nevertheless recognized that the commandment came from the Lord. They understand God's
covenant made with the tribe of Levi.

The Covenant of Levi

The next three verses describe the Levitical covenant:

Malachi 2:5-7: "My covenant was with him of life and
peace; and I gave them to him for the fear wherewith he

348

feared me, and was afraid before my name. 6 The law of truth was in his mouth, and iniquity was not found in his lips: he walked with me in peace and equity, and did turn many away from iniquity. 7 For the priest's lips should keep knowledge, and they should seek the law at his mouth: for he is the messenger of the LORD of hosts."

(See) Numbers 25:12; Deuteronomy 33:8-9; Psalm 119:142; Jeremiah 23:22

There was a time when Levi feared the name of the Lord, when truth came forth from his lips, and when many were turned to righteousness. Levi was the "messenger of the LORD of hosts." Now Malachi, which means "messenger of the Lord," is proclaiming this judgment upon Israel, particularly upon the house of Levi.

Malachi 2:8-9: "But ye are departed out of the way; ye have caused many to stumble at the law; ye have corrupted the covenant of Levi, saith the LORD of hosts. 9 Therefore have I also made you contemptible and base before all the people, according as ye have not kept my ways, but have been partial in the law."

(See) Nehemiah 13:29; Jeremiah 18:15; Ezekiel 44:10

The prophet mercilessly exposes the sins of Levi. Instead of fearing the Lord and leading people toward righteousness, they had "corrupted the covenant." The priests had become "partial in the law." No longer was "thus saith the Lord" the deciding factor, but the interpretation of it became the primary message and action of the priest.

They did their own thing according to their own evil heart.

Three Questions

Malachi identifies himself with the sins of the people, when he asked the following three questions:

Malachi 2:10: "Have we not all one father? hath not one God created us? why do we deal treacherously every man against his brother, by profaning the covenant of our fathers?"

(See) Isaiah 63:16; 64:8; Jeremiah 9:4-5; 1 Corinthians 8:6; Ephesians 4:6

We saw in the previous verse that the priest had become partial when it came to the law. They played favoritism, as if God would apply the law differently to different people. This becomes clear by the words, "deal treacherously...against his brother." There was no unity among the brethren. They altogether failed to love one another. Did not Moses instruct them, "Thou shalt not avenge, nor bear any grudge against the children of thy people, but thou shalt love thy neighbour as thyself: I am the LORD" (Leviticus 19:18)?

Thus we see, "Love thy neighbor as thyself" is not intellectual property of the New Testament alone. This reveals the fatal error of some well-meaning teachers, who instruct that we should embrace ourselves, love ourselves more, build up our self-esteem. That apparently is unnecessary, because by nature we love ourselves. Self-love and self-esteem do not need further encouragement, for we read in Ephesians 5:29, "For no man ever yet hated his own flesh; but nourisheth and cherisheth it, even as the Lord the church." True love includes those we dislike.

The Tribe of Judah

Malachi 2:11: "Judah hath dealt treacherously, and an abomination is committed in Israel and in Jerusalem; for Judah hath profaned the holiness of the LORD which he loved, and hath married the daughter of a strange god."

(See) Ezra 9:1-2; Jeremiah 3:7-9

The burden of the Word of the Lord is now expanded from Levi to Jerusalem, Judah and Israel. This obviously does not speak of one person, but collectively of the whole nation. Serving the Lord, based on religious practice, is missing the point. Israel was not only to enjoy the blessings of God, but also to wholeheartedly serve God and glorify Him. As a result, the Gentiles would honor the God of Israel.

We read the testimony of Rahab in Joshua 2, "And she said unto the men, I know that the LORD hath given you the land, and that your terror is fallen upon us, and that all the inhabitants of the land faint because of you...And as soon as we had heard these things, our hearts did melt, neither did there remain any more courage in any man, because of you: for the LORD your God, he is God in heaven above, and in earth beneath" (Joshua 2:9, 11). The people of Jericho recognized that "the Lord your God, He is God in heaven above and in earth beneath." The attention of Jericho shifted from the armies of Israel

351

to the God of Israel. Here in Malachi, however, the center is self, the priests, the Levites, Judah, Jerusalem, and Israel. Not surprisingly, we read that Judah "hath married the daughter of a strange god."

Holy and Unholy Mixture

Here we are reminded of the words in Ezra 9:2, "For they have taken of their daughters for themselves, and for their sons: so that the holy seed have mingled themselves with the people of those lands: yea, the hand of the princes and rulers hath been chief in this trespass." Mixing with unbelievers was the first step on the way to total apostasy. The result? Verses 12-13 answer:

Malachi 2:12-13: "The LORD will cut off the man that doeth this, the master and the scholar, out of the tabernacles of Jacob, and him that offereth an offering unto the LORD of hosts. 13 And this have ye done again, covering the altar of the LORD with tears, with weeping, and with crying out, insomuch that he regardeth not the offering any more, or receiveth it with good will at your hand."

(See) Jeremiah 11:14; 14:12; Ezekiel 24:21; Hosea 9:12

In the midst of this horrendous apostasy, the mixing of the holy with the unholy, Israel continues to practice their religion, even with tears and weeping. But all of it is rejected by the Lord. During Ezra's time, there was at least acknowledgement of sin. "And after all that is come upon us for our evil deeds, and for our great trespass, seeing that thou our God hast punished us less than our iniquities deserve, and hast given us such deliverance as this" (Ezra 9:13).

Not following the Lord's Word will always lead to catastrophe. Moses verbalizes the one commandment that stands above and beyond any, "And thou shalt love the LORD thy God with all thine heart, and with all thy soul, and with all thy might" (Deuteronomy 6:5).

God Hates Divorce

Malachi 2:14: "Yet ye say, Wherefore? Because the LORD hath been witness between thee and the wife of thy youth, against whom thou hast dealt treacherously: yet is she thy companion, and the wife of thy covenant."

(See) Isaiah 54:6; Jeremiah 9:2

One notices Israel's attitude is like a misbehaving child, who would continuously question the authority of his parents with the word, "Why?" or in this case, "Wherefore?"

With this we come to our times, when marriage is considered old-fashioned. A large percentage of people, young and old, conveniently ignore the bonds of marriage to which they have sworn, "Until death do us apart." When confronted, it is always the same answer, "You see, it was not my fault...it's because...because..."

Malachi 2:15: "And did not he make one? Yet had he the residue of the spirit. And wherefore one? That he might seek a godly seed. Therefore take heed to your spirit, and let none deal treacherously against the wife of his

353

youth."

(See) Genesis 2:24; Exodus 20:14; Leviticus 20:10; Ruth 4:12; 1 Samuel 2:20; Matthew 19:4-5

Here we are shown that the spirit of man recognizes his wrong, yet deliberately and persistently refuses to heed the Spirit.

Malachi 2:16: "For the LORD, the God of Israel, saith that he hateth putting away: for one covereth violence with his garment, saith the LORD of hosts: therefore take heed to your spirit, that ye deal not treacherously."

(See) Psalm 73:6; Isaiah 59:6; Matthew 19:6-8

Here we have the plain words, "God...hateth putting away [divorce]."

Again, the same words are used to warn, "take heed to your spirit." The priests deliberately rebelled against God, misinterpreting His Holy Word, and caused this behavior to be passed on to the families, the tribe, and to Israel. That is the progression of spiritual pollution.

The Ultimate Rebellion

We must emphasize here that God is pronouncing judgment; He is proclaiming His burden upon the people concerning their relationship to Him. Thus, He uses these fitting examples to show how horrible the sin of separating one's self from God's covenant is for His people.

Malachi 2:17: "Ye have wearied the LORD with your words. Yet ye say, Wherein have we wearied him? When ye say, Every one that doeth evil is good in the sight of the LORD, and he delighteth in them; or, Where is the God of judgment?"

(See) Job 9:24; Isaiah 5:19-20; 43:22, 24; Jeremiah 17:15;
Zephaniah 1:12; 2 Peter 3:4

This is diabolical rebellion. The people have become so dull to the Word of God and so used to religious activity, that they are incapable of perceiving what their own spirit has to say about their behavior.

Not only are they doing wrong, rebelling against God, but now they are twisting the truth, calling good evil and evil good. That is the foundation of Antichrist, of which we read in 2 Thessalonians 2:4, "Who opposeth and exalteth himself above all that is called God, or that is worshipped; so that he as God sitteth in the temple of God, showing himself that he is God."

Chapter 3

Introduction

The challenge to return to God is connected to His promise, "Jerusalem be pleasant unto the Lord," with the goal that "all nations shall call you blessed." Even agriculture will experience renewal.

"Prepare the Way"

Malachi 3:1: "Behold, I will send my messenger, and he shall prepare the way before me: and the Lord, whom ye seek, shall suddenly come to his temple, even the messenger of the covenant, whom ye delight in: behold, he shall come, saith the LORD of hosts."

(See) Isaiah 40:3; Matthew 11:10; Mark 1:2; Luke 1:76; 7:27; John 1:6-7

This is a clear prophecy of the coming of the Lord, preceded by the messenger who will prepare the way.

Messenger or Angel?

Of interest is that Luther translates the word not as messenger, but angel. Here we are reminded of Revelation, where the first sentence of chapter 2 reads, "Unto the angel of the church of Ephesus...." An angel is understood to be a heavenly messenger. He may appear in human form or as a spiritual being, as stated in Hebrews

1:7, "And of the angels he saith, Who maketh his angels spirits, and his ministers a flame of fire."

I take the liberty to call an angel a messenger and a messenger an angel. But there is a difference, and we may see that in John the Baptist.

John the Baptist

The messenger we are concerned with here in Malachi is doubtless John the Baptist; an earthly creature, born of man, whose father was Zechariah the priest, and mother Elizabeth. However, his actions, behavior, and appearance were rather unearthly, as we read in Matthew 3:4, "And the same John had his raiment of camel's hair, and a leathern girdle about his loins; and his meat was locusts and wild honey." His life was consumed with his office: messenger of God, the herald of His coming.

When reading 2 Kings 1:8, we find a similar description of Elijah the prophet, "He was a hairy man, and gird with a girdle of leather about his loins." In other words, the prophet or messenger was "in the world, but not of the world."

John the Baptist's task was preparing the way of the Lord. It was necessary for him to be fully human, because God would send His Son in human flesh. In other words, God came down to earth. When Jesus began His office, He continued the same message His predecessor John the Baptist proclaimed, "Repent ye: for the kingdom of heaven is at hand."

Judgment against Religion

John the Baptist did not mince words. When those responsible for teaching God's Word came to his baptism, he totally insulted their expectations, "But when he saw many of the Pharisees and Sadducees come to his baptism, he said unto them, O generation of vipers, who hath warned you to flee from the wrath to come? Bring forth therefore fruits meet for repentance: And think not to say within yourselves, We have Abraham to our father: for I say unto you, that God is able of these stones to raise up children unto Abraham" (Matthew 3:7-9).

John the Baptist, and later Jesus Christ Himself, declared judgment against traditional religion unsparingly. Jesus pronounced the eightfold "woe" specifically against the scholars and religious leaders in Matthew 23:

1. "But woe unto you, scribes and Pharisees, hypocrites!" (verse 13).
2. "Woe unto you, scribes and Pharisees, hypocrites!" (verse 14).
3. "Woe unto you, scribes and Pharisees, hypocrites!" (verse 15).
4. "Woe unto you, ye blind guides" (verse 16).
5. "Woe unto you, scribes and Pharisees, hypocrites!" (verse 23).
6. "Woe unto you, scribes and Pharisees, hypocrites!" (verse 25).
7. "Woe unto you, scribes and Pharisees, hypocrites!" (verse 27).
8. "Woe unto you, scribes and Pharisees, hypocrites!" (verse 29).

Then in verse 33, he summarizes the religious community with the following condemnation, "Ye serpents, ye generation of vipers, how can ye escape the damnation of hell?"

The religious people had the knowledge of the Word of God, but they did everything according to the imagination of their own evil hearts.

The Coming of the Lord

There are those who were waiting for the Lord, "The Lord, whom ye seek, shall suddenly come to his temple." He surely did come unexpectedly. When He was born in Bethlehem, attention was called to His birth by Gentiles, "wise men from the east." Bible scholars in Jerusalem identified the place where Jesus should be born, "...In Bethlehem of Judaea: for thus it is written by the prophet" (Matthew 2:5). But they did not in reality believe Scripture; they did not go to worship the newborn King of the Jews.

When Jesus was eight days of age, He appeared in the temple, "And, behold, there was a man in Jerusalem, whose name was Simeon; and the same man was just and devout, waiting for the consolation of Israel: and the Holy Ghost was upon him" (Luke 2:25). Simeon was waiting for the Lord.

Another one is mentioned, Anna, a prophetess of the tribe of Asher. We read in Luke 2:38, "And she coming in that instant gave thanks likewise unto the Lord, and spake of him to all them that looked for redemption in Jerusalem." Note the words, "that looked for redemption." Anna did not proclaim the arrival of Jesus, the Messiah of Israel, the King of the Jews and Savior of the world, to people everywhere, but to a distinct group of people: those who were looking for the Messiah. Trying to proclaim the prophetic Word to the church at large is in reality wasting time. They will not listen; they will not react.

The Judge Is Here

Malachi 3:2: "But who may abide the day of his coming? and who shall stand when he appeareth? for he is like a refiner's fire, and like fullers' soap."

(See) Isaiah 33:14; Ezekiel 22:14; Zechariah 13:9; Matthew 3:10-12; 1 Corinthians 3:13-15; Revelation 6:17

Certainly, this speaks of Jesus' first coming, His appearance as "refiner's fire...fullers' [launderer's] soap" against the deception and lies of the religious authorities in Jerusalem.

Yet doubtless, this also speaks of the future. Isaiah made reference to the coming of the Lord in chapter 1:25-27, "And I will turn my hand upon thee, and purely purge away thy dross, and take away all thy tin: And I will restore thy judges as at the first, and thy counsellors as at the beginning: afterward thou shalt be called, The city of righteousness, the faithful city. Zion shall be redeemed with judgment, and her converts with righteousness."

We know that the beginning of the Church consisted only of the children of Israel. Many were converted to the Lord, but the full restoration of Zion is yet to come. We read of this in the next two verses:

Malachi 3:3-4: "And he shall sit as a refiner and purifier of silver: and he shall purify the sons of Levi, and purge them as gold and silver, that they may offer unto the LORD an offering in righteousness. 4 Then shall the offering of Judah and Jerusalem be pleasant unto the LORD, as in the days of old, and as in former years."

(See) 2 Chronicles 7:1-3; Psalm 4:5; 51:19; Isaiah 1:25; Daniel 12:10

We cannot spiritualize these promises and apply them to the Church, because names are mentioned—Levi, Judah, and Jerusalem.

Once again, we learn from the prophets that when they speak about the future, they identify the Lord's first and second coming in one breath. The Messiah's coming and the Messiah's return are sometimes intermingled in the prophets' statements. First, He came as Savior, as the perfect sacrificial Lamb of God, but at His return, He will be the "refiner and purifier."

Irrevocable Judgment

Malachi 3:5: "And I will come near to you to judgment; and I will be a swift witness against the sorcerers, and against the adulterers, and against false swearers, and against those that oppress the hireling in his wages, the widow, and the fatherless, and that turn aside the stranger from his right, and fear not me, saith the LORD of hosts."

(See) Exodus 22:22-24; Leviticus 19:13;
Deuteronomy 18:10; Jeremiah 5:2; 7:9; Zechariah 5:4

Unrighteousness, sin, and rebellion will be dealt with swiftly. Note particularly the words, "oppress the hireling in his wages." Compassion for the less fortunate and the working class was lacking; it was one of Israel's cardinal sins.

Success or Blessing?

Unfortunately, this truth is being denied in the proclamation of the gospel in many churches. Success has become the new god and is praised quite frequently. Apparently without thinking, many pastors exclaim, "When you trust the Lord, believe in Him, He will bless you abundantly. He will cause you to be successful because He wants the best for His children." That sounds quite natural, but is contrary to Scripture.

In the New Testament, the word "poor" appears 35 times (KJV). Reading those verses, one notices that the poor are comforted. The word "rich" is found 40 times, and virtually in every case the rich are condemned.

The assumption that blessings translate into health, wealth and happiness is the gospel of another Jesus, the gospel of the great deceiver.

Social Gospel

Some well-meaning churches have recognized this important message; subsequently, they involve themselves wholeheartedly in social activity, at the cost of proclaiming salvation in Jesus. The primary purpose for the existence of a church is the message of salvation. That is why it is important to proclaim the whole Bible, from Genesis to Revelation, which reveals God's love for mankind, but also His irreversible judgment upon those who reject salvation offered in Christ Jesus.

Malachi 3:6: "For I am the Lord, I change not; therefore ye sons of Jacob are not consumed."

(See) Numbers 23:19; James 1:17

Note the name Jacob. This is Israel in the flesh, and it was in the flesh when Jacob-Israel received the promise, "...in thy seed shall all families of the earth be blessed" (Genesis 28:14).

"Return unto Me"

Malachi 3:7: "Even from the days of your fathers ye are gone away from mine ordinances, and have not kept them. Return unto me, and I will return unto you, saith the LORD of hosts. But ye said, Wherein shall we return?"

(See) Jeremiah 7:25-26; 16:11-12; Zechariah 1:3

This verse in particular reveals God's persistence; His accusation against Israel's disobedience on the one hand, but His compassionate pleading on the other, "Return unto me, and I will return unto you."

But this invitation falls on deaf ears, "Wherein shall we return?" That is like a slap in the face of God. It reveals stubborn disobedience to the utmost.

Apparently, Israel was so sure of their position as God's chosen people, exhibited by the glorious temple in

Jerusalem, that they outright rejected God's accusation against them, which He proclaimed through the prophet Malachi.

Malachi 3:8-9: "Will a man rob God? Yet ye have robbed me. But ye say, Wherein have we robbed thee? In tithes and offerings. 9 Ye are cursed with a curse: for ye have robbed me, even this whole nation."

(See) Nehemiah 13:11-12

Judgment was already pronounced against the sorcerers, adulterers, and the oppressors of the poor. Now all of Israel is cursed due to the failure of giving God His due: "tithes and offerings."

Deception

A word of explanation may be helpful with the words "rob God." The *Tenakh* reads "defraud God" and Luther writes "deceive God." We do not know whether they refused to pay the tithes or used deception. For example, the priests practiced deception, "offer polluted bread upon my altar...offer the blind...ye offer the lame and sick...." We must therefore assume that the whole nation continued their practice of religious law to pay their tithes, but it was a deception; they did not bring the best of their produce, the most treasured part of their blessings, but robbed God by not following His orders.

God's Blessings

Malachi 3:10: "Bring ye all the tithes into the storehouse, that there may be meat in mine house, and prove me now herewith, saith the LORD of hosts, if I will not open you the windows of heaven, and pour you out a blessing, that there shall not be room enough to receive it."

(See) Leviticus 26:3-5; 27:30; Numbers 18:21-24; Psalm 78:23-29;
Ezekiel 34:26

True sacrifice and true giving of the tithe would result in blessing from above so abundant that the storehouses would overflow.

The words "open...windows of heaven" must be taken very literally. That, incidentally, is the most essential ingredient for life on earth to exist. This fact is totally ignored not only by the world at large, but also by most of Christianity. They seem to neglect the fact that life depends on God's blessings. Often we assume that life continues to exist because of our Christian service, our prayers, and our compassion for other people. In reality, it is exclusively due to God's grace, "While the earth remaineth, seedtime and harvest, and cold and heat, and summer and winter, and day and night shall not cease" (Genesis 8:22).

When the Lord blesses, He goes beyond the rain that comes out of heaven. He will cause the destroyer of agriculture to be hindered:

Malachi 3:11: "And I will rebuke the devourer for your sakes, and he shall not destroy the fruits of your ground; neither shall your vine cast her fruit before the time in the field, saith the LORD of hosts."

(See) Joel 1:4; 2:25

Pre-fulfillment

Since the return of the Jews to the Promised Land and the establishment of the State of Israel on 14 May 1948, the land is indeed producing an abundance of "the fruits of [the] ground." This is primarily due to Israel's technology and inventiveness; Israel's agricultural scientists have fine-tuned their work to produce the most with the least water available. But it is our opinion that today's Israel does not fulfill all the requirements of the promises given in Scripture. That will be fulfilled when Jesus returns.

Malachi 3:12: "And all nations shall call you blessed: for ye shall be a delightsome land, saith the LORD of hosts."

(See) Isaiah 61:9; 62:4

We all agree that the nations of the world do not call Israel "blessed," and they are not a delight in the land. As a matter of fact, Israel's neighbors would rather see the nation cease to exist. Iran, for example, publicly declares that Israel should be wiped off the map. The rest of the world pays lip service and agrees that Israel should live in secure borders, but those borders are dictated by the nations. They all have determined that Israel should exist, but only within parts of the Promised Land.

Nevertheless, we insist that the Jews' return to the land of Israel and the amazing success they have achieved is part of the pre-fulfillment of Bible prophecy. It is a shadow of things yet to come.

Stubborn Rebellion

Malachi 3:13: "Your words have been stout against me, saith the LORD. Yet ye say, What have we spoken so much against thee?"

Again, Israel despises God's statement with their words, "What have we spoken...against thee"? Quite amazing is that God, in His long-suffering and patience, answers their question:

Malachi 3:14: "Ye have said, It is vain to serve God: and what profit is it that we have kept his ordinance, and that we have walked mournfully before the LORD of hosts?"

(See) Isaiah 58:3; Jeremiah 2:25; 18:12

These are the words of the people of Israel. They are simply telling God it is useless to serve Him: there is no advantage to keeping His ordinances or mourning before the Lord. That is the epitome of hardness of heart.

Calling Good Evil and Evil Good

Next they call good evil and evil good:

Malachi 3:15: "And now we call the proud happy; yea, they that work wickedness are set up; yea, they that tempt God are even delivered."

(See) Isaiah 2:22; Jeremiah 7:10

The *Tenakh* reads, "And so, we account the arrogant happy; they have indeed done evil and endured; they have indeed dared God and escaped."

Israel had sunk so low in their relationship with the living God that they were incapable of recognizing true happiness and true deliverance.

Salvation for the Remnant

Malachi 3:16: "Then they that feared the LORD spake often one to another: and the LORD hearkened, and heard it, and a book of remembrance was written before him for them that feared the LORD, and that thought upon his name."

(See) Psalm 34:15; Isaiah 4:3; Jeremiah 31:18-20; Daniel 12:1

In the midst of apostasy, rebellion, even blasphemy, there is a remnant, those that "feared." Nothing is mentioned about their sacrifice or the giving of tithes, but very specifically that they "feared the Lord." They spoke often about the Lord, and they "thought upon His name." These faithful ones were part of Israel, but not of rebellious Israel. They were the true servants of the Lord. Only they will partake of the reward:

Malachi 3:17: "And they shall be mine, saith the LORD of hosts, in that day when I make up my jewels; and I will spare them, as a man spareth his own son that serveth him."

(See) Exodus 19:5; Deuteronomy 7:6; Psalm 103:13; Isaiah 4:2; 43:1

The ones that occupy themselves with the Lord will become His jewels. But it will be an act of His grace, as Psalm 85:2 proclaims, "Thou hast forgiven the iniquity of thy people, thou hast covered all their sin. Selah."

Malachi 3:18: "Then shall ye return, and discern between the righteous and the wicked, between him that serveth God and him that serveth him not."

(See) Genesis 18:25; Amos 5:15

Only those who fear the Lord, hearken to His voice, and contemplate on His holy name will be able to distinguish between the righteous and the wicked, between those who truly serve God and those who do not.

Chapter 4

Introduction

The final chapter in the Old Testament declares the absolute judgment of the wicked, and the wonderful restoration of those who fear the Lord, with the words, "Unto you that fear my name shall the Sun of righteousness arise."

400 Year Silence

The six verses of chapter 4 constitute the end of the Old Testament.

The book of Malachi is appropriately listed as the last book because after Malachi, there is about a 400 year silence; no word was received, no prophet spoke and no prophet wrote.

Fiery Destruction

Malachi 4:1: "For, behold, the day cometh, that shall burn as an oven; and all the proud, yea, and all that do wickedly, shall be stubble: and the day that cometh shall burn them up, saith the LORD of hosts, that it shall leave them neither root nor branch."

(See) Psalm 21:9; Isaiah 5:24; 9:18-19; Obadiah 18; Nahum 1:5-6; 2 Peter 3:7

This is total destruction. We note the word "proud," which appears 48 times in our Bible. Except for Psalm 31:23, it is always an indication of lofty arrogance, rebellion against the living God.

If we were to use one word to define Israel's attitude toward the God of heaven and earth, it would certainly be the word "proud."

Going back four verses in chapter 3, we read of the arrogance expressed by Israel, "...we call the proud happy; yea, they that work wickedness...." Israel's thinking, behavior, and attitude were diametrically opposed to God. They actually stated that the Lord delivered the proud and the wicked. But now God gives the answer: the proud that do wickedly will be incinerated. The statement, "it shall leave them neither root nor branch," shows there will be no more descendants; they will be eradicated from the land of the living.

This Scripture also reminds us of the words the Apostle Peter wrote, "But the day of the Lord will come as a thief in the night; in the which the heavens shall pass away with a great noise, and the elements shall melt with fervent heat, the earth also and the works that are therein shall be burned up. Seeing then that all these things shall be dissolved, what manner of persons ought ye to be in all holy conversation and godliness, Looking for and hasting unto the coming of the day of God, wherein the heavens being on fire shall be dissolved, and the elements shall melt with fervent heat?" (2 Peter 3:10-12).

No Future without Jesus

We know that this will take place at the very end; that is, after the Thousand-Year Kingdom of Peace has expired.

But the spirit of the message is applicable today. There is no future for any of us on planet earth; there is no future for our city, state, or country. We may involve ourselves for the betterment of mankind or our nation, but in the end, it's all in vain. Only what is done in the name of Jesus and through His Spirit will remain for eternity.

Speaking of fire, we are also reminded of the Church. Here we must read the words Paul wrote in 1 Corinthians 3:12-15, "Now if any man build upon this foundation gold, silver, precious stones, wood, hay, stubble; Every man's work shall be made manifest: for the day shall declare it, because it shall be revealed by fire; and the fire shall try every man's work of what sort it is. If any man's work abide which he hath built thereupon, he shall receive a reward. If any man's work shall be burned, he shall suffer loss: but he himself shall be saved; yet so as by fire." Nothing, absolutely nothing, will be left that is earthly; all will be gone.

But there is a distinct difference between those who rebelled against the God of Israel, who were annihilated, and the believer in the New Covenant. Those who build on "wood, hay, stubble" will suffer loss, yet will not be annihilated: "but he himself shall be saved; yet so as by fire."

Often I have marveled at the words "suffer loss." What does it entail? We read in Scripture that believers will be in the glorious presence of the Lord for all eternity; yet in this case, the person who has built on "wood, hay, and stubble" will "suffer loss." That is an extremely serious warning for believers, particularly in our days, as we see the process of fulfillment of Bible prophecy before our very eyes. So, what does "suffer loss" mean? One thing is sure: that person will lose his reward.

Sun of Righteousness

Malachi 4:2: "But unto you that fear my name shall the Sun of righteousness arise with healing in his wings; and ye shall go forth, and grow up as calves of the stall."

(See) 2 Samuel 23:4; Isaiah 35:6; 60:1; Jeremiah 30:17; 33:6

Here we have the opposite of pride defined: "fear." Specifically, fearing the name of the Lord. Such a person will prosper spiritually; he will experience "the Sun of righteousness"; that is, the glory of the Lord. We note again that the believer, the one that fears the name of the Lord, experiences a direct relationship with the Son.

"Wailing and Gnashing of Teeth"

No wonder so many churches deliberately neglect the study of the whole Bible, particularly the prophetic Word. It has become popular to preach, proclaim and teach the advantages of believing in Jesus Christ, the benefits of being a Christian. However, the other part of the message—judgment, eternal punishment, separation from God—is often left out. We need to take the words of Jesus seriously, "The Son of man shall send forth his angels, and they shall gather out of his kingdom all things that offend, and them which do iniquity; And shall cast them into a furnace of fire: there shall be wailing and gnashing of teeth" (Matthew 13:41-42). That is also part of the gospel.

The Day Star

Although it speaks of the "Sun of righteousness," it does not mean the literal sun. Note something specific: "healing in his wings." The Apostle Peter explains it this way, "We have also a more sure word of prophecy; whereunto ye do well that ye take heed, as unto a light that shineth in a dark place, until the day dawn, and the day star arise in your hearts" (2 Peter 1:19). The prophetic Word is identical with the "light that shineth...and the day star." Without the prophetic Word, the Bible is not complete. Revelation 19:10 says, "the testimony of Jesus is the spirit of prophecy."

This is a strong admonishment to heed the prophetic Word; not to neglect it, not to conveniently leave it out, but to receive it personally: "the day star arise in your hearts." This light, the Day Star, is identical with the Son of righteousness John speaks about in 1 John 3:7-8: "Little children, let no man deceive you: he that doeth righteousness is righteous, even as he is righteous. He that committeth sin is of the devil; for the devil sinneth from the beginning. For this purpose the Son of God was manifested, that he might destroy the works of the devil."

Saints Will Judge

Malachi 4:3: "And ye shall tread down the wicked; for they shall be ashes under the soles of your feet in the day that I shall do this, saith the LORD of hosts."

(See) Job 40:12; Isaiah 26:6; Ezekiel 28:18; Micah 5:8

Salvation includes judgment. That means the believer

will participate in the execution of judgment. The Apostle Paul asked the question, "Do ye not know that the saints shall judge the world? ...Know ye not we shall judge angels?" (1 Corinthians 6:2-3). That is the other side of salvation.

The Other Side of the Lamb

In Revelation 6, we read in verses 15-16, "And the kings of the earth, and the great men, and the rich men, and the chief captains, and the mighty men, and every bondman, and every free man, hid themselves in the dens and in the rocks of the mountains; And said to the mountains and rocks, Fall on us, and hide us from the face of him that sitteth on the throne, and from the wrath of the Lamb." In vain, the people on earth try to hide themselves "from the wrath of the Lamb." That is strange because the lamb is a picture of meekness and innocence; a lamb would do no harm to anyone.

But this speaks of "the Lamb of God, which taketh away the sin of the world." Something else is happening here: the world sees the Lamb of God, not as the Savior, whom they rejected, but as the executor of God's righteousness, "Behold, the lion of the tribe of Judah, the Root of David, hath prevailed to open the book, and to loose the seven seals thereof" (Revelation 5:5).

Something significant is revealed in Revelation 5:12, "Saying with a loud voice, Worthy is the Lamb that was slain to receive power, and riches, and wisdom, and strength, and honour, and glory, and blessing." These are the attributes of the Lamb of God. The Lamb of God is salvation to those who believe, but judgment to the unbeliever.

The Law of Moses

Malachi 4:4: "Remember ye the law of Moses my servant, which I commanded unto him in Horeb for all Israel, with the statutes and judgment."

(See) Deuteronomy 4:23; 8:11

The prophet puts the Law of Moses on a pedestal. The law was given to the children of Israel. They were supposed to be obedient. Actually, the people promised to be submissive to the law, "And all the people answered together, and said, All that the LORD hath spoken we will do. And Moses returned the words of the people unto the LORD" (Exodus 19:8). We note that it says, "all the people" and, "all that the Lord hath spoken we will do." Israel solemnly promised to obey the Lord. Reading the Old Testament, we have an abundance of documentation showing that Israel repeatedly violated the Law of Moses, and often deliberated turned to the idols of the surrounding nations.

However, in the end, Israel is destined to be above all the people on the earth—under one condition: "Now therefore, if ye will obey my voice indeed, and keep my covenant, then ye shall be a peculiar treasure unto me above all people: for all the earth is mine" (Exodus 19:5). Will Israel be obedient in the end? Yes, but it will be based on God's grace exclusively.

The Coming of Elijah

In the third from last verse of the Old Testament, the prophet Malachi challenged Israel to remember the law, with its statutes and judgments. That admonition was extremely important, because those who remembered the Law of Moses were also able to recognize the herald of His coming: the one who would come in the spirit of Elijah, "For this is he that was spoken of by the prophet Esaias, saying, The voice of one crying in the wilderness, Prepare ye the way of the Lord, make his paths straight" (Matthew 3:3).

Malachi makes this announcement about four centuries before the coming of John the Baptist:

Malachi 4:5: "Behold, I will send you Elijah the prophet before the coming of the great and dreadful day of the LORD:"

(See) Matthew 11:4; 17:10-13

We note "the great and dreadful day of the Lord" is part of the Great Tribulation. However, to designate the fulfillment of that verse solely to the end of the end times is an error, because the prophetic Word is often timeless. The prophets frequently incorporate thousands of years into one sentence.

Progressive Fulfillment

As an example, let's look at Isaiah 61:1-2: "The Spirit of the Lord GOD is upon me; because the LORD hath anointed me to preach good tidings unto the meek; he hath sent me to bind up the brokenhearted, to proclaim liberty to the captives, and the opening of the prison to them that are bound; To proclaim the acceptable year of the LORD, and the day of vengeance of our God; to comfort all that mourn." Note that the "acceptable year" and the "vengeance of our God" is uttered in one breath. Now look at the fulfillment in Luke 4:18-19, "The Spirit of the Lord is upon me, because he hath anointed me to preach the gospel to the poor; he hath sent me to heal the broken-hearted, to preach deliverance to the captives, and recovering of sight to the blind, to set at liberty them that are bruised, To preach the acceptable year of the Lord." The Lord is reading from Isaiah 61, but He only reads part of verse 2, "to preach the acceptable year of the Lord." What next? "He closed the book...and sat down." That's it; there was no more to say. Then He explains, "This day is this scripture fulfilled in your ears." The Scripture that ends with "the acceptable year of the Lord," was fulfilled at that very moment, but "the day of vengeance of our God" is yet to come.

Jesus spoke of John the Baptist in Matthew 11, and He says something peculiar, "And from the days of John the Baptist until now the kingdom of heaven suffereth violence, and the violent take it by force. For all the prophets and the law prophesied until John" (verses 12-13). Here Jesus makes the distinction about the prophets and the law until John. He is definitely speaking of a new dispensation. He makes the following statement in verse 14, "And if ye will receive it, this is Elias, which was for to come." Here John the Baptist is identified as the pre-fulfillment of the coming of the prophet Elijah.

Later, in chapter 17 He explains further: "And his disciples asked him, saying, Why then say the scribes that Elias must first come? And Jesus answered and said unto them, Elias truly shall first come, and restore all things. But I say unto you, That Elias is come already, and they knew him not, but have done unto him whatsoever they listed. Likewise shall also the Son of man suffer of them. Then the disciples understood that he spake unto them of John the Baptist" (verses 10-13).

Elijah or John?

Has Elijah the prophet come? Yes and no. Yes, in the person of John the Baptist, who prepared the way for the Messiah. And no, because he is yet to come. Although Elijah is not mentioned by name, we read in Revelation 11:3-4 the following, "And I will give power unto my two witnesses, and they shall prophesy a thousand two hundred and threescore days, clothed in sackcloth. These are the two olive trees, and the two candlesticks standing before the God of the earth."

Malachi 4:6: "And he shall turn the heart of the fathers to the children, and the heart of the children to their fathers, lest I come and smite the earth with a curse."

(See) Isaiah 11:4; Luke 1:17; Revelation 19:15

Elijah has to come to restore the family, to restore God's original intention. Here we should read the message of Gabriel to Zechariah, the priest, the father of John the Baptist, "And he shall go before him in the spirit and power of Elias, to turn the hearts of the fathers to the children, and the disobedient to the wisdom of the just; to make ready a people prepared for the Lord" (Luke 1:17).

The Cross Separates

Was this prophecy fulfilled in the days of John the Baptist? Or later when Jesus began His ministry? Absolutely not! Jesus makes it clear that something must take place first before the final fulfillment can be implemented. Luke 12:51-53 says the following, "Suppose ye that I am come to give peace on earth? I tell you, Nay; but rather division: For from henceforth there shall be five in one house divided, three against two, and two against three. The father shall be divided against the son, and the son against the father; the mother against the daughter, and the daughter against the mother; the mother in law against her daughter in law, and the daughter in law against her mother in law."

That is the separation of the family unit, due to the cross. Yet when Elijah comes, the fruit of the cross will be presented. Elijah shall "turn the heart of the fathers to their children, and the heart of the children to their fathers." What is the alternative? "Lest I come and smite the earth with a curse." Thus, we come to the conclusion that the coming of Elijah is part of the process of reestablishing the family unit in preparation for the Thousand-Year Kingdom of Peace.

Conclusion

Malachi thunders his prophetic message against Judah/Israel, to show their utter failure to do and practice the Law of God as given to Moses. The failure of the priests and the temple service is highlighted. He foretells of the Great Tribulation and the coming of Elijah, and concludes with the restoration of the family with the words, "...turn the heart of the fathers to the children, and the hearts of the children to their fathers." The absoluteness is expressed with one word: "curse." There is no alternative; either remember the Law of Moses or the curse.

It is of comfort that the New Testament ends with the words, "The grace of our Lord Jesus Christ be with you all. Amen" (Revelation 22:21).

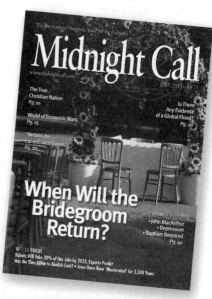